A STUDENT'S GUIDE TO THERAPEUTIC COUNSELLING

Sara Miller McCune founded SAGE Publishing in 1965 to support the dissemination of usable knowledge and educate a global community. SAGE publishes more than 1000 journals and over 800 new books each year, spanning a wide range of subject areas. Our growing selection of library products includes archives, data, case studies and video. SAGE remains majority owned by our founder and after her lifetime will become owned by a charitable trust that secures the company's continued independence.

Los Angeles | London | New Delhi | Singapore | Washington DC | Melbourne

A STUDENT'S GUIDE TO THERAPEUTIC COUNSELLING

KELLY BUDD, SANDRA MCKEEVER
TRACI POSTINGS & HEATHER PRICE

SAGE

Los Angeles | London | New Delhi
Singapore | Washington DC | Melbourne

SAGE

Los Angeles | London | New Delhi
Singapore | Washington DC | Melbourne

SAGE Publications Ltd
1 Oliver's Yard
55 City Road
London EC1Y 1SP

SAGE Publications Inc.
2455 Teller Road
Thousand Oaks, California 91320

SAGE Publications India Pvt Ltd
B 1/I 1 Mohan Cooperative Industrial Area
Mathura Road
New Delhi 110 044

SAGE Publications Asia-Pacific Pte Ltd
3 Church Street
#10-04 Samsung Hub
Singapore 049483

Editor: Susannah Trefgarne
Assistant editor: Ruth Lilly
Production editor: Martin Fox
Copyeditor: Christine Bitten
Proofreader: Jill Birch
Indexer: Silvia Benvenuto
Marketing manager: Dilhara Attygalle
Cover design: Sheila Tong
Typeset by: C&M Digitals (P) Ltd, Chennai, India
Printed in the United Kingdom by Hobbs the Printers Ltd, Totton, Hampshire

First published 2020

Library of Congress Control Number: 2019939801

British Library Cataloguing in Publication data

A catalogue record for this book is available from the British Library

ISBN 978-1-5264-0829-7
ISBN 978-1-5264-0830-3 (pbk)

This book is dedicated to our students, who often taught us as much as we taught them about dedication, resilience and commitment to counselling work.

Contents

About the Authors

KELLY BUDD

Kelly is an experienced person-centred counsellor, supervisor and tutor. She took up the role of Head of Qualifications at CPCAB after having worked in the FE sector for many years. She has a particular interest in supporting practitioners taking their first steps into the field of counselling and found her years teaching diploma programmes hugely inspirational.

SANDRA MCKEEVER

Sandra is a counsellor, psychotherapist, supervisor and trainer currently working in private practice. She has delivered all CPCAB qualifications up to Level 5 in both FE and private centres and was qualification leader of the Level 4 Diploma at CPCAB head office. She has also delivered counselling training in HE. She has a particular interest in alternative approaches to mental health and spirituality along with the role of personal development in training programmes and its impact on the therapeutic relationship and the prevention of burnout and vicarious trauma.

TRACI POSTINGS

Traci is an experienced counsellor, supervisor and tutor who has also worked extensively in homelessness and addiction settings. Over the years she has taught counselling at all levels and worked at CPCAB for over ten years to promote high standards in counselling training and qualification development. Traci currently works at BACP (British Association for Counselling and Psychotherapy) as a strategic project manager within the professional standards team.

HEATHER PRICE

Heather is a very experienced counselling tutor, having delivered Levels 2 to 4 for many years in an FE College. She is also a counsellor and supervisor, with a particular interest in bereavement work. Her role at CPCAB has involved managing the Levels 4, 5 and 6, enabling centres to produce tailor-made qualifications, approving CPD programmes, and carrying out external verification visits.

Introduction

This book is a comprehensive and coherent core text book for trainee counsellors on a practitioner counselling course with a placement in an agency setting. This will appeal to learners on diploma courses at Level 4 and above. It maps to widely adopted counselling courses at Level 4 and Level 5 on the Regulated Qualifications Framework which are delivered mainly in Further Education colleges, but is also applicable to all practitioner counselling courses in Further Education, Higher Education and the private training sector.

As authors of this book we have drawn on our experiences delivering diploma qualifications to trainee counsellors for many years and the questions that we have been asked during that time, to create an accessible and easily referenced resource text for all students.

Our aim is to locate the learning within a research-informed practitioner model focused on what makes counselling effective. The model values the significance and role of research findings both in application to and for improvement of practice.

The book is structured in three parts with a common introduction which locates the book within a research-informed counselling paradigm, drawing on the factors that contribute to therapeutic change. The first part is divided into seven chapters which reflect the seven processes of the Counselling and Psychotherapy Central Awarding Body (CPCAB) model of practitioner development. Although supported by the CPCAB training model, this book is equally applicable to qualifications from other awarding bodies in the UK.

PART I

The first part is aimed at supporting learners to gain an understanding of the content of counselling practitioner courses at Level 4 and above. It is a combination of underpinning knowledge, advanced use of skills, integration of theory into client work, and includes subjects for reflection and self-challenge. The emphasis is on safe and ethical practice within a range of counselling agency settings with different client groups, and encompasses contracting, risk assessment, deeper aspects of the therapeutic relationship, client factors and observed and inferred, therapist factors. There is a focus on the importance of reflection and evaluation of practice. Practical case examples will be given throughout to enable readers to engage with the subject matter and explore their own developing knowledge.

PART II

The second section is devoted to practice issues. It focuses on finding a suitable placement, including what an agency might require from a student. It addresses how to access supervision and understand the use of personal therapy for the developing practitioner. This section also covers how to utilise self-care throughout the training experience, and carry this forward to prevent counsellor burnout. Other academic support issues are also covered such as analysing a recorded transcript, and writing a case study.

PART III

The third section addresses other professional issues such as 'What next?' This includes how to decide when you are ready to work in independent practice. It covers the rudiments of professional body registration and accreditation schemes. There is also a helpful 'What if?' FAQ (Frequently Asked Questions) chapter covering such queries as: touch in counselling, meeting clients outside the therapy room, attraction in the therapy room, dress codes, use of social media, and dual relationships or other conflicts of interest.

The questioning terminology is intended to replicate the conversation between a practitioner level student and their tutor who is guiding them through the learning process, while empowering them to challenge the process with the natural passion of a diploma student. This guidance is supplemented by reflections, activities, examples, and case studies, to enable the reader to connect with the material and engage in additional critical thinking around the subjects presented.

The terminology used throughout the book has been chosen to represent the body of students accessing this text. We have primarily used the terms counsellor, practitioner, trainee, and student interchangeably to indicate those engaged in counselling practitioner level training.

THE UNDERPINNING MODEL

Background

The first version of the CPCAB model was developed during an educational design research programme in the late 1980s and early 1990s that sought to identify the core elements of counsellor proficiency and their development in counselling training. Since then the CPCAB model has been updated to reflect: (1) a broad range of research findings, including for example the various factors that contribute to therapeutic change; and (2) a wide range of practice insights gained from the model's application across thousands of counselling courses. This latest version of the model is therefore informed by both contemporary interdisciplinary research and extensive educational practice.

Overview of model

Counselling was originally founded in the 1940s (Rogers, 1942) as a direct challenge to the traditional medical model – a model that reduces client problems to specific symptoms, each requiring specific treatments. This 'reductionist' approach necessarily excludes the *context* of client problems together with a range of contextual factors that have been shown to be critically important elements of the counselling process.

The counselling approach challenges, therefore, the reductionism of the traditional medical model by providing an alternative 'whole systems' perspective in which client problems, client change and the process of supporting client change (the counselling process) are all inextricably connected to their context (see Figure 0.1).

Following on from this, the CPCAB model sets out the essential elements of practice that are common to all counselling approaches. It describes how counsellors can support clients to change and consists of three parts:

- *Part 1: Three levels of client problems.* This defines the broad categories of client problems for which counselling has proved helpful:
  - Service Level A: Everyday life problems
  - Service Level B: Common mental health and other psychological problems (which, the model proposes, may have both an explicit and implicit aspect)
  - Service Level C: Severe and complex mental health problems.

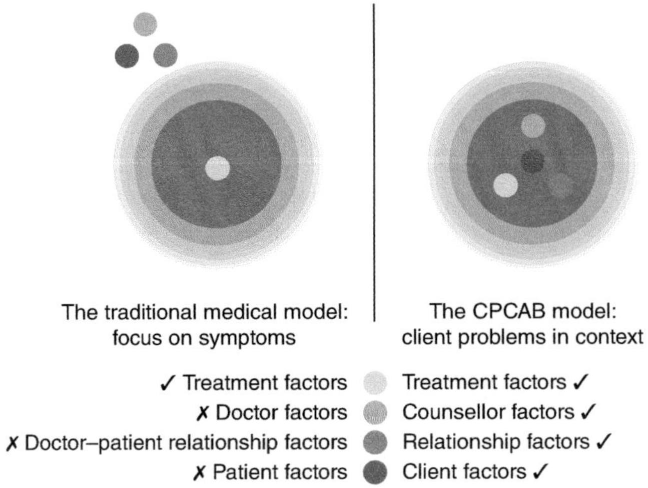

FIGURE 0.1 Focus of the models

- *Part 2: Three dimensions of client problems.* This describes how client problems can be best understood, and worked with, in the *context* within which they arise. For everyday life problems the context is (1) the person's thoughts and feelings in (2) their relationships and (3) particular life stage. For common mental health and other psychological problems the model proposes a similar three-dimensional psychological context within which those problems have developed.
- *Part 3: Seven helping and counselling processes.* This describes how the process of supporting client change is associated with a range of contextual factors – including those concerning the client, the counsellor and the relationship that they form. Following on from this, and drawing on a wide range of research, Part 3 of the model describes seven processes that weave together to form the counselling process as a whole.

Parts 1, 2 and 3 of the model fit together into a coherent matrix (see Figure 0.2).

Part 1: Three levels of client problems (service levels)

All professions define a set of real world problems which they aim to manage and which therefore delineate their professional domain. Counselling has proven to be effective with the following broad categories of client problems:

Service Level A: Everyday life problems

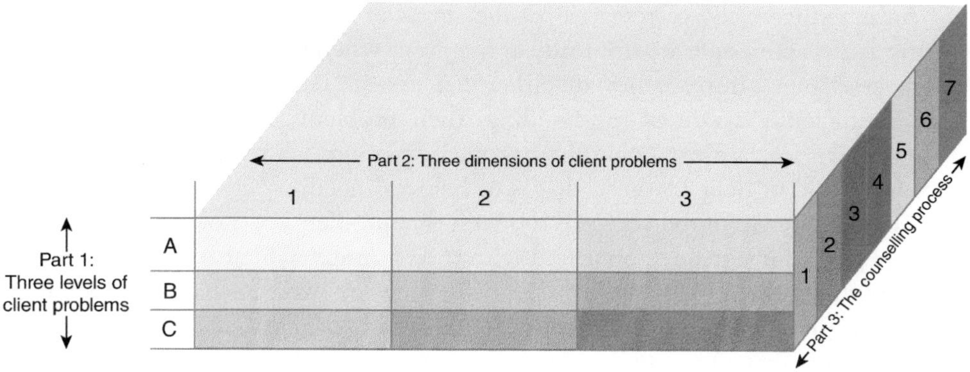

FIGURE 0.2 Overview of CPCAB model

Service Level B: Common mental health and other psychological problems

Service Level C: Severe and complex mental health problems.

Service Level A – Helping work and counselling: Everyday life problems

Problems with our parents, or when we first become a parent … problems with our partner, or with the loss of our partner … problems with our work, or with not having work … problems with our lifestyle such as our weight, our drinking or our smoking … problems that gradually build up over time (because we ignore them), or problems that suddenly 'hit us in the face' … life is full of these everyday life and lifestyle problems.

In the past, researchers tended to assume that we faced all these problems alone. However, recent research on everyday problem-solving[1] has shown that not only do we often seek help from friends and family, but also that partners regularly solve problems together. So most of the time with a little help from our friends and family, we cope reasonably well with our everyday life problems. Sometimes, however, we can get overwhelmed and 'stressed out'[2] and in these kinds of situations a helper or counsellor can provide much needed support.

---

[1]See, for example, various research publications by Cynthia A. Berg (and colleagues) on 'everyday problem solving in context'.

[2]This section of the CPCAB model on everyday life problems is informed by research on stress, coping and resilience.

An extensive body of research on the stages of change[3] has concluded that as many as 80% of people are not ready, at the point when they seek professional help, to make changes. Instead, they are either in a 'pre-contemplation' stage where they are insufficiently aware of (or avoiding) their problems, or in a 'contemplation' stage where they are exploring their problems but not yet ready to make changes. So what kind of help do these clients or helpees[4] need?

The perspective of the CPCAB model is that problems do not exist in isolation, but are instead intimately connected with their context. Clients need, therefore, to explore this context before they are ready to focus on making changes – they need to explore how their problems arise from, and are connected to, themselves and their life (see Part 2).

An important aspect of this context is the client's stage of change, and one of the key recommendations of the research cited above is that the counselling service can be usefully tailored to this – that is, that clients who are in (1) the pre-contemplation stage can be supported to develop their awareness of themselves, together with the advantages of changing, while those in (2) the contemplation stage can be supported to:

a. Explore their thoughts about themselves, their life and their problems with the aim of developing associated insights and self-re-evaluations.
b. Explore their feelings about themselves, their life and their problems with the aim of developing emotional understanding and awareness together with readying themselves to emotionally move forward and change.
c. Develop a belief in their ability to change together with an associated commitment to change.

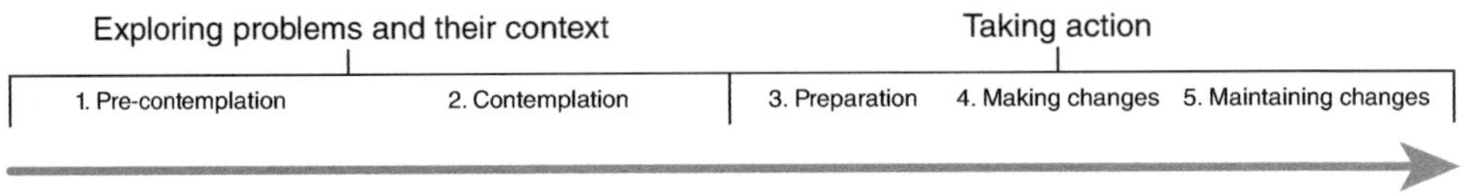

FIGURE 0.3 Stages of change

[3]The stages of change model was originally developed by Prochaska & DiClemente in 1977 and has been extensively researched over nearly four decades. See, for example, Chapter 14 in Norcross, 2011.

[4]The term 'client' refers to people working with a counsellor while 'helpee' refers to those working with a helper.

Once a person has made a firm commitment to change they can then be supported to (3) prepare for and then (4) make the necessary changes. Finally, they can be supported to (5) maintain those changes (see Figure 0.3).

Informal helping work may be able to provide the support needed to cope with everyday life problems, but sometimes a person will need to see a counsellor, who can provide a more in-depth supportive relationship. Additionally, some people who are not yet ready to make the (Level A) life or lifestyle changes[5] may first need to work with a counsellor on an underlying psychological problem (Level B – see below). For example, a client and counsellor might agree on the goal of stopping smoking, but as the counselling progresses it becomes clear that smoking is not only a *problem* but also a *solution* in that the client uses smoking to soothe their social anxiety.[6] The client and counsellor both realise, therefore, that to achieve the (Level A) goal of stopping smoking they will first need to deepen the level of work (to Level B) and focus on the underlying social anxiety.

Service Level B Counselling: Common mental health and other psychological problems.

Sometimes, as in the example above, the core problem is not so much in our life but within ourselves ... and many clients come to counselling for help with these *psychological* problems. The traditional medical model defines these as mental health problems, which are normally divided into *common* mental health problems (such as anxiety and depression) and *severe and complex* mental health problems (such as bipolar disorder and schizophrenia: see Level C below). The CPCAB model proposes that, rather than simply focusing on the treatment of symptoms, these psychological problems are best understood, and worked with, in the context of the particular person within whom they develop.

As mentioned above, one important aspect of this context is the client's stage of change, including the level of awareness of their problem. Drawing on the research

---

[5]Counselling has proved effective for a range of health issues and lifestyle changes and is therefore becoming a key element of health service provision.

[6]Much of the research on the stages of change concerned smoking cessation. A strong link between mental health problems and smoking has also been identified: a 2010 NatCen report, for example, found that one-third of people with common mental health problems and 57% of people who attempted suicide were smokers, while a 2015 Public Health England survey concluded that mental health patients smoke three times as much as the general population and that smoking is the primary reason why these patients have a lower life expectancy of 15–20 years.

on the stages of change, together with research on the 'explicit' and 'implicit' nature of our thoughts and feelings, relationships and memory,[7] the CPCAB model proposes that working with psychological problems can involve both an explicit (B1) and implicit level (B2).

In the above example the client begins counselling wanting to stop smoking (Level A) but also with an implicit psychological problem (Level B2) and therefore in the pre-contemplation stage with respect to this underlying problem. Later in the counselling process, when it becomes clear that the underlying problem is their social anxiety, this implicit problem moves to the explicit, contemplation stage (Level B1) and client and counsellor are then able to explore it together.

It is important to note that when working at the explicit level with a client it may be possible to proceed in a goal-directed way towards change, but the process of supporting clients to change implicit aspects of themselves (that they may be avoiding) can be more complex. Together with developing their awareness of themselves and the advantages of changing, this level of work may also, for example, involve the client developing a deeper level of trust, not only with their counsellor but also within themselves.

Service Level C – Severe and complex mental health problems

This aspect of the CPCAB model is informed by research on early childhood development during which time the *foundations* of the person are developed. The model proposes that these foundations include experiences such as the person's core sense of being-at-home-in-themselves and being-in-the-world-of-others, together with their core sense of their own development process (that is, their 'ontogeny' as a person).

The model proposes that clients categorised with severe and complex mental health problems may be helped by working on aspects of the foundations of themselves, but only with a counsellor who is trained and experienced to work with this level of client problems and normally in conjunction with other services. Clients with severe and complex mental health problems will normally, therefore, need to be referred to, for example, the psychiatric provision of secondary mental health services.

---

[7]This research includes explicit/implicit emotions and cognition, dual process theory, explicit/implicit social cognition, explicit autobiographical memory and implicit emotional memory.

Tailoring helping and counselling to the level of client problems

The CPCAB model proposes that helping and counselling can be usefully tailored not only to the client's stage of change, but also to the *level* of client problems. However, it's important to note that this 'map' is only a map and not the 'territory'. Clients may present, for example, with a mixture of interconnected problems at differing levels and the stages may be more spiral in nature than linear. In other words real life, and real-life counselling, can be much more challenging, and profound, than this map (see Figure 0.4).

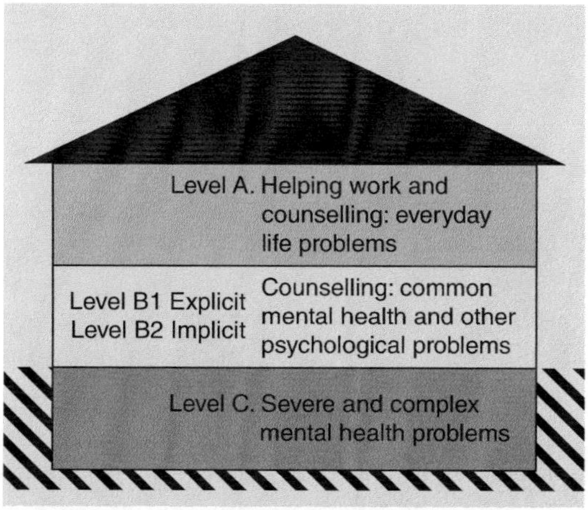

FIGURE 0.4 The three service levels of client change

Part 2: Three dimensions of client problems

Part 2 of the CPCAB model is based on a 'whole systems' approach to understanding client change in relation to both everyday life problems and psychological problems. From this perspective client problems both arise from, and remain connected to, their context. Client problems are 'context-dependent' and client change requires, therefore, working with both problems and their context. The CPCAB model proposes that this context consists of three dimensions (see Figure 0.5).

Service Level A: Everyday life problems[8]

With everyday life problems counsellors can support client change by working with the:

---

[8]This section of the CPCAB model is informed by, for example, research on (1) emotional regulation; (2) social problem-solving; and (3) the life course.

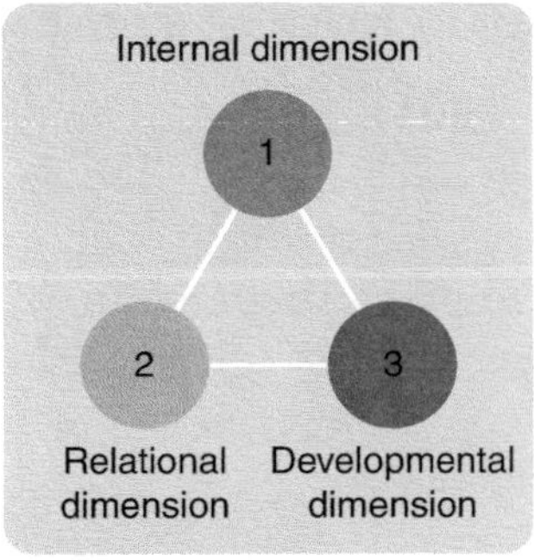

FIGURE 0.5 Three dimensions of client problems

1. Internal dimension – thoughts and feelings
2. Relational dimension – relationship issues
3. Developmental dimension – life stage issues

When, for example, someone has an accident they have to cope with the physical effects. There are often, however, 'knock-on' effects on relationships and the ability to cope with the challenges of the particular life stage. A young mother with a physical injury, for instance, might find it much harder to care for her child, and her relationship with her partner might also deteriorate (relational dimension). As a result of her injury she might also have to give up her work and associated career (developmental dimension). All of this also has profound effects on her inner life – on her thoughts and feelings (internal dimension).

Service Level B: Common mental health and other psychological problems[9]

With common mental health and other psychological problems counsellors can support client change by working with:

1. The internal dimension: changing the way clients relate within themselves

Clients may not be able to change who they are, but they can often change the ways that they relate within themselves – changing, for example, an internal conflict between the 'head' and the 'heart' into a more collaborative inner dialogue.

[9]This section of the CPCAB model is informed by, for example, research on (1) emotional and cognitive systems; (2) social neuroscience; and (3) explicit autobiographical memories and implicit emotional memories.

Different theories and techniques offer different ways of understanding and working with this dimension. The Freudian model of id, ego and super-ego is one such theory, but there are many others. In Transactional Analysis, for example, the counsellor might help the client to uncover a conflict between an angry internal parent and an anxious internal child and then work to change this internal relationship for the better; a CBT counsellor, on the other hand, might support the client to change their habitual thinking patterns; but a person-centred counsellor might work with the client to understand the conflict between different parts of themselves; whilst a transpersonal counsellor might support the client to use mindfulness, meditation and contemplation to develop a greater sense of inner peace.

As clients learn to relate more collaboratively within themselves, they develop a more resilient sense of themselves – enabling them to cope more effectively with their everyday life problems.

2. The relational dimension: changing the way clients relate with others

Clients may not be able to change other people, but they can often change their ways of relating with others – their habitual patterns of perceiving, communicating and behaving with their partner, parents, children, friends or colleagues.

These changes often need to initially take place within the safety of the counselling relationship, where the client can test out new ways of relating. By changing their unhelpful patterns of relating, clients develop better ways of coping with difficulties in their relationships and are consequently able to develop more open, supportive and resilient relationships that directly contribute to their health and wellbeing.

3. The developmental dimension: changing the way clients relate with their past

Clients cannot change the past, but they can often change the ways that they relate with their past. They can, for example, change the autobiographical stories that they tell themselves about their development across the life course or change their implicit emotional response to past traumatic events.

As clients change the ways that they relate with their past, they become more resilient within themselves through, for example, letting go of blaming themselves or feeling less overwhelmed in the present by emotionally painful memories from the past.

Importantly, the model also proposes that the theories and techniques (the treatments) that have been developed across the broad range of counselling approaches can be usefully organised into these above three dimensions.

Part 3: Seven helping and counselling processes

All clients come to counselling because they want to change something. Recent research has demonstrated that counselling works best when the client instigates change supported by a particular kind of therapeutic context in which the counsellor utilises, not just their theoretical understandings and skills, but themselves and the counselling relationship, together with an ethical and reflective approach to their work.

Factors common to all counselling approaches

Contemporary research has confirmed that the primary contribution to effective counselling is made, not by any specific treatment, but rather by the context-dependent factors that are common to all the approaches.[10] These context-dependent factors are known, in the counselling and psychotherapy research literature, as the 'common factors'. They consist of:

1. Client factors – which can be divided into those which can be observed (the difference and diversity of every client, including their community and culture) and those that can only be inferred (the client's subjective experience, stage of change, expectations, characteristics and preferences, e.g. motivation, hope, etc.).[11]
2. Counsellor factors – these can also be divided into observed and inferred factors. The counsellor's observed factors again concern their difference and diversity (e.g. gender and ethnicity), while the inferred factors include, for example, their level of 'healing involvement'[12] and their use of self-awareness in the counselling process.
3. Relationship factors – the quality and effectiveness of the counselling relationship.

Evidence for the importance of these categories of common factors comes, for example, from a recent American Psychological Association Research Task Force (Norcross, 2011). Their meta-study encompassed 100,000 clients across more than 400 quantitative research studies and concluded that 'the common factors make the greatest contribution to client change – with client factors being the most important of all' (CPCAB, 2015).

4. Treatment factors – the above study, together with other research, also concluded that treatment factors make an important contribution to therapeutic change. The CPCAB model proposes, however, that there are

[10] Wampold and Imel (2015) propose a contextual model of therapeutic change.

[11] This distinction between observed and inferred factors was proposed by Castonguay and Beutler (2006).

[12] This is a measure of some key aspects of the counsellor's contribution to the counselling process – see, for example, Ronnestad and Skovholt (2012).

important aspects of treatment factors that are common to all the counselling approaches – and the second part of the CPCAB model (as described earlier) provides a generic framework for organising these commonalities.

So taken together there are four categories of context-dependent factors that contribute to therapeutic change.

Drawing heavily on the research into the factors that contribute to client change, the third and final part of the CPCAB model proposes a 'whole systems' approach to the counselling process in which a broad range of factors support client change (see Figure 0.6).

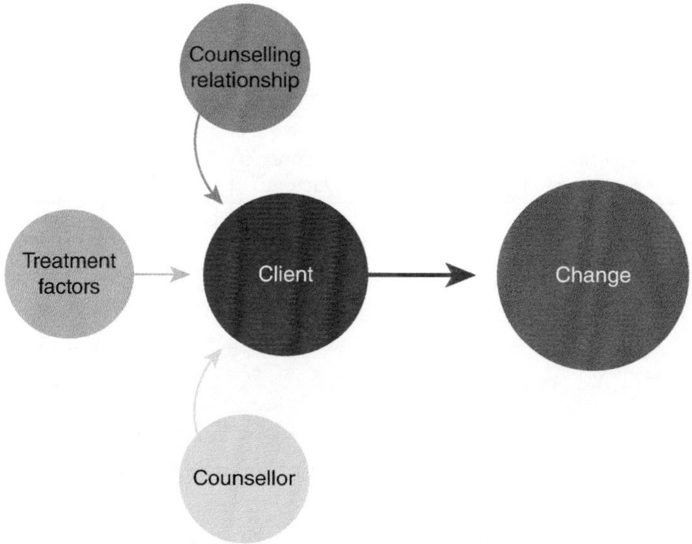

FIGURE 0.6 Supporting the client change process

- Client factors – the client as the primary agent of change. The counsellor seeks to understand the client in terms of, for example, their difference and diversity, their unique subjective life and their stage of change (etc.), in order to support the client's change process.
- Counsellor factors – this is the contribution that the particular counsellor makes to the counselling process (as distinct from the counselling relationship or the use of specific theory and techniques). It includes, for example, the counsellor's level of healing involvement (see research cited above) together with their ability to use self-awareness in the counselling process.

- Relationship factors – a broad range of research has concluded that the counselling relationship makes a major contribution to client change.
- Treatment factors – the theory and techniques of the specific counselling approach.
- Professional factors – two other key elements of helping and counselling practice:
  - working within an ethical and professional framework
  - working as a reflective practitioner.

The model proposes that these two professional-practice processes support and contain the counselling process (see Figure 0.7).

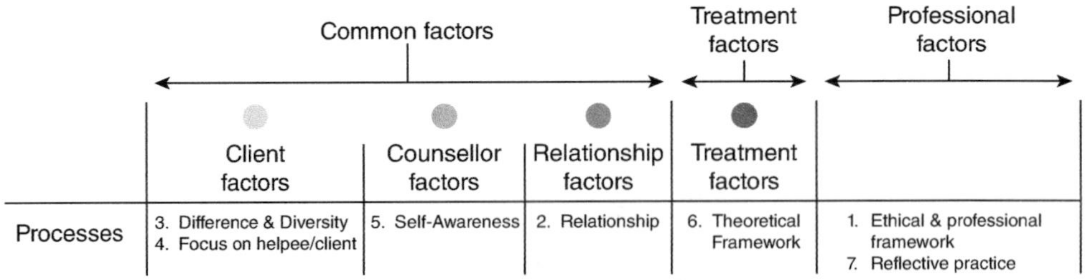

FIGURE 0.7 Counselling factors and processes

Taken together, the factors listed above form seven helping and counselling processes – seven processes that support client change (see Figure 0.8):

1. Working ethically and professionally (professional factors)
2. Working with the relationship (relationship factors)
3. Working with difference and diversity (observed client factors)
4. Working with a primary focus on the client (inferred client factors)
5. Working with self-awareness (observed and inferred counsellor factors)
6. Working within a coherent framework of skills and theory (treatment factors)
7. Working reflectively (professional factors)

These seven processes do not exist in isolation from each other, but continually interact. They are, therefore, a bit like seven 'balls' which the helper or counsellor 'juggles' when supporting their helpees, or working with their clients. Helpers can work with these seven processes to enable a person to reflect on themselves and their life, get clearer about their everyday life problems and identify better ways of coping. Counsellors can work with these same seven processes to support clients to change aspects of their lives and themselves.

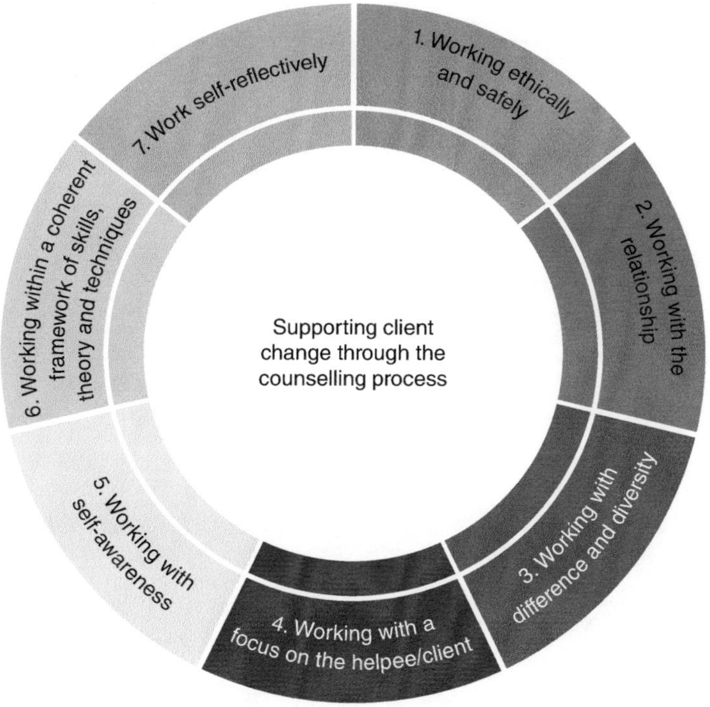

FIGURE 0.8 The seven processes

When a helper or counsellor uses these seven processes to help someone explore their everyday life problems or to change themselves, they are working in a way that is supported by the latest research on what's effective. Additionally, at each level of the CPCAB's counselling qualifications progression route, the seven processes reflect the depth and focus of that level of training and articulate the associated increase in the learner's skills, proficiency and autonomy (see Figure 0.9).

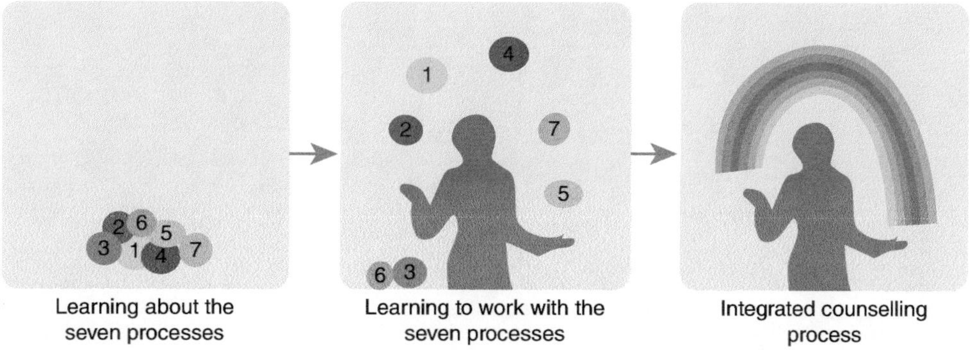

FIGURE 0.9 The juggler

PART I

TRAINING TO BE A COUNSELLOR

1 Working Ethically and Safely as a Counselling Professional

This chapter is about working ethically and safely with clients as a counselling professional.

ETHICAL FRAMEWORKS

Q Oh no, not ethics again, we did that last year, and the year before! Why do we have to do it again?

A Well the clue is in the sentence above – can you see that it says, 'counselling professional'? That's the difference. Towards the end of this year you will begin to work with real clients in an agency placement. You will be joining the counselling profession. So as well as all your skills and theory, your knowledge about ethics will be called upon because it will be so important to work safely with your clients in a professional manner.

> **REFLECTION**
>
> So take a moment to think about working with clients – that's quite a responsibility isn't it? Just jot down anything that concerns you about working professionally, safely and ethically.

So I expect you have listed things like not letting my clients down, keeping their confidentiality, holding the boundaries, doing the right thing, not harming the client, being competent, managing suicide threats, making referrals, getting on with other people at the agency, using supervision.

Let's start with what you know already. You have learnt that there are such things as Ethical Frameworks and that they exist to protect the client and counsellor, to ensure that the counsellor is accountable to a professional body and that the client has access to an avenue for making a complaint if necessary.

OK, so far? We'll come back to some of these things later, but at this stage of your training it is about learning to apply and extend the skills and knowledge you already have in order to work with clients, within an ethical framework. This is the next step on from just carrying out practice sessions with your peers in class.

Q What do we mean by working ethically with clients?

A The word ethical is used in various ways – you will probably have come across some of them. For example 'ethically farmed', 'ethically sourced', and 'ethically invested'. If you consider each of these phrases you will see that they all have something to do with doing good and/or causing least harm.

> **EXERCISE**
>
> Jot down as many words as you can think of that define 'ethical' for you.

Here are some of the more common ones – equitable, honourable, just, morally right, accepted standard of conduct, right minded.

Q So are morals and ethics the same then?

A The word 'moral' implies conforming to accepted or established notions of right and wrong in a community, country or culture. The word 'ethical' suggests the more complex and subtle exploration of fairness, rightness or equity and might need to be considered for each individual case, for example, a family's ethical consideration of the pros and cons of having a Do Not Resuscitate order for their elderly mother.

REFLECTION

Consider the following: It may be scientifically possible to clone human beings, but is it ethical?

Q So, coming back to counselling, what exactly is an ethical framework?

A It is a set of guidelines which aim to lay down a broad standard or benchmark for working as a counsellor. An ethical framework is produced by a professional body in the field of counselling and determines how a counsellor should conduct themselves, and what a client can expect when they enter into a counselling agreement. The reason for this is so that there can be a generally accepted standard for counselling work all across the country, in all types of agency, dealing with all kinds of clients and a whole range of issues. The standards usually include reference to values, principles and moral qualities and how these relate to good practice, that is, putting the client first.

Q I understand all that, but how does it impact on me working as an individual counsellor in an agency?

A You need to know which ethical framework your placement adheres to so that you can work according to the same guidelines as everyone else in the agency, so that you are conducting yourself in a way which conforms to the same standard of behaviour as the other counsellors, and so that the clients know what to expect from you and all the counsellors in the agency.

ACTIVITY

Find out which Ethical Framework is adhered to at your agency placement. Does it differ from the framework you have already signed up to? Print out a copy and familiarise yourself with all its main points. Consider how easy (or difficult) it might be for you to keep within these guidelines in this placement – what might you find challenging?

(You might want to refer to it when looking at the ethical dilemmas in Part III.)

Q What would be the consequences then of not having an ethical framework to work within?

A Most people who come to a counsellor do not know much about professional organisations for counselling or about standards and ethics. They tend to be driven to seek help from a counsellor when they are going through a difficult emotional time which often means that they are distressed and in a vulnerable state. When anyone is in a vulnerable place they could easily be exploited – emotionally, financially, sexually or physically. They need to trust that the counsellor will do the right thing by them – but what if the counsellor doesn't?

REFLECTION

Think about how a vulnerable person seeking counselling might be exploited in any or all of these ways – emotionally, financially, sexually or physically. Here are a few examples, see if you can think of some more:

A young female client who has just suffered a relationship break up could be taken advantage of sexually by an unscrupulous male counsellor who finds her physically attractive.

A counsellor could exploit a client who they know has plenty of money by suggesting they have another six sessions when in fact the counselling work is done.

An un-boundaried and inexperienced counsellor might be tempted to give a client a hug when in fact it is their own need to have that physical closeness.

A counsellor could be drawn into telling their client what to do, as clients so often want us to just give them an answer. But that might be totally the wrong thing for that client, with disastrous consequences.

So a client could be physically or sexually abused, emotionally scarred and/or be drained of their money if there were no safeguards, if the counsellor was not answerable to a professional organisation, and if the client had nowhere to take any complaints.

Q I know about the BACP ethical framework but are there others?

A Yes, the BACP one is called the *Ethical Framework for the Counselling Professions* (2018). Other well-known ones include those from UKCP (UK Council for Psychotherapy), ACC (Association of Christian Counsellors), NCS (National Counselling Society), BABCP (British Association for Behavioural and Cognitive Psychotherapies).

ACTIVITY

Compare and contrast the key points of the ethical framework which is used in your agency with the ethical framework from one other professional body (or compare the BACP framework with one other if you have not yet started agency work). Do you think you would find one of these more comfortable to work within than the other and why?

Q Now, I know all about the importance of an ethical framework, but how do I introduce my client to this?

A This is a very good point, as knowing it yourself is one thing, but introducing it to a client in a way that they can understand it, is another.

REFLECTION

So imagine that you don't know anything about how counselling works and you have plucked up courage to see a counsellor for the first time. You have a personal issue that you want to talk about that is very private to you and you are afraid that you will get very upset. You have limited funds and can't afford to attend for endless weeks. What would you want to know that would reassure you on that first meeting?

I expect you would want to know that the counsellor you are seeing is part of a wider network with professional standards, not just one solitary person operating in a little room on their own. Just like when you need a plumber, you could ring up the 'man with a van' round the corner and he might do a reasonable job and not charge you too much. But if anything goes wrong it may transpire that he is not actually a qualified plumber at all, therefore he may not be accountable to any professional standards or have any insurance, then it could cost you a lot of money and a lot of wasted time.

The agency placement might introduce the idea of an ethical framework in the initial assessment meeting, but it is your job as part of making a therapeutic relationship with your client to reassure them that you are trustworthy, that you will respect their confidence (within certain limits which we will look at later on), that you will do your best for them and do your very best to do them no harm. They need to know that you will treat them fairly, not showing favouritism or judgement, that you will be 'strong' enough to hold their distress without breaking down, and that you will be consistent and reliable, you will be there every week when you say you will. It is important too that you take care of your own wellbeing so that you can be there for them.

> **REFLECTION**
>
> Why do you think it is that they say on an airplane to put your own breathing apparatus on first before you attempt to help a child or another person in need? How does this link to self-care in counselling?

Q How will a client know that I am committed to conduct myself like this, with integrity?

A Well you could just say all this to a client – but just saying it does not necessarily guarantee that you will carry it out. So a client would need a safeguard, and the safeguard is knowing that you are accountable to a nationally accepted framework of standards, that they have somewhere to go if they have a complaint about you and what you offer, and that there would be sanctions against you if you do not meet the professional standards you have signed up to, for example, the worst scenario could be that you would be removed from the membership list of the professional body – this could affect your chances of qualifying, practising and/or gaining employment.

Q Do I just say all this then when I first meet my client?

A It could overwhelm them on the first session, they may not take it all in, especially when they are feeling distressed. The key points are to name your ethical framework, in full, not just the initials because most clients won't know what the initials stand for – you could liken it to any other profession or trade. Explain briefly what adhering to an ethical framework means for you – doing your best, doing no harm, etc. Mention that there is a complaints vehicle, and refer to supervision. Also check with your agency what it is that they want you to cover and what might be referred to in the agency literature which is given to new clients.

REFLECTION

It is important to remember that any ethical framework is a set of guidelines, as no framework could cover every possible eventuality. If there is a complaint against you the complaints committee would consider the facts from all angles and refer to different aspects of the guidelines to determine if you acted ethically given the circumstances at that time with that client.

Q I'm just wondering where my theoretical approach fits in here, does that have any impact on how I practise ethically?

A It could well do, because as any framework is merely a set of guidelines, then these guidelines can be open to interpretation and different theoretical approaches could consider the same scenario in slightly different ways.

Q I don't really understand that, surely rules are rules?

A They are not rules as such with a definite black or white, yes/no answer. Remember we said at the beginning of the chapter that ethics is about the 'more complex and subtle exploration of fairness, rightness or equity'. These are subjective notions – not everyone would come to the same conclusion given the same scenario. For example, a classical psychodynamic counsellor tends to portray 'a blank canvas' and would not necessarily bring the client back to a safe place at the end of a session. They might consider this to be rescuing, whereas a person-centred counsellor might be more mindful of ensuring their client is composed and ready to go back into the outside world. What would you do?

APPLICATION OF ETHICAL AND LEGAL PROCESSES AND PROCEDURES

Q OK, so I understand about ethical considerations, but in practice what exactly do I have to do?

A Well, partly this depends on the ethical framework adhered to by your agency placement and by their own policies and procedures. So first of all familiarise yourself with that framework and with their other policies and ask your placement manager how they apply to you as a trainee counsellor.

REFLECTION

Some things to think about are:

- Does the agency require you to undergo their own specialised training?
- Do you have to have insurance, and if so what kind of insurance?
- How do you and your client make contact with each other, initially and on-going?
- What are the confidentiality guidelines?
- How many clients per week are you allowed to see?
- What are the record keeping arrangements?
- What are the risk assessment procedures, who would you disclose to for child protection or other safety concerns?

Q I remember from skills triad work last year we had to mention certain legal restrictions. Is this still the case and why?

A Yes, very much so. Now that you will be working with real clients then you need to think about the implications of some of these legal requirements.

ACTIVITY

Look up the following areas of legislation and consider how each one could impact on your work as a counsellor in your chosen agency.

- Mental health legislation
- Data protection regulations
- Child protection
- Counter terrorism and security (Prevent)
- Equal opportunities legislation
- Anti-discrimination legislation
- Health and safety
- Confidentiality
- Human rights
- Duty of care
- Safeguarding
- Adoption
- Disability
- Money laundering

Q This seems like an alarming list – do I really need to know all these?

A Well you don't have to know them all off by heart, but you do need to know which statutory guidance applies to your specific client work, and where to look for guidance should an issue arise. If something goes wrong it is no defence to say, 'I didn't know about that'.

Q I'm getting a bit confused now about the difference between what is ethical and what is legal. Can you help?

A Ok, so here is a little exercise to help you think about the differences.

EXERCISE

Consider these definitions:

Legal and ethical – following a just law

Legal and unethical – following an unjust law

Illegal and ethical – breaking an unjust law

Illegal and unethical – breaking a just law

Alegal and ethical – doing good where no law applies

Alegal and unethical – doing harm where no law applies

So which of the above terms would fit each of the following circumstances?

- A man gets out of his car and directs traffic away from an accident on the road
- An able bodied person parks in a space reserved for disabled drivers
- Keeping to a designated footpath when walking on private farmland
- Shooting at a burglar who enters your home
- Setting up as an independent counsellor having done a 10 week introductory course
- Moving UK savings to an offshore investment account
- Not mentioning to a client that you are a trainee counsellor

Q It's quite tricky isn't it, but I think I get the picture. Legal is when an actual law has been passed which covers that area, but ethical is about considering all aspects and weighing up the balance of good and harm.

A Yes, you've just about got it, and as you can see it is not clear cut. Just remember that all these policies, procedures and laws are there to protect you and your client.

Q Is there a minimum amount that I must say to my client regarding legislation?

A It depends on the agency in which you are working. It is generally considered good practice to highlight terrorism, money laundering and safeguarding of children and vulnerable adults.

Q You mentioned that my agency will have a set of its own policies and procedures. What might these be?

A One of them might be for example a policy about lone working, that is, being the only other person in a building when working with your client.

EXERCISE

Which legislation or agency policies do you think apply in each case below?

- Between assessment and the first session with you, your client has broken his leg and rings reception to say he is waiting outside at street level and cannot get up the stairs. What are your/the agency's responsibilities?
- A female client can only come to the agency after 7 pm in the evening. As a male counsellor you will be alone in the building as everyone else will have left by 6.30 pm. What are your agency guidelines?
- Your client talks about a time some years ago when they worked at a garage forecourt where they thought that money laundering was going on. What do you have to do?
- Whilst you are in reception a 14-year-old boy comes in and asks to see a counsellor at the agency. Does he need parental/adult consent?
- A client you have been working with for five sessions asks to see all the notes and information you have on them. How do you handle this?
- Your client has had six of the agreed eight sessions and is now asking for an additional four. How do you make a decision about this?
- You strongly suspect that the teenage client you are working with is involved with a gang of men grooming underage girls for sex. What do you do with this information?

As you are realising, sometimes the issues can be quite complex and have to be looked at from more than one side.

CASE SCENARIO

Your son went off to University in September. It's a long way from home – you drove him there and saw him settled into his room in the Hall of Residence and he seemed very perky. The following weekend you phoned him on his mobile, had a chat and he reported having made some new friends and had a good week. Since then you have phoned every weekend and now more recently two or three times a week and can't get hold of him. You have left messages but he doesn't ring back. You remember that he had a wobbly time when doing his A levels at Sixth Form College – he needed some additional learning support and went to see a counsellor for six weeks. This week you rang the University to try to speak to his lecturers or tutor, but they would not give you any information, saying that it would contravene the Data Protection Act as he is over 18. You've asked them to check if he is going to lectures, if he is coming out of his room, if he is unwell, if he is in counselling. They have said they will make enquiries but will not be able to report anything back to you. You are beside yourself with worry.

Explore this scenario from the point of view of each party – the parent, the son, the University tutors and the University counsellor.

CONTRACTING AND BOUNDARIES IN DIFFERENT AGENCY CONTEXTS

Q Last year we had to practise our 'opening' with each other in our triads, so what happens now?

A The same principles apply and yet of course one of the differences is that once you are working with real clients you will become part of a team of professionals – very different from practising skills in triads with your peers. Also many clients will never have experienced any counselling and know nothing about how it works and the client's best interests must always be at the heart of what we do.

REFLECTION

Think about how you feel about working as part of a team. Are you a good 'team player' or do you generally prefer to do things alone? What role do you play in teams – are you the one who naturally takes the lead, or are you a follower, do you wait to be told what to do, are you the ideas person but not good at following things through, do you like structure or prefer a relaxed way of working? What might be the personal challenges for you when working as part of a team?

Q How do my feelings about being a team member relate to agency boundaries?

A As part of the agency you will be 'signing up' to adhere to the boundaries which they set.

Q I'm happy to do that, what's the problem?

A There could be a problem if you don't quite agree with the agency boundaries – for example that a client pays for a missed session. Also, to widen your experience you may be working in more than one agency, and find that their boundaries are different.

Q I see, so what boundary issues do I need to be aware of?

A We'll run through some of them:

Ethical Framework – we've mentioned before that you need to know and be able to convey to your client which ethical framework informs your work. This and your theoretical approach are what inform many of the boundaries.

Legal requirements – Where it is the law, as noted above, you have to obey these legal requirements. These will also link in with the agency's own policies and procedures.

Assessment, allocation and referral of clients – as a trainee you will not be the first point of contact for a new client coming to the agency. Someone else will be responsible for conducting an initial meeting (face to face or by phone) and allocating that client to a counsellor. You need to be clear about your limits of proficiency and be prepared to refer the client elsewhere if necessary. There will be more about this in a later chapter.

Q What do you mean by 'limits of proficiency'?

A It means only practising when and where you have the appropriate qualifications, experience and training to work with certain clients or client issues. Your first few clients are likely to present with concerns at what CPCAB designate as Service Level A (clients experiencing difficult life events and life crises) or maybe just going into Level B (clients experiencing common mental health problems). Of course clients do not always tell the whole story at assessment, and other deeper issues may become apparent as the work progresses. Knowing when to refer is something to be discussed with your supervisor.

Time – you are used to managing sessions of 20 or 30 minutes in class – but in placement this will increase to an hour. Some agencies operate a

'50 minute hour', that is, you see your client for 50 minutes and then have 10 minutes for writing up notes. What does your agency do?

Number of sessions – the client contact may be open ended or time limited. If the latter, then how many sessions can you offer a client? Is this a rigid boundary? What if you disagree and want to offer more, who can you negotiate this with?

Confidentiality – you will be used to saying 'everything that we talk about will be confidential except …' So you need to be very clear now about your agency's confidentiality policy, what the exceptions are, when you can or must disclose and to whom. The client must know what these exceptions are and the reasons for disclosure.

Q Won't I just talk to my supervisor?

A No, not necessarily – there may be times when you might have to go straight to someone else such as the agency manager, a safeguarding officer, the police or a GP.

Q Oh, do you mean when there might be a suicide risk?

A Yes, but also in different scenarios. It might be a month until you see your supervisor so who does your agency say you should talk to? What is the line of accountability?

Q I've heard about something called 'team confidentiality' – what's that?

A Some agencies believe that in the best interests of their clients some information about a client must be shared across the team, for example, in an addictions unit this could include the group facilitator, key worker, activities manager, doctor. A case conference could involve a number of people needing to know about the progress of the client's counselling. This is sometimes called a multidisciplinary team. How do you feel about sharing information about your client?

ACTIVITY

Find out what the limits of confidentiality are in your agency. Discuss these with your supervisor so that he/she is fully aware of the boundaries within which you are working.

Payment – It must be clear in your counselling agreement what the fees are, if any, who takes the payment and when.

Q I'm not very happy about handling other people's money – will I have to do that?

A You may have to, if this is the agency's policy. So how will you handle this?

Supervision – your agency might provide supervision for you. They may require you to have more than the BACP minimum amount of one and a half hours per month. You might have to pay for this. This could be a boundary conflict for you if you do not agree with the amount of supervision required.

Record keeping – every agency must keep to the rules on Data Protection, yet within these they may have their own procedures. Here are three different ones:

- The agency just needs to know the start date, the end date and the number of sessions carried out.
- You must fill in weekly client notes containing brief details of the session and leave them in a locked filing cabinet in the agency. You can make process notes at home.
- Any and all notes you take must be left on the premises.

Q What if I want to write a case study on one of my clients?

A That's a good point. Again each agency has their own policy on this, so check with them and with your professional body, as to how you manage this course requirement.

Q There's quite a few things here to think about – anything else?

A It's worth thinking about 'touch', for example, handshakes, touch on the arm, a hug. Depending on the agency policy, interpretation of the ethical framework and your theoretical approach there can be variations in what is acceptable. See Chapter 15 for more details and find out what is applicable at your agency.

Gifts – clients sometimes like to show their appreciation for your services by bringing a present.

Q That's alright isn't it?

A Again it depends on the factors mentioned above.

REFLECTION

What message do you think the client is giving if they bring you a box of chocolates, a bunch of flowers or a Faberge egg?

Power and authority – clients tend to seek counselling when they are distressed and vulnerable. It could be easy for a counsellor to take advantage of this by exerting power and control and denying them their autonomy.

Q I wouldn't want to do that, so how might I do that accidently?

A It could be by the way you greet them, how you usher them into the room, where you invite them to sit, what you wear, how you 'manage' the session.

Q Can you give me an example of where I might break the boundaries around power and authority?

A The most common fault, particularly for a trainee, is to veer into advice giving, fixing it, and telling the client what to do. This could work against the ethical principle of promoting autonomy, may not be beneficial and could cause harm.

Relationship boundaries – the next chapter looks at the relationship between counsellor and client, how this relationship can be established, maintained and sometimes broken. Clients may have had bad experiences of relationships so it is up to the counsellor to maintain strong boundaries around the therapeutic relationship.

Q I've heard about clients testing boundaries, what does that mean?

A Clients can sometimes unconsciously test the boundaries by repeating ingrained patterns of behaviour, or purposefully trying to manipulate their counsellor to get the outcome they want. So it is up to the counsellor to be on the alert for when this is happening, and use it as part of the therapy.

Fitness to practice – counselling is demanding work and if we feel in any way diminished by lack of skills, knowledge, resilience, or health (physically or emotionally) to practise safely and effectively our ethical framework will inform us that we must not work with clients. Specific agencies may have their own guidelines around this too. For example if working in a specialist bereavement agency it is very likely that you will not be allowed to see clients for quite some time if you have had a significant bereavement in your own life. The amount of time out depends on the agency. Coupled with this, you might have to attend a 'return to practice' interview when you wish to resume client work.

Q So if a client has needs which seem to be beyond my professional capabilities, or if I don't feel well, either physically or mentally, then I must stop working and/or refer my client on to someone else?

A Yes that is right, and this is where good supervision comes in as your supervisor will be able to help you determine if you are fit to practise or not. Also other people at the agency, remember what we said a while back about working as a member of a team – so enlist the support of others and draw on your team mates' expertise and experience.

Q If I have an emotional problem myself, say like a bereavement you mentioned, or a relationship breakup, or something my client is working through which triggers old behaviours of mine, what should I do?

A This is where personal therapy comes in, that is, your own counselling. Your training course will require you to attend a specified number of personal therapy sessions, and there might be times when you need additional counselling to work on a particular area that has cropped up.

REFLECTION

Consider the differences between supervision and personal therapy for a practising counsellor. What is the role of the supervisor, and that of the counsellor? Think about what you could take to each and why.

Reflect on the relationship between your use of personal counselling and the effectiveness of your client work.

RISK ASSESSMENT AND REFERRAL

Q We've already looked at this haven't we?

A Yes, we have discussed some of this above, but there are a few other things to think about. We mentioned that someone else in your agency will carry out the initial assessment of a client.

Q They do this so that I can be allocated someone who is within my level of competence – is that right?

A Partly yes, it is to assess the needs of the client such as what their concerns are and what help they are seeking. It is also about their readiness to enter counselling and assessing risks, for example, if they are posing a risk to themselves or others, or if they are heavily medicated or misusing substances.

Q How does that happen then, does someone just ask them a load of questions?

A It does tend to be quite question orientated because it is a fact finding session, yet also it can be the beginning of a counselling relationship.

Q Yet you said that it would not be the counsellor doing the assessment.

A That's right, but if the potential client has a bad experience of the assessment then they might never come back and engage in actual counselling sessions. In that respect it is the beginning of their relationship with counselling.

Q Who carries out the assessment?

A It is usually a more experienced counsellor in the agency, or it might be the practice manager, or the placement manager or an assessment officer. Different agencies call them different things, but the role is the same – to discuss with the client what it is they are seeking and to determine if they are in the right place emotionally and physically to engage effectively with counselling. Then to allocate (or refer) them to the most appropriate counsellor who is available.

Q How is this done then?

A This depends on the agency, the type of client issues being dealt with, and the theoretical modality favoured by the placement. It might be through a fairly informal two way chat, or it might be done by using a structured written form that the assessor will work through with the client.

It usually entails taking a personal history of the client, that is, what has brought them to this place at this time, what are their concerns, what support do they have in their life and what are they expecting out of counselling. It will probably include making a note of their GP, and discussing any medication they may be taking. Some theoretical approaches, as well as funding applications, will favour a risk assessment questionnaire where the client's details feed into a scale or table which ranks them in terms of a number of factors, including the likelihood of risk. This may be computerised.

ACTIVITY

Find out about assessment tools such as Core, PHQ-9, GAD-7, DSM-V, the bereavement compass and any others which may be used in your agency. Compare and contrast them with 'informal' assessments and consider which ones fit best with your theoretical approach.

Q So the assessment is a bit like a doctor making a diagnosis.

A Yes, it is a bit. It is about gathering information and making an informed decision as to what should happen next in the best interests of the client. You may have heard of the 'medical model' which is very much about assessment, diagnosis and treatment. It is not always quite so clear cut in counselling and this is where making a team decision can be very helpful.

Q How does the person doing the assessment decide who to allocate the client to?

A This depends on a number of factors – some of them might be the nature of the client's problems and which counsellor is most experienced or best qualified to work with these, the availability of client and counsellor and how these match up, agency waiting lists, geographical area if clients are seen at home.

Q As the counsellor, when I am allocated a particular client, how much of this assessment will be made available to me?

A Again this depends on the agency – you might get a copy of the full assessment, or just a brief referral note with the bare bones of the issue and essential details about the client. However assessment is commonly believed to be an on-going process so you will be finding out more about the client and their issues all the time when you are working together, and discussing this with your supervisor or others in a multidisciplinary team.

Q I'm a bit worried about risks to self or others. I'm really concerned that a client of mine might be self-harming or even might take their own life.

A Sadly this can be a real concern with quite a few clients. However that is why an assessment is carried out. The assessor is using their skills, knowledge and experience to determine the likelihood of a client taking their own life, and as a novice counsellor you should not be allocated clients where there is a known history of suicide attempts or a high probability of your client taking their own life. Of course that is not to say, as mentioned before, that this possibility could still happen.

REFLECTION

It is very useful to reflect on your thoughts and feelings about suicide.

- When the word suicide is heard what does that conjure up for you – what images come to mind, what feelings do you have, are any specific thoughts triggered?
- Have there been any suicides in your family or amongst close friends? How did these affect you and what impact will it have on your counselling work?
- If you have no personal experience of suicides, what are the challenges for you? Do talk about these in your training group and with your supervisor and agency manager.

Q What do I do if I think my client is at risk of serious self-harm or suicide?

A Your agency will have its own specific procedures and there will be a line of accountability.You will receive training in your own training group, and hopefully at the agency too, on how to react if a client tells you they are considering taking their own life. This can come quite naturally during your contracting when discussing harm and self-harm. The usual advice is to be open about this with the client, gently find out the extent of their wish to end their life, for example, is it a natural reaction to losing a loved one, that they don't want to go on living without them, or an enduring struggle to cope with life's challenges and a need to find peace?

Q How would you suggest I do that? It sounds very daunting.

A This is one of the reasons why establishing a sound therapeutic relationship from the beginning is so important. If the client feels held and heard by you they are more likely to trust you and disclose what is happening for them.

Q Do I need to know what they plan to do?

A It is helpful to establish if they have made a plan, if they have gathered the resources to carry it through (for example, been collecting tablets), and what their trigger points are. You can then find out what support is already in place or what needs to be put in place.

Q What sort of support might that be?

A It could be that they alert family or friends when they recognise that they are in a very vulnerable state. It might be asking or giving permission for you to ring their GP or the mental health services when you sense they need additional support. You will want to talk to your supervisor when this is happening, and it could be urgent.

Q I only see my supervisor once a month though, so the next appointment might not be soon enough?

A Most supervisors will agree that you can contact them between appointments. Otherwise talk to your agency manager straight away, and/or ring the GP directly or a mental health worker, or the police if you feel that the client is in immediate danger. Remember the guidelines in your ethical framework – you are committed to doing the best for your client and doing no harm. Sometimes this might include referring the client to an alternative service and this can be discussed with the client and with the placement.

NB – different agencies may take a different view about clients taking their own life, so do check out the guidelines in your particular placement.

> **REFLECTION**
>
> It is not now appropriate to use the term 'committed suicide', rather that a client has taken their own life. Why do you think this is the case? What difference does it make – to you as a counsellor, to the client, to family and friends of someone affected by a suicide?

Q Can I do specific training around working with suicide ideation?

A Your agency may well offer their own training, and many other organisations do deliver short trainings on this area of work. Some parts of the country have an 'Applied Suicide Intervention Skills Training' (ASIST) programme delivered by the NHS which is open to anyone working with vulnerable people.

Q I notice you said 'refer' just then, can referral mean different things?

A It can be a bit confusing yes. When a client is initially assessed in an agency they can then be referred to an appropriate and available counsellor. Perhaps allocated might be a less confusing term. If the counselling has started and a different service or professional support is felt to be more appropriate then a client can be *referred* to that other service. So in both cases it means passing people on in some way. Of course a client may ask to be referred because they don't get on with you, they prefer a different sort of help, or their issues change.

Q 'Passing on' a client sounds a bit cold and could be seen as rejecting them couldn't it?

A You would always be doing it for the client's best interests and in collaboration with the client themselves, the agency you are in and the service or professional receiving them. It is good to think of them as a precious gift to be given rather than a tiresome package to be got rid of!

WORKING AS A PROFESSIONAL

Q It seems to me that I will not be working on my own in the agency placement. Is that right?

A You will have gathered from what we have been saying that other people are involved in many aspects of the work. These include your supervisor, agency placement manager and a range of other professionals, for example, GP, mental health team, client employer, other closely linked support agencies.

ACTIVITY

Find out who else your placement has links with in terms of other professionals, services and organisations that they might commonly refer on to. Find out what the protocols are for seeking help or advice from these, or for referring a client on.

Q You mentioned protocols there and I have heard that there's something called codes of conduct too. What are these?

A Just as your ethical framework gives you guidance on ethical conduct, your agency will likely have *codes of conduct* relating to how you behave and interact in the agency and with others. These guide you on how to keep to professional standards of conduct.

EXERCISE

Imagine that you are embarking on your personal therapy for your training course. You have had your assessment appointment and been allocated a counsellor. You have been sitting in the waiting room of the agency ready to be called into one of the small rooms for your first appointment. It is now ten past the appointed hour. Suddenly the outer door opens with a flourish and bangs back against the wall causing you to jump. When you look up you see a rather wild haired young man in ripped jeans wearing a vest top and sporting tattoos on his shoulder. He is talking quite loudly and angrily on his phone and you gather he is talking about an agency client, you hear a name but don't recognise it. Then he drops his papers on the floor and they scatter near your feet. In an effort to be helpful you bend down to pick them up and notice your name on the top of one of them. Then you realise that this is your counsellor!

List everything that goes against professional standards of conduct.

You have probably listed issues around punctuality, behaviour, dress and appearance, confidentiality, competence, respect.

Q So would I not be able to wear what I want then?

A It is more a question of keeping to the norms of the agency and wearing what is appropriate for the client group, the location of the agency and the work itself. Remember that you are in a working environment and although you may be volunteering it is still work and must be treated as such. Your clients deserve your respect in whatever way that presents itself. See Chapter 15 for more information.

REFLECTION

What might be the conflict, if any, between you 'being yourself' and maintaining a professional manner and appearance? Consider how codes of conduct compare in various agencies in your training group.

Q That makes me think back to my ethical framework. Are there links here?

A Yes, there are – self-respect and respect for others is referred to in all frameworks. Integrity is also important – you have responsibilities to others, to your clients, to the agency, to your supervisor and wider professions in the community. Working as part of a team can be enormously supportive and enjoyable, and it is essential to collaborate with others to get the work done efficiently and effectively for the good of the client. Don't think you can go it alone.

REFLECTION

You have lived in your local community for a long time and know a lot of people. The church counselling service offered you a placement. Last Saturday you celebrated a friend's birthday at the pub and next day discovered that someone else had posted pictures on social media which included you looking worse for wear. How does this fit with presenting a professional standard of behaviour in front of clients?

Q All this sounds very grown up, what can I do to not feel so nervous?

A You are right, it is grown up, you are entering a profession and an adult world of work. The most important thing to do is communicate – talk to everyone who can help you and give you advice inside and outside the agency (whilst respecting confidentiality of course). Make sure that all your communications are clear and concise whether that be face to face, email or telephone. Ensure that you know the protocols for having contact with clients inside and outside the agency, and vice versa. Make a record of any action taken before you forget it. If in doubt seek help and err on the side of caution and safety rather than carelessness.

Q Anything else?

A Counselling is quite a unique occupation in that you are the only one coming face to face with your client on a regular basis, so if there is a team meeting or case conference, or you are discussing your client with your supervisor you will often have to make professional judgements based on what you know, as others may not have had the same opportunities to get to know the client so personally. This is part of your responsibility to clients so don't be afraid to say what you think and feel based on your professional opinion.

SUMMARY

In order to work safely and ethically as a counselling professional you need to:

- Identify and abide by the ethical framework adhered to in your agency placement.
- Familiarise yourself with the legalities around counselling in your placement(s) and work accordingly.
- Find out about any other agency policies, procedures and professional standards of conduct relevant to you as a counsellor in this agency.
- Make yourself aware of and adhere to the boundary limitations in your agency placement.
- Understand and work within the assessment and referral processes in your agency.
- Ensure you know what to do if there is a risk of suicide or any other emergency with a client.
- Monitor your fitness to practise and limits of proficiency.
- Demonstrate team work skills with others.

2
The Therapeutic Relationship

The following chapter looks at how to establish and maintain a therapeutic relationship, and looks at its importance in counselling. When you read Chapter 4 on the user-centred approach, you may find that there are some overlaps to the ideas here as both areas are very connected. Differing modalities and theoretical approaches work with the relationship in slightly different ways, but research shows that the relationship between the client and the counsellor has a significant impact on successful outcomes of therapy. Different agency settings will also influence the nature of the therapeutic relationship.

Q What do you mean by the therapeutic relationship?

A The therapeutic relationship is the relationship that exists between the client and their counsellor. It is this relationship that allows the client to make the changes they need, and is shown, whatever theoretical approach is used, to be of significance in positive client outcomes.

Q So what kind of things do I need to be aware of in relation to the therapeutic relationship?

A Research has shown there are a number of different factors, some of which relate to the client and some which relate to the counsellor. It's important to always remember that this is a relationship and, as with all relationships, more than one person is involved. What are called 'client factors' and 'therapist factors' are both important and both need to be taken into account. The relationship needs to be collaborative and involve both individuals from the very beginning.

Q So it sounds like getting the relationship right is very important?

A Yes. Mick Cooper in his book *Essential Research Findings in Counselling and Psychotherapy* states:

> The quality of the therapeutic relationship is closely associated with therapeutic outcomes, across both relationally orientated and non-relationally orientated therapies. (Cooper, 2008: 125)

This means that it doesn't matter what your theoretical model is, it's the therapeutic relationship that makes the difference.

It can be useful to think of the therapeutic relationship as the container in which the work takes place. So if we are able to provide a container that feels safe, and one that allows us to trust our client and the client to trust us, then the work of therapy can really take place.

Q If we trust the client? I hadn't thought about that. Do you mean that we feel safe in the room with them?

A It's partly that. If we are working alone in a building at night with a client of the opposite sex who is maybe very flirtatious, or just seems very angry, then we may feel unsafe and untrusting and it's going to be difficult to fully relax and really listen to what the client is saying. But I was really meaning in a more therapeutic way. Do we trust our client to engage with the work? Do we trust our client to be honest with us and to like us enough to keep coming back to us? And if we don't, we need to be talking to our supervisor about our feelings. The relationship is a two way thing, and I will keep saying this through this section.

Q Ok. So how do I begin? It sounds like the first session may be really important. Are there things I need to be particularly aware of?

REFLECTION

Think about what makes you feel comfortable when you meet someone for the first time. It may be such factors as:

- Tone of voice
- Their welcoming manner
- Their smile
- Their friendliness
- Their willingness to put you at your ease
- Their confidence and comfortableness in their own skin

> Many of these factors can be difficult to pin point – quite often they are a felt sense, rather than anything we can directly identify, but it is still worth giving them some consideration. However we also have to maintain our professionalism within this role, so being friendly is different from becoming our client's friend.

A The relationship begins on the first contact with the client whether this be in person, by email or on the phone. This will be influenced by your agency placement and how they set up initial contact between you and your client. It can be worth thinking about those qualities that we reflected on above and how you present yourself in this initial contact. I would imagine you will want to come across as professional, but also appear warm, welcoming and friendly. Your prospective client may be feeling very anxious and scared about coming into therapy. It can feel very scary to talk to a total stranger about something that is possibly very personal, and that the client may not have talked about to anyone else. It's a great privilege to be in this place of trust. It could be that you as the counsellor also feel some anxiety. You are about to meet someone you have never met before, and you may feel unsure what to expect, even if you have some details about the client and their reason for being referred to you by your line manager.

Q Mm mm … I'm beginning to see what you mean now. I had some counselling a few years ago and the first counsellor I saw was so scary. She reminded me of one of my teachers who was always supercritical. I found it really hard to talk to her. And she was so prim and proper! I just felt really silly and felt I had to mind my p's and q's.

A We will talk more later about what happens if we remind our clients of someone they used to know, or still do know, or our client reminds us of someone we once knew. But it sounds like this person you saw made you feel quite inadequate without even saying anything. You say your first counsellor – did you see someone else?

Q Yes, I did. They were lovely. As soon as they opened the door for me, they smiled and shook my hand. They showed me where to sit, and asked if I was comfortable and introduced themselves and asked how it felt to be there. They were very normal, and seemed quite relaxed. And they seemed really happy to see me – not in a noisy excited way, but just in a very welcoming manner.

A It sounds like they behaved like a normal human being – just being warm and friendly and it sounds like you felt they cared about you.

Often the first session is about setting the contract with our client and establishing the professional boundaries of the working relationship. So it can be worth thinking about how we do that – we need to involve our clients in this process, and not just dictate a whole heap of information to them. Some areas may not be up for negotiation as your agency may have very clear rules on cancellation policies, etc. And it may be that you too have limitations around when you can see your clients. If you are only available Wednesday afternoons, then obviously you cannot negotiate another time with your client. However, if Wednesday afternoons are a problem for your client, it does mean that you take that on board and discuss with them the practicalities of attending counselling with you. It may be that there are other alternatives available (your agency may have other counsellors available on other days). Exploring client concerns and ensuring that clients really understand the contract enables the relationship to get off to a good start, allowing the client to be heard, acknowledged and empowered.

Different agencies sometimes have different boundaries, sometimes depending on the client group. Whilst you need to work within the boundaries set by that particular agency, you do also need to find where the boundaries sit comfortably with you, and where they don't, and it can be really helpful to explore with your supervisor the issues raised or anything you might feel uncertain about. This is particularly important if there is something in the contract that is different from what you have been taught in your training. It may be that the agency rules do not sit comfortably alongside what you are being taught on your course, but exploration with tutors and supervisors can help you to work in a way that sits more comfortably with you. If it's too far out of your comfort zone then it may be worth looking for a different placement.

REFLECTION

Maybe you have had some personal therapy yourself. (It's certainly very useful for all trainee counsellors to have this experience and to feel what it is like to be the client!) If so, think back to what it was like for you when you first met your therapist. How easy was it to tell them about why you were coming into counselling? What kind of thoughts did you have? Did you worry that the counsellor may think you were being silly or stupid? Or maybe you are someone who is so used to not talking about things that it was just hard to say what you needed to say. Or did you worry about upsetting the counsellor? And how did the counsellor respond to you – did you feel comfortable with them or uncomfortable? And what were the contributory factors that left you feeling like that? If you felt uncomfortable what could they have done to make you feel better about talking to them?

Q We have talked a great deal about boundaries within counselling throughout all my training. I think I understand what they are quite well now, but could you clarify in case I'm missing anything.

A One of the most basic boundaries is the time boundary – what time will you meet, what day of the week and how often. Then it can be useful to discuss what contact is permissible outside of the session, when might you contact the client and how, and when can the client contact you, and how. Also what happens if you were to unexpectedly meet somewhere outside the therapy room? Would your client expect you to greet them? What happens if they feel really depressed and want to talk to someone – clients do not always understand we are not available outside the session and it can be useful to make it clear within the initial contracting that this is the case. Other areas that are covered by boundaries, are cancellation policies, what happens if the client keeps not turning up for sessions, or what happens if the client turns up under the influence of drugs or alcohol. Different agencies have different policies on all of these areas so to some extent you will be guided by this, but also there may be areas your tutors have insisted that you cover and your professional body requires you to cover, such as disclosing the fact you are a trainee counsellor. Another important area is confidentiality and its limits – again this can vary from agency to agency, but it is important to be very clear and accurate in explaining to your clients what can be kept confidential and what can't, and to whom you would break confidentiality. As stated in the previous chapter, good practice would suggest that you make clear that you work within an ethical framework, and with which governing body you are aligned, and that you have supervision and what information would be shared with your supervisor. Whilst all of these are very important areas, it's also important to remember that when you are discussing these with your client you are also establishing a relationship. This part of the proceedings is often referred to as a working alliance.

Q We have spent quite a lot of time looking at this in class. And I think I have some understanding around it but I hadn't related it to the therapeutic relationship. In fact during triad sessions it often feels it gets in the way!

A It can feel like that during a skills session. However, it is actually intrinsic to the formation of a healthy and safe therapeutic relationship. Petruska Clarkson in her integrative approach refers to this as the 'vas' or the container. If this is not 'solid' then the client is not being held in a safe manner, and it becomes more difficult to maintain the relationship.

Q What if I make the boundaries really clear when we first meet, but then the client ignores them? I'm thinking about how they may try and contact me outside the session so they can have a chat, or if we meet at the pub or in the street.

A Clients sometimes test the boundaries or push against them as you say. It is your responsibility to find a way of dealing with this, but supervision can be a useful place to begin to explore what is actually happening and different ways of dealing with it. Sometimes we need to go back to our clients and explain again, and try to help them understand that it isn't optional and is for their safety, and yours.

Q What about the boundaries within the agency? What if there are other people who I have to share information with?

A The role of the counsellor can vary slightly in different agencies. This can relate to whether you get paid, whether your expenses are paid, the type of clients you might see and the presenting issues that are dominant, and whether there are other people in the agency who do different work than the counsellors. It may be that at times you have to work with other people in the agency in some capacity or share certain information. The agency should make all of these areas clear to you when you start your placement with them.

REFLECTION

Now we have talked about confidentiality and the different areas it needs to address, have a think about what it is you know you need to cover, from the information here, and from the suggestions by your tutors, and from the agency if you have already begun your placement. Then think about how you might explain this to your client in a way that builds the relationship. It can also be useful to think about what your own needs are in this area too. So if you were to meet a client out of the therapeutic space, what would be comfortable for you? What contact outside of sessions would you find comfortable, and what is it about yourself you would want to keep confidential? It can be worth looking at the ethical guidelines of your professional body for further information about what they see as good practice, but it is also important to check in with our own boundaries and what we as practitioners feel is ok. Where this doesn't meet with ethical practice, see how you feel you can work and explore with your supervisor and tutors.

Q It sounds quite a big thing to get right. What if I do something that upsets the client or get something really wrong?

A Counsellors are human and will get things wrong. Even very experienced counsellors still mess up now and again. It's how we handle the ruptures that is the key and often when well-handled these ruptures can enhance the relationship rather than damage it. Our humanness in turn gives the client the permission to get things wrong too. This, however, is not an excuse to be careless and assume that it doesn't matter. It does. So often our clients will have been damaged by relationships where others appeared to be careless in their treatment or them, and we don't want to create further feelings of rejection, or abandonment, or that we don't like them or care about them. It is also important that when we do get things wrong, we do explore this with our supervisors. It can be indicative of our own unconscious processes coming in, or something with our client we are not fully aware of. Again, it can be a source of valuable information!

Q Suppose everything is going well but then I get sick and have to take time off, or I go away on holiday. Or my client does?

A Breaks need to be well prepared for and when possible advance notice should be given when it's the counsellor who is going on holiday or when you know you are not going to be available at the usual time for the client. Many clients will have the experience of people in their lives being unreliable and if we don't give advance warning they may think we just don't care about them, or they have upset us, or we are bored with them. None of those things are going to help our clients to trust us and sometimes much of the work we do with clients is what is called 'reparative'.

Q We talked about that in class recently. My tutor said it's like being the good parent or carer that the client never had.

A Yes. That's right – but also any other relationship that maybe did not work out well for the client and has left them mistrustful of others. It may even be that if you are only able to work short term with the client, the only real work that you are able to do is to show them that counselling is an ok place they can come to and be supported and held within the relationship. This will then leave them in a place where counselling has been a positive experience and something they will feel good about accessing again when they are able to.

Q So what happens if the client takes a break from the counselling? I can imagine that I would struggle if the client just suddenly stopped coming or missed a session – I might feel it was my fault and I had done something wrong.

A In the initial contracting, cancellation policies and how DNAs (did not arrive) will be treated, should have been fully addressed, usually with agency guidance. This means that when the client doesn't turn up for a session you have a firm foundation to begin to address what has happened. If the client does not show up again, supervision can be used to explore your own feelings of unfinished business (self-care) and what has happened. It's very easy to feel that you somehow got something very wrong in this situation, but there can be any number of reasons a client doesn't show, including that they are just not ready to go into counselling yet or if they have attended a few sessions, they have gone as far as they are able at this point in time.

If the client does return, explore what happened, remind them of the contract, and look at what can be put into place in the future, if necessary, if a similar situation occurs. This can also be a good time to explore how they are finding therapy – is it what they expected? How are they finding working with you? All of these things can be used to strengthen the relationship, and to deepen understanding of your client. Earlier in the book, we talked about boundaries, and boundaries are important for the relationship and again can strengthen it, by keeping you and your client safe. There is a reparative element to this too as many clients will not have had clear boundaries, or may not have had any boundaries that were understanding of their needs.

Q What happens if I say something wrong in the session? I am thinking if I can see that I have upset the client, or if I have worded things badly and it comes out in the wrong way.

A These moments can be very uncomfortable for both client and counsellor. It can be the client's body language, the expression on their face, their tone of voice which changes or a flash of anger in their eyes, their lack of engagement for the rest of the session, all of which can indicate that the client is not happy with something we have said. Whatever happens, don't ignore it but acknowledge it. If you know you just said something wrong – apologise instantly. This could be as simple as getting a family member's name wrong, mishearing something they said, or it could be something much more serious like getting your client's name wrong. Or it could be that the client just did not like what you said in response to something they said. Whatever it is, it can be really useful in building the relationship, and understanding the client, to check it out thoroughly. And as always in these situations, explore with your supervisor to gain further understanding.

EXAMPLE

In my early days I was working with a client who spoke at some length about a painful issue. I paraphrased back what I thought I heard, but at one point, as the words came out of my mouth, I realised it sounded super critical and offensive. I stopped mid-sentence and was totally congruent, saying how that came out totally wrong and I was so sorry, it sounded really offensive and that wasn't what I had

> meant at all! My client initially looked startled – understandably – but then started laughing at my embarrassment. It turned out what I had said gave him a different perspective on the situation, and my embarrassment shifted the power balance to one where we became more equal. (We will talk more about power later.) The relationship became much more relaxed and he clearly was much more at ease with me from that time.

It can be worth remembering that everything that happens in the room can be used to deepen the relationship. As I said earlier, this isn't an excuse that anything goes – or that it is ok to make mistakes. To continually paraphrase in a way that sounds offensive would not only be damaging to the client, but would destroy any therapeutic relationship.

Q That sounds like the kind of thing I would do, then try to make a joke out of it!

A In the above example I gave, I mentioned laughter. Laughter in therapy can be healing. If a client comes from a family background where laughter is seen as 'silly' then learning to laugh and be silly can be an essential part of the therapy. And laughter can be important in developing a relationship. However there is a big difference between appropriate laughter, and laughter that is avoidance of painful subjects. When clients escape into laughter or make a joke every time something uncomfortable is mentioned, this needs exploring. But only when the relationship is well enough established to be able to do this. And making jokes can be ok, but only if we have a strong sense of our client and how they work, and what they are likely to find humorous and not. And only once there is a strong relationship in place.

Q I was told off in class for making inappropriate jokes. I think it's something I do when I am uncomfortable but I am beginning to understand it is not always ok to do that. This relationship thing sounds more and more complicated.

A As with much in counselling, on one level it is very, very simple. And yet at another level, it is anything but. With all of these areas, supervision needs to be used to monitor our responses and to look at any underlying issues, and to examine where we might be struggling in our relationships with our clients. This might mirror our own struggles in relationships with people outside of the therapy room. However it is really worth working on these areas, more than anything else, because a strong therapeutic relationship allows us to challenge our clients and take them to uncomfortable areas and work at a much deeper level.

Q All of this is making me think how difficult it could be when I get to the point of finishing work with the client. If we have a relationship, that could feel quite difficult for both of us.

A Yes, it could. Sometimes it can feel sad to say goodbye to our clients, knowing that we may never see them again and it would be inappropriate to have any other contact. It is important however, that the endings are well handled and not avoided. So often clients have not had an experience of 'good endings' in their lives. People for whom they have cared for have suddenly left and never said goodbye. And that can also be true for the counsellor. It is therefore really important that the ending of therapy is well managed so clients have some understanding of how that can feel, and can in future manage other endings as they arise. This is something that should ideally be discussed in the very first session and then regularly checked up on in the work, so the client knows when the ending is going to come. It can be worthwhile thinking about how the ending can take shape, what it is the client needs from the ending for it to feel ok. This is a really good time to review, and check what the client is taking away from the work you have done together. And to check that they feel ok about the work finishing – if they don't, what support can be put into place, where else can they get support and maybe who else can they talk to. Before it gets to the point of ending it may be worthwhile to check out their past experiences of ending. Sometimes clients tend to avoid endings at all costs, and if you know this in advance, you can possibly put something in place to encourage the client to attend their final session.

REFLECTION

Think about your own experiences of endings and, if you have had therapy before, how was the ending managed there. What would be your ideal way of finishing work with a client? How might you feel when ending the work together? What kind of feelings might come up for you? What might it remind you of in your own life?

Q You said earlier that different theories work with the relationship in different ways. Can you say more about that?

A Yes, different theoretical modalities do work slightly differently with the therapeutic relationship, placing emphasis on different areas. I like what John McLeod says in his *Introduction to Counselling* which is that:

> It is useful to think about the different types of style of therapeutic relationship in terms of images, rather than as lists of attributes or theoretical models. (2003: 297)

He goes on to say that all of these ideas, whether of Rogers or Freud, come from the imagination and are just different ways of describing something intangible, or implicit that is happening in the relationship. To me that means that if we put on our Freud glasses we will see it in one way, but if we put on our Rogers glasses then we will see it differently, but neither are wrong or an absolute truth.

Q That helps me to think of it in those terms. It feels easier to understand why people have different opinions. My core theory is Person Centred, so I think the approach of that is very much that the relationship is everything.

A Yes you are right. In Person-Centred approaches, and other humanistic approaches such as Gestalt, the emphasis is on the relationship between counsellor and client above all else. Rogers' theory was that if certain conditions were put into place – the core conditions of congruence, empathy and unconditional positive regard – then individuals would move towards self-actualisation. The core conditions are now recognised across all theoretical models as being important in establishing the basis of any therapeutic relationship. And whilst this sounds quite a simple idea, to do it well, is actually quite difficult and requires a lot of work on the self to develop self-awareness and understanding of our own reactions and responses.

Rogers believed that if these conditions were met, and all expectations of the client were left out of the room then the client would find their own way through their problems. It puts the emphasis on the client as expert, not the therapist. The therapist's role is to walk alongside and be with, a way of being rather than doing.

Q Yes, sometimes it can be difficult to just sit with the client and to hold those core conditions. It seemed such an easy idea when I first learned about it, but I'm realising it is really not that straightforward. One of the ideas I really struggle with is transference. It seems so complicated and yet we talk about it a lot in class.

A Transference is one of the most important ideas in psychodynamic theory, and was also recognised by Rogers. Psychodynamic theory tends to emphasise the therapist as the blank screen on which other relationships can be projected. This means that unresolved issues from other relationships can be played out in the therapeutic relationship. Here the importance of transference and counter transference is stressed. Earlier you mentioned how your first therapist reminded you of your teacher whom you found scary. Whilst transference is more of an unconscious process than this, and it would be a situation where you would not understand, or maybe even be aware that you were reacting to the person as you would have reacted to your teacher. In this situation the therapist would pick up that something odd was happening in the relationship, and bring it into the client's awareness. Then through exploration, an understanding could be gained of why that reaction was occurring. Counter transference would be when the therapist responds to you out of character, as if they were your teacher. They would then hopefully pick up that something was out of sync and again explore this with the client. It's important to recognise that this is an unconscious process, but one which can impact on the relationship quite profoundly. If our client perceives us in some way as someone in the past who betrayed their trust, this is obviously going to make it harder for them to trust us, and if they struggle to fully trust us, then it can make it difficult for them to really engage with the work in the sessions. This is why transference, and counter transference is such a big deal in the therapeutic settings.

Q Can you quickly say something about counter transference?

A Yes that can impact on the relationship too. So if for instance we find ourselves reacting in an unusual way to our client, it may be because we are responding to the way they are responding to us, for example, if they are really angry with a parent, and we remind them of that parent, unconsciously, then we might find ourselves reacting to them as if they were a stroppy child! If however we can recognise what's happening and explore it with the client 'I have a sense that you are really angry with me, and I wonder what is happening. Do I possibly remind you of someone?' This then allows the client to explore what was previously unconscious material, and it will also make them feel really seen and understood which will deepen the therapeutic relationship.

Q Wow! That sounds very powerful, but also like I have to really know myself and how I react to things. It seems I have to understand what my own triggers are.

A Yes, I would say that is true. I would say it is really significant in developing a strong therapeutic relationship, whatever modality you are coming from. Should we look at some other theories? How about Cognitive Behaviour Therapy?

Q I hear a lot about that in different settings but mainly in the NHS. It seems like that is not so dependent on the relationship, is that right?

A No, relationship is just as important here as it is in any other theoretical approach, although because of the work load that many therapists who work in this way carry, and the limited time they have available, it can seem like it is not as important. However, there is a growing recognition that without the relationship in place it is less successful. At the end of the day, if you don't like the person in front of you, or if you feel they don't care about you, or are not very friendly, then it's going to be difficult to really talk to them or take on board anything they say to you.

Q When we studied psychodynamic theory in class we looked at Object Relations theory and Attachment theory. From what I remember they could be useful in understanding the therapeutic relationship.

A Absolutely. In Object Relations theory, the therapist becomes the transitional object or the secure base from which our clients can finish their growing up. Attachment theory was developed by John Bowlby and became influential within psychodynamic counselling but because of its importance, many modalities also recognise its value in helping us in understanding an individual's ability to relate to others. Bowlby talked about secure attachment, insecure avoidant attachment and insecure ambivalent attachment. As a therapist it can be very useful to have some understanding of our own attachment patterns because they are likely to be mirrored within the therapeutic setting. It can also be useful in understanding our client's ability to form some sort of attachment to us and what to look out for within the relationship to avoid a possible rupture to the therapeutic alliance.

Q We've talked about using more than one theory in class. How would that impact on the relationship ... If I have two different theories that work differently that could be very confusing couldn't it?

A Yes, it could be – both for yourself and your client. That's why it can be useful to work with a model of integration that allows us to weave different theories together in a cohesive way that allows us to make sense of what is happening in the room. One of the most well-known integrative models (we talk about integrating different theoretical models in Chapter 6) is Clarkson's therapeutic relationship integrative model which stresses the different relationships present in the client–counsellor interaction. This is also a useful model for understanding the therapeutic relationship and the many different aspects that it contains. The different relationships she talks about are the working alliance between client and counsellor, the I–Thou relationship, the reparative relationship, the transpersonal relationship and finally the transferential/counter-transferential relationship. Placing emphasis on these differing relationships then allows the use of differing theoretical models to enhance that particular type of relationship that is taking place A more recently developed model of integration that very much focuses on the relationship with the client is Pluralistic Therapy, developed by John McLeod and Mick Cooper.

Q I am getting a real sense of the differences but also the things that are similar. Are there other theories that are different?

A There are so many, many theories now, but many overlap and just as Object Relations and Attachment could be seen to fall under the psychodynamic approach, other theories would fall under the same umbrella as Rogers, which is Humanistic. It might be worth just mentioning three more approaches here. Firstly Transactional Analysis, which again places great emphasis on the relationship as does Person Centred. However, an awareness of the different ego states and transactions that take place within the therapeutic setting can be used to enhance the relationship. An example would be that clients would be encouraged to be in adult ego state throughout the contracting process. Or the therapist may see the client behaving in quite childlike ways when challenged by the therapist. This could then be used to inform the relationship, but also give a sense of how the client responds in the outside world in other relationships. Gestalt works very much with the here and now, and what is most in the field at any point, along with using imagery and body work. Some techniques in Gestalt are very powerful, as in other theories, and for them to be used successfully, the client needs to feel very safe and held, so again the relationship is essential.

Q Someone in my class is really into the spiritual side of things and keeps mentioning something called the transpersonal.

A This sometimes is classed under the Humanistic umbrella, but also can include the ideas of Carl Jung who was a student of Freud. In the transpersonal there is a recognition of something much bigger that brings you and your client together and that there is a sense of 'other' that can be worked with. There is a lovely quote from John Rowan,

> If we once admit that we are spiritual beings then the whole game takes another turn. Instead of patching wrecks, or even realising potentials, we are dismantling the barriers which are keeping us away from the divine. That which separates us from our spiritual centre has to be questioned, seen through and transformed. (Rowan, 1993: 2)

With all theories, there is information present in the interaction between client and counsellor, which informs the nature of the therapeutic relationship, and in turn reflects how the client may be in other relationships outside of the therapeutic encounter.

Q It seems like the therapist has many different roles within the relationship.

A Sometimes it can be that our role feels more educational, sometimes more as a parent, sometimes more as a friend. And it is all of these things, whilst also being none of them.

EXERCISE

Think about the theory or theories you have learned within your training group. What is your understanding about the importance of the therapeutic relationship within that theory, and what does it focus on in the therapeutic encounter? Are there areas where you feel a little confused? And if so, how can you clarify your understanding?

Q Earlier you said there was evidence to back up the importance of the therapeutic relationship. What does it actually say?

A One of the best summaries is in Mick Cooper's book which I mentioned earlier. In this book he has taken all the most recent research from a wide range of sources and neatly and concisely brought it together in an easily understandable way, even for those who may be apprehensive about looking at research articles and the language used. He gives a Summary of Key Findings:

- The quality of the therapeutic relationship is closely associated with therapeutic outcomes, across both relationally orientated and non-relationally orientated therapies.
- The strength of the therapeutic alliance – in particular, the extent to which clients and therapists agree and collaborate on the goals and tasks of therapy – has consistently been shown to relate to therapeutic outcomes, and seems important to establish prior to more challenging interventions.
- Therapists' levels of empathy are closely associated with the outcomes of therapy.
- Therapists' levels of positive regard are modestly related to the outcomes of therapy.
- In some instances, therapists' levels of congruence have been found to relate to the outcomes of therapy.
- There are indications that therapists' abilities to manage counter-transferential reactions are related to therapeutic outcomes.
- Moderate amounts of self-disclosure, particularly as positive self-involving statements, may be more helpful to clients than systematic non-disclosure.
- Feedback, particularly positive feedback, can be useful to clients.
- Indirect evidence indicates that the capacity to repair alliance ruptures is associated with positive therapeutic outcomes.
- High frequencies of transference interpretations should be avoided, particularly as a means of dealing with alliance ruptures or with highly dysfunctional clients; but low concentrations of accurate interpretations may be helpful. (Cooper, 2008: 125)

It can be really useful to look at this book in some depth to gain a greater understanding of the nature of the work we do and what works and what doesn't!

Q I am really getting a sense of how important the relationship is now. It feels like it's a big responsibility and it seems much of it is down to me to make it happen.

A Whilst it's certainly not all about the counsellor, and if the client is not able to engage in the relationship or is unwilling, there can be little we can do about it.

However, we can make sure that we do all we can to make that happen – after all we are the therapist, and we are the ones who understand what the process is about, which may not be the case for our clients. Self-awareness becomes very important in this area, a subject we will be looking at in more detail further on in the book.

And that does not just apply to the client but to the therapist too.

To be in relationship with our clients we need to understand how we function in our own relationships. We also need to be able to put to one side our own needs and expectations, our own assumptions and prejudices. It's a big ask and to do it well we come back to self-awareness and our ability to be comfortable in our own skin. If we fear intimacy, how can we be in the most intimate of intimate relationships? Ultimately in counselling, our own self is the principal tool, and like any tool that we may use in another area of life, it needs to be kept in good condition.

Q That reminds me of the ethical principal of self-respect in the BACP Ethical Framework. I am guessing we need to do quite a bit of work on ourselves to hold the relationship well and not get burned out.

A Absolutely. Self-awareness touches in on many, many areas of counselling and is ultimately about client safety. If we are not able to recognise our own process and our own issues in the counselling room, and be brave enough to own them, then we are not able to make the best use of supervision. This need for a high level of self-awareness is ultimately what probably distinguishes counselling and psychotherapy from any other profession. Chapter 5 covers self-awareness in some depth but for now, in the context of what we are discussing here let's just reflect for a moment.

REFLECTION

Think about what it is you could do to increase your own self-awareness. Personal therapy is a requisite of many counselling courses. How do you feel about this? Is it something you welcome, or something you resist, finding lots of reasons why it would be difficult for you to attend personal therapy. What other activities, outside of your training, may enhance your self-awareness?

Q It's all very well talking about relationship, and equality in the relationship but what about clients who come along and want me to be the expert and to fix them?

A This is a good point because clients will do just that. And it's really important that we understand how powerful we can be in the role of counsellor. Power is a difficult word in society and too often implies power over or power under. Undoubtedly when clients come to us they come from a place of vulnerability and many will want us to be the expert who can fix them, or whatever is wrong in their lives. Within this it is important that we own the power we carry. We know the rules, the boundaries, what is ok and what is not ok. If you were to think of it as a game, we understand the rules in a way our clients do not. And this is one reason why clear contracting is so important. We also need to fully own the power we carry in this situation. If we do not, if we pretend to ourselves, for whatever reason, we do not have power, then we are creating a situation that is unsafe for ourselves and our clients. If we fully own our power, we can then work with it and recognise how we are using it. This is why it can be so important to make sure that power is shared, through contracting and negotiation, through checking in with the client and reviewing the work together. It is also why it is important to be congruent and be very clear with our clients that we are not the experts, and do not have all the answers.

REFLECTION

Think about how power could be misused in the counselling room. It can be useful to think about the power the client does have – if they are unhappy with us, then they could complain to our ethical organisation, to our tutors, to the agency. And then think about the power you have in this situation or how it would be possible to misuse that, and what may be the temptations in misusing it.

Q I feel confused about using self-disclosure – we are told not to do so, but I have also read that it can be used to enhance the therapeutic relationship. Is this true?

A Self-disclosure is a vital skill within counselling and when used well can enhance the therapeutic relationship. However, it is very definitely a case of less is more, and should only be used with the utmost discretion. Some theories tend not to use self-disclosure at all, notably psychodynamic theories in which the therapist maintains themselves as the blank screen. The most important question any counsellor can ask themselves when thinking about self-disclosure is 'who is this for?' How will it benefit the client – if at all? And how will it enhance the therapeutic relationship? And finally how will I feel if the client knows this about me (if it's personal)? When it is used well it can move the relationship forward. It shows that we trust and respect our clients enough to share something of ourselves with them. It can also show our own humanness, particularly if we share something of our own vulnerability. And of course self-disclosure is also strongly linked to the skill of immediacy – it could be that in the session we feel it is appropriate to share something of how we experience the client. Again this can be quite tricky and needs to be well thought out.

Q I can see that could be reassuring. So what may not be helpful?

A Anything that may be distressing for the client to hear. Anything that they do not need to know – the session is about them not you. Anything that makes the session about you and not about the client. And anything that may lead the client to want to take care of you or protect you. It can be useful to think about if you were to share something, where might it take the session? If the client begins to ask you questions, which results in you sharing something you would rather the client did not know, it could be a way of the client distracting themselves from their own discomfort in the session.

REFLECTION

Just spend a few minutes thinking about what it is you would want the client to know about you, and what you would not want to share with them. Then think about what it would be like to share any of those things with the client and what would be your reason for doing so? What is it you feel you could share that would enhance the relationship? And what kind of things might get in the way? If you have had therapy, what did you know about your therapist – and was that useful?

A How are you feeling about the therapeutic relationship now?

Q It has really made me think about how I need to be in the room with my client and how I can come across as warm and welcoming enough, but to still hold all those boundaries. There is a lot to think about.

A Yes there is. Shall we move onto the next section now?

SUMMARY

- The strength of the therapeutic relationship has a significant impact on the successful outcome of therapy.
- A number of different factors impact on the therapeutic relationship.
- Clear boundaries allow for both the safety of the client and the counsellor.
- All theoretical approaches now acknowledge the significance of the relationship but may approach it slightly differently.

3
Working with Client Diversity in Counselling Work

In this chapter we will be exploring the importance of recognising difference and diversity within counselling settings. To work successfully with clients we need to have an awareness of how difference and diversity issues impact both societally and within the individual relationships we have with our clients.

Q I really struggle with this. We are taught that we need to be non-judgemental with every client and leave our assumptions out of the room because everyone is different. And yet at the same time you get this whole thing about difference and diversity all the time. Surely if everyone is different, then everyone is different?

A It's a valid point. But we also know there are certain groups in society who because of the colour of their skin, their sexuality, their gender, or their religious beliefs do not automatically get the same benefits of living in our society as others who are part of what is seen as the 'norm'. So as therapists, although we may attempt to treat everyone as equal, and may be appalled by racism, sexism and all the other isms, we may find ourselves working with people who have found themselves on the receiving end of prejudicial behaviour. Alongside that, we need to be aware of where our own prejudices lie and what it is we may have unconsciously absorbed either from society or from our family or community as 'normal'. And some of those prejudices may not be negative stereotypes but overly positive. We may be so keen not to be racist, we over compensate by assuming all people who are not of the same race as ourselves are good – when clearly like everyone else, the majority are neither all good nor all bad.

Q I think one of the things I struggle with is that I love diversity – I am fascinated by other cultures and how they live and it's hard to see why some people have such a problem with it.

A I do know what you mean. I remember going to visit my daughter in London, and as I walked towards her flat there was a man and woman sat on a bench in the park talking. Both were dressed in what appeared to be the national dress of one of the African countries. I don't know enough about African culture to be able to say which country, but I loved the rich bright colours of their garments and thought how incredible they looked sat there – way more interesting than all the business men in their suits. I remember wondering what their lives are like, in what ways their lives may be different from mine, and even asking myself if they were different. And I was aware how much I wanted to be a fly on the wall and find out about their lives ... and I find that happens often when I visit places both in the UK and abroad – I really want to learn about all these different ways of living because I think I may learn something. As a result, I really struggle to see how some people are unable to see those who are different from the mainstream dominant culture as a problem. But there in itself is a difference – I know I would really struggle to be with someone who voiced strong opinions disagreeing with my point of view around this and would find it really offensive. And yet in that moment aren't I becoming as judgemental as they are? And maybe some would argue that there is an inbuilt prejudice in assuming other cultures are more interesting than my own.

Q I know I couldn't stand to work with someone who made sexist or racist remarks. I would really struggle to have any sense of compassion for someone like that.

A And yet this is something as counsellors we may have to do and have to manage, and in some instances challenge. And yes, it's really difficult. How can we stay empathic but also true to our values? When is it appropriate to speak out and when not? These are important but difficult questions. And it's important to remember this works every which way – if you are not from the dominant white culture, how does it feel to work as a therapist with someone who is? And as a therapist what might it feel like to be rejected because your client sees you as different from them, and not in a way that is positive – so it's important to remember that this is not just about a counsellor's attitude to difference, it's also how counsellors handle their clients' attitudes to diversity issues.

> **REFLECTION**
>
> 'The ultimate tragedy is not the oppression and cruelty by the bad people but the silence over that by the good people.' Dr Martin Luther King Jr
>
> Think about how this relates to your role as a counsellor. Where might the challenges be? And what might be your resources when faced with these challenges?

Q So I am already seeing that difference opens up a whole can of worms where there are often strong opinions. But isn't that true outside all the 'isms'?

A Totally. As I write this, Brexit is a huge deal and has caused many family disagreements. If you had to work with someone whose opinion was different from yours, how would you feel? Or, as another example, I have been a vegetarian for over 40 years, working with someone who talked about killing animals either for sport or as part of their job, maybe because they were a butcher, I may find really uncomfortable. Would I be able to park my vegetarianism outside the room? I really don't know and guess it would depend on the individual person and what was shared in the room and ultimately the relationship I had built with that client. So yes, we are not just talking about the big societal stuff here, we are also talking about where our own individual opinions get challenged in the room.

Q So this is sounding like it can be something personal or something that impacts on everyone. But what happens when there is no obvious difference?

A I often think 'sameness' is much harder to work with. So I am a white, middle class, middle aged woman with three grown up kids and single. If another woman in similar circumstances, of a similar age, who talked about similar life experiences was my client, I may find myself making all kinds of assumptions based on my own experience. This can sometimes be much more difficult to manage and more subtle than having to manage glaring differences.

But let's do a little fun exercise around difference to check where your prejudices may lie. This was one I used to do with my own students and resulted in some fabulous discussions.

EXERCISE

First of all let's make a list of people with different life circumstances:

A teacher, an MP, a judge, an unemployed homeless man, a banker, a single mother with four young children, a TV presenter, someone who works for the rubbish collection, a student, a writer, a doctor, a heroin addict.

Now, I would like you to list those individuals in the order of importance or status that you think society would put them in. When you have done that, if you wish, you can put them in the order of importance/status that you would allocate to them. Are there differences and if so why?

Now we are going to add another factor. The teacher has been convicted of tax fraud, the MP is a war veteran, the judge is a lesbian, the unemployed homeless

(Continued)

> man is titled and inherited a stately home, the banker works with refugees, the single woman with four young children is a heart surgeon, the TV presenter is serving a prison sentence for abusing young children and the guy who works for rubbish collection has a PhD in astrophysics. The student is an Islamic refugee, the writer a Nobel laureate, the doctor has HIV, and the heroin addict works in Hollywood as a film producer.
>
> How do you believe society would line these people up now? Has anything changed concerning their social positions? What about how you see them? Has it changed how you would view them?
>
> You can play with this and add other factors and just be aware of how you would react and how you feel society would change its view of the individuals concerned.

Q That is quite powerful – I was surprised by how I instantly found myself making judgements and each time a different factor was included how that changed my opinion of where that person would sit in society or with myself.

A Yes – it's quite shocking isn't it? The important thing to remember is that our very survival is built on making snap judgements on everyone we meet. Our old brain relies on that to keep us safe. This isn't about giving ourselves a hard time, it's just about recognising when the old brain clicks in and checking with ourselves whether it is a fair judgement and on what information we are basing that judgement, and is it helpful in the current circumstance. Some years ago, just after the 7/7 bombings in London, I was on a bus when a young man got on who had a back pack. I was day dreaming and people watching as I tend to do on public transport, and noticed my body tense. I realised I was having a reaction to the young man with the back pack. It was totally unconscious and as soon as I noticed it and realised what was happening, it disappeared. But this is why we need to be very aware of our own reactions to different people and different situations.

Q It's a helpful reminder to think of it in terms of the old brain needing to make snap judgements. It makes me feel better about myself.

A Yes, it can be helpful. But it's also important to remember, that even when it's the old brain kicking in, it's not always helpful or ok. The importance of self-awareness and critically evaluating our own reactions is vital here.

Another way of thinking about difference, particularly in the wider social picture, can be around where power in society lies. If you remember, we began to touch on the issues of power when we talked about the therapeutic relationship in an earlier chapter. In very simplistic terms, who holds the top jobs, who makes the big decisions about our lives and where society places individuals in the social strata is about where power is placed. The exercise we did above is a great illustration of that. And one of the biggest areas of difference is still around class in this country.

The recently (January 2018) released *Power Threat Meaning Framework* issued by the British Psychological Society states:

> The Power Threat Meaning framework demonstrates that distress may be experienced by anyone, including those whose social status is more privileged. Everyone is impacted by the negative operation of power in one form or another, and no one is immune from social and relational adversities. Higher social status can bring exposure to its own characteristic negative operation of power. However, as a generalisation, some identities offer much greater compensatory power, status, control and access to social capital in the face of distress than others, along with more options for support, escape, protection, safety and healing. This is confirmed by the evidence about class, 'race' and gender gradients in mental health, criminal justice and other welfare systems. (Johnstone and Boyle, 2018: 47)

Q I had never thought of it in those terms, but that really helps. Yes, I can see that – and I'm thinking even those that have power, like judges and MPs, have lots of assumptions and judgements placed on them by the public.

A Yes they do – and if you imagine working with someone from one of those groups, how would you feel? Would you be comfortable with them? Or might you feel intimidated? Jo Cox, the Yorkshire Labour MP murdered in a racist attack, said 'We are far more united and have far more in common with each other than the things that divide us.' And it is what we have in common as human beings that allows us as counsellors to get alongside our clients, whatever their experience in life and however they may be different from us. To be able to do that well, we need to be clear where the differences lie and also to have some understanding of how wider society perceives the difference carried by our client.

Q I struggle with the word power, it's a word I feel very uncomfortable with.

A So do many people and yet in some ways it's the essence of the work we do. Too often people feel very disempowered when they come into therapy. Too often someone is struggling because they do not feel in control in some area of their life. And in turn they come to us in the hope we will have the power to make it all ok. Yet many therapists become very uncomfortable when talking about power – but it's really important that straight away we recognise that we have a major power imbalance in the room, and that this is the first big difference. One person is the therapist and one is the client and by its very nature, whoever is the therapist holds much of the power. They know the rules of therapy and they are in charge of the session even if it's no more than saying when the session commences and ends.

Q But I don't feel at all powerful when I do skills sessions either in college or with clients. I feel anything but!

A But even though you feel like that, it doesn't change the fact that you are. But also, on a very basic level, power not only influences who has easy access to counselling, but it is also shown to influence an individual's mental and emotional health. Power here means who is judged by society as better, or more important.

EXERCISE

If we are to think about power, where would you put yourself? Where do you feel you have power in your life? And where do you feel you don't?

Q I often think in my agency placement how, if I was working in private practice, I may not get to work with many of the clients I work with – most of the clients who come have too little money to be able to pay for therapy, and those who can pay can only pay a very small amount.

A Yes, this is very true – there are big differences between agency work and private practice. There is a big divide in society around who can afford to access personal therapy and those that can't. There too is another major area of difference – if we have too little money to pay for therapy, then we are at the mercy of what, if anything, we can access through agencies and the NHS. We therefore have less choice concerning how long we stay in therapy, who our therapist will be and what kind of therapy we can access. Another way of thinking about difference and diversity can be around the issue of privilege. One of the most useful statements I read when studying the area of difference and diversity, was from one writer, whose name I no longer remember, who said if you are white, when was the last time you got turned down for a job and walked away wondering if it was because of the colour of your skin? As a white woman, it is not a thought that has ever gone through my head – I have walked away thinking I did not have the right level of experience, or the right level of qualifications, or even that someone was just better than I was. But never once was it because of the colour of my skin. And for those who are not white, that may be a major difference in life experience. If we live in a society that is predominately white, that is predominately ruled by white individuals, I therefore am automatically in a place of privilege, although less so than white men who still dominate the top positions in careers and in society.

EXERCISE

Where do you feel you fit into our social strata? If you think of the exercise we did earlier, where would you put yourself, and where would you see society putting you? Has this changed throughout your lifetime – are there times when your social status may have been perceived differently? And if so, what were the differences for you on a day-to-day level?

A Over recent years attempts have been made to recognise and acknowledge where difference and diversity lie in society, as an attempt to create greater equality. The 2010 Equality Act (see www.gov.uk/guidance/equality-act-2010-guidance) talks about 'protected characteristics' which are listed as age, disability, gender reassignment, marriage and civil partnership, pregnancy and maternity, race, religion or belief, sex, and sexual orientation. Individuals who would class themselves as belonging to one of these categories are protected by law should discrimination take place, for example, if your training centre refused you a place on the course because of your religious beliefs then you would have the right to use the law to prosecute the centre. Whilst no one would argue that protecting all individuals was a bad thing, it's also made many people worried about getting it wrong. As a result, some diversity issues are deliberately ignored or avoided.

REFLECTION

What is your understanding of each of these protected characteristics? Is there more information you need to fully understand any of these areas? If so how could you begin to find the information you need? Are there any areas where you know you have strong opinions or prejudices? Which of these characteristics would you feel is most relevant to you? Have you experienced prejudice due to one of these characteristics?

Now think of them in relation to yourself. Take each one and think how it might impact on you, e.g. if we think of age, what prejudices, if any, are you aware of that society may have around age, but also what do you have? What are your perceptions of people older and younger than yourself? Do you feel at whatever age you are, there are expectations about how you should dress, or behave? That maybe your life should be a certain way, or are there times ahead which concern you – if you are female you may be approaching the menopause, or if male, have retirement approaching ... what are your assumptions around these things?

Q This is an area I always find worrying. I feel anxious I am going to say something wrong, use the wrong terminology and upset someone. Sometimes it just feels quite overwhelming.

A I have spoken to many trainees, and also many well qualified and experienced counsellors who also feel the same. It's almost like they are so eager to not get it wrong, and often feel so guilty about the prejudices that are out there, they are overly keen to make it right and end up tying themselves in knots. Rogers talked about unconditional positive regard but he also talked about congruence. Maybe sometimes we need to be just that and express our concern – if of course it is appropriate.

Q What do you mean? Tell the client I am not sure what to say?

A Yes! Say that you recognise that there are diversity issues present and you really want to get it right for the client. If it's an issue around skin colour, then ask the client how they see themselves and what is their preferred terminology?

Q Would I need to mention it if I see it or experience it?

A Again this varies from client to client. For some clients it could feel like they are being labelled and that all that is being seen about them is the colour of their skin, their race, their sexuality, their gender or whatever the difference is. And if the issues they are presenting are not related to the difference, it may not be appropriate to raise it. If we were to bring it in unnecessarily it may be that our own agenda starts to get in the way of the client work. However, for other clients it may be absolutely appropriate. Again, it is important not to make assumptions.

Acknowledgement of difference when appropriate and an exploration of that within the counselling room can play a significant part in developing the therapeutic relationship. In naming it and asking how it is for the client, we are making the client as powerful as we are. As I said earlier, as 'the counsellor' we automatically have more power than our client. If the client is someone who lacks power out in society, it can be incredibly helpful and healing to attempt to equal out the power in the therapeutic space.

Q How much do I need to know about language and the protected characteristics?

A Making yourself familiar with politically correct language, which is important and also can be thought provoking, can be really useful. There are government websites that address this clearly (I have chosen not to address this here because the language changes). An example would be 'a wheelchair user' rather than someone in a wheelchair. It's also useful to simply ask your client, IF it is relevant, how they like to be referred to as again this addresses any power imbalance.

Q We talked about the therapeutic relationship earlier, I guess this is where it becomes important again?

A Totally. Bringing difference into the room may enhance the relationship, but if it's inappropriate, may in fact damage it. And where difference, or sameness, do exist in the room it can be used to deepen the relationship. Many years ago when I was first beginning my client work, I had a client who like myself came from the North of England. She was expressing her frustration that her friends in the south, where we were both living, didn't understand how different it was in the north and how hard that sometimes was to put into words. I made the decision to self-disclose that I too was from the North of England, and also had a similar experience. My client visibly relaxed and became more open in the session. (Self-disclosure is a powerful tool in some situations and should always, always be used very carefully – it's a tool where less is always more! It needs to be well thought out and with a very clear reason of why you are doing it, and what the impact may be on your client, and what it is you hope to achieve by sharing. Ultimately it should always be about developing the relationship.) In this instance sharing our sameness was useful in opening up the work in the session and helping the client to feel understood.

Q We also spoke in another chapter about self-awareness and I can see how really relevant this is here – it feels as we work through this that I really have to be very aware on so many levels.

A One of the most important areas within this is self-awareness and a willingness to be totally honest with yourself and where your own struggles lie. Who is it out there you have problems with? As I write this the UK is very divided – the gap between the wealthy and the poor is getting wider and we have areas of terrible social deprivation. How do you feel about the super-rich and how do you feel about the poor, about those who claim benefits? How do you feel about food banks and about the homeless? Muslim groups have had a particularly bad press since 9/11 – how do you feel about people whose faith is different from yours, and if you have no faith or religion how do you feel about those that do? How do you feel about individuals who drink heavily, or use recreational drugs? What are your assumptions and understandings in all of these areas and how much contact have you had with any of these groups? And how do you feel if you find yourself out of your familiar environment? I can quickly become overwhelmed in a busy city environment, because I have spent most of my life in rural settings, where I feel very comfortable. However, I have city friends who quickly become overwhelmed by the countryside, its silence and the lack of signposts and clear footpaths!

EXERCISE

Once you have begun to work out your own beliefs and values, think about where they have come from. Have they come out of your own experience? Was that experience a one-off or was it through many experiences? Is it still valid to have that belief now or if you think about the experience, could you interpret it differently from the understanding you have today? Have those beliefs come from your parents or significant others? If so where did they get those beliefs from, and are they still applicable? (It can be worth remembering that sometimes our parents' beliefs are based on their parents' beliefs and their experiences, which may no longer have relevance in the world we live in now.)

A One big influence on all of us, is the impact of the media and society as a whole. TV, social media, advertising, etc. all impact on us and often subliminally, leaving us with ideas and beliefs that we may not have consciously taken on board. Monitoring yourself around these can be really useful – what is it you expose yourself to and how balanced and well informed are the viewpoints you hear, or have heard.

Once we have worked out where our beliefs and values lie then it can be useful to check their validity and what evidence we have that backs up that belief.

EXERCISE

So having done this, think about the type of client you would most struggle with at this point in your training. Write a description of what kind of client might it be really difficult for you to empathise with and why.

Q We did an exercise like this in class early in training and it was surprising how many of us came up with the same things – people who were paedophiles, people who were racist, sexist, domestic abusers.

A I think those are the common ones and yet we need to remember that none of these people come into the room with that label stamped on their forehead! But it can be worth thinking if you have started working with clients (and if you haven't then maybe play with this idea), then suppose someone came into the room and you built a relationship with them, and you found you really liked them. And then they began to drop comments into the conversation that indicated maybe they carried some of the traits you have just mentioned. How would that be? This isn't always about what our clients may have done, but about the person they are and what has happened to them to bring them to the place they are now. This is not to excuse their behaviour or opinions, but sometimes when we hear a person's story and life experiences, it can lessen how appalled we are. There are times when I have really struggled with the appalling behaviour that a client has been exposed to, and my supervisor has reminded me that babies aren't born 'bad'. In my experience it's always surprised me what I have struggled with and it's never been the big issues, but always what appear to be the smaller more insignificant differences that touch a nerve, usually related either to my own beliefs or to my own issues.

Q I guess this is where good supervision and good personal therapy are essential.

A Absolutely. It's also why it's important to have the class room environment to support you in the early days of working with clients. Having as much support as possible, and this includes tutors and peers, is an absolute must and can help normalise some of your own struggles, or get a sense of where you need more support.

REFLECTION

Think about the area in which you are currently living, and where you intend to be practising as a counsellor.

What distinguishes this area from other places in the country? Is it predominately rural or urban? Is it wealthy, or is there a great deal of poverty and social deprivation? Is there much ethnic diversity, or very little? And if there is, how would you describe that diversity?

What kind of agency placements are available to you? Is there a variety of places or is it quite limited? And in what way do they mirror the local society? And think about yourself, do you feel you reflect the local society in which you will be practising, or are you in some way 'different'?

A You mentioned earlier personal therapy, and one of the first things as counsellors we need to do is to have a strong sense of who we are and how we fit into the dominant society, both of the country as a whole and also the area in which we live and in which we practise. If we cannot see our own differences and uniqueness, along with our own 'sameness' then it can be very difficult to see how we are different from our clients, other than the glaringly obvious.

Q I've always seen myself as pretty ordinary and boring and at college I feel like I just blend into the background. But in my group there are some who appear to be very different from most of the people I am used to being around.

A Difference and diversity often focuses on the protected characteristics – and they are undoubtedly very significant. However, it is important to recognise other areas too. The way people dress can indicate which sector of society they feel they belong to, how they wear their hair, the music they listen to, and with whom and how they spend their spare time. Words like 'Chav', 'Punk', 'Emo', 'Hippy', 'Hipster' all denote different social groups. However class in the UK is still of great influence and significance and is often unrecognised or ignored despite the fact it has a huge influence on how much power we have.

Q I remember how important it was at school to have a certain skirt because that meant I was part of the group that was seen as 'cool'. I haven't really thought about that too much, other than there is one woman in the class who seems very posh, you know really well spoken and well dressed and drives an expensive car.

A The findings of a piece of research published in the *Counselling & Psychotherapy Research* journal by Trott and Reeves,

> show that where there was social class disparity, it was the explicit recognition and acknowledgment of disparity that were shown to have a positive impact on the client; improving equality, increasing rapport and enabling greater psychological growth. ... Therapists' lack of awareness of social class was shown to lead to inadvertent oppressive and/or classist behaviour. For a client to take full benefit from therapy, the therapist must recognise the importance of social class and classism and their impact on the therapeutic relationship and be prepared to attend to these dynamics when appropriate. This study illustrates that social class was a silent but powerful force affecting client's feelings of equality and the effectiveness of therapy. (Trott and Reeves, 2018: 166)

In the same article it was stated:

> class differences and similarities are apparent through more subtle factors, for example; accent, language, appearance and manner, reinforcing both the client's and the therapist's internalised classism. (p. 166)

Even though the UK is very small, there is an incredible variety of accents – do you have a favourite, and if so why? And is there an accent you don't like, and again, why? What is it you associate with certain accents? You mention your fellow student and how she is very well spoken, how does that impact on you, if at all?

Q I did feel a little intimidated by her actually. Thinking about it, I assumed she must be very clever if she sounded like that, but she is no cleverer than anyone else in the room.

A Interesting isn't it how we make assumptions based just on the sound of someone's voice? That might be something worth watching in yourself and just bringing into your awareness any assumptions when you begin listening to someone. And then of course there are people's individual beliefs about what is right and wrong, and their political beliefs. All of these can be areas that impact on the therapeutic space and as a therapist areas we may have to work with – and you may be able to think of others.

We spoke earlier about Rogers, and the significance of UPR and about how easily or not, we can empathise with someone else's experience of living in the world. And to really hear our client we need to really 'see' what their lived experience is like, and we cannot do that where our own prejudices and assumptions begin to get in the way.

REFLECTION

If you have started client work in an agency placement, can you think of a clear example where a new client came into the room and you instantly made assumptions? (Students at this point often say no, of course not, and claim they always use UPR!) If you have not begun client work, think about your training group and the first day you met them. What were the stories you told yourself about your peers – were there some members of the group you were instantly drawn to, and were there others you instantly wanted to pull away from, felt a little nervous of, or just quite simply didn't like. How accurate have your assumptions and initial judgements proven to be? What surprises have you had from group members?

Q One of the most uncomfortable areas for me was when one member of the group disclosed they were an ex heroin addict and had been a sex worker to pay for their addiction. I had never met anyone who had been an addict or a sex worker before – the thing was they looked really like anyone else and seemed quite prim and proper. I would never have associated them with such a thing.

A So there is a really good example of how we can have little sense of someone's personal history from just looking at them, and may make all kinds of assumptions as a result. I wonder how knowing that information changed how you interacted with them.

Q I was aware that when I spoke with her after her disclosure, I swore and didn't feel uncomfortable, but had prior to the disclosure, so yes it did make a difference. I was also aware that I felt a certain level of disgust with her initially and then felt ashamed of myself for feeling like that! I guess the other thing that was shocking was someone who came in and talked about their experiences of psychosis within the mental health system and within her own family. I was shocked by how much prejudice and intolerance she was exposed to.

A It's great to hear you recognising your own reactions so clearly and owning how you felt. That is the important bit – if we don't do that, we can't begin to reflect and change our own attitudes.

Mental health is still one of the big taboos. Whilst attitudes have changed and people are more open about their mental health in some instances, and there is a much greater level of awareness in society as a whole, it is still something that many people feel unable to discuss with family and friends. It is great there is so much more publicity around it all, but it still causes strong reactions. Many clients will bring these issues into the room and there are still many who will not let their family know they are having counselling.

Q I know in my own family, there have been mental health problems and no one talks about them. There is a great sense of shame, and embarrassment when it comes up in the family. And it's made worse by the fact that one individual who has struggled the most is now on benefits and lives in terrible housing, having been homeless in the past. Some members of the family behave as if they have let the whole family down!

A Another quote from the *Power Threat Meaning Framework* feels appropriate here:

> As a general rule, all mental health diagnoses are more common in people with devalued identities, especially when they belong to several devalued groups. For example, people from minority ethnic backgrounds living in the UK have much higher rates of both common and severe diagnosed mental health problems than their white British counterparts. This holds whether they were born in the UK or moved to the UK from other parts of the world. It also holds for some white minority groups in the UK such as the Irish. Other marginalised groups, including women, Gypsies and travellers, people with disabilities, people identifying as gay, trans and disabled, and people of any background with low

socio economic status, are more likely to be diagnosed as having both common and severe mental health problems in proportion to their numbers. (Johnstone and Boyle, 2018: 4)

Q That's interesting – I find that phrase 'devalued identities' useful. I hadn't thought of it in those terms before.

I've had quite a reaction around training as a counsellor. Some family members see it as something really weird or they are frightened I am going to read their minds! And it's surprising how many think that they have to be a little 'crazy' to see a counsellor!

A This is not an uncommon reaction. One of the biggest ironies of course in all of this is that counselling and psychotherapy have been dominated by the white middle classes. There are few jobs out there, although that is beginning to steadily improve. Counselling training is expensive – even if you are fortunate enough to have your course fees funded, you will still have to pay for your own therapy, and will have to work for free. Sometimes your supervision, insurance and travel will be paid for, but often it is not, in which case these will have to be self-funded. Because of the demands of counselling training which involve not only time in your training centre, but time doing your personal therapy, your placement and your supervision, for the majority of students it will mean losing a day or more at work, and seeing a cut in wages. It is not difficult to see that this automatically excludes a significant percentage of the population who would not be in a financial position to make that commitment.

Q We have talked about this in our breaks in college – it's all so expensive and some of the group are really worried about how much it is costing them, but then also whether they will be able to get a job at the end of it.

A These are common anxieties amongst trainees and understandably so. The majority of counsellors once qualified set up in private practice due to the few number of paid jobs available, often whilst also continuing to work for free in an agency to accrue enough hours for accreditation, which is a demand of many of the paid roles out there. But private practice is also expensive – not everyone is in a position where their living circumstances mean they can work from home, or indeed would want to – private practice can then mean room hire along with insurance, supervision, advertising and the costs of running a practice. It can be quite shocking to work out the costs and how many clients a therapist will need to see before they begin to break even. So we end up with a profession dominated by the middle classes who can afford to makes these sacrifices. The profession therefore does not accurately represent the make-up of our society. And if we look further into this, even deeper divisions can be seen in the theories used by therapists which have been developed by white, middle class, well-educated Christian or Jewish men from western cultures. There are a number of discussions around how well these theories meet the requirements of those who come from cultures where there is less emphasis on the individual, and more emphasis on the wellbeing of the group.

Q I hadn't really thought of that before. It seems ironic that there is so much emphasis on difference and diversity, and yet most of my training group are white women. And as you say, all the theories we have looked at have been developed by white western men!

A There has been a great deal in the media recently about the feminist movement and sadly there is evidence of those wider societal issues within our own profession. Despite the fact that it's still the case there are many more women therapists than men, and more women access therapy than men, the profession is still dominated by men who sit in the positions of power, as with any other profession in our society. Working as a trainer, with groups of 12–14 students, the most men I ever had in a class was three – yet the men always had fewer problems getting placements. Because men were in short supply they were snapped up, whatever their level of ability.

And going back to what I said earlier about theorists, the women such as Anna Freud, Petruska Clarkson, Melanie Klein and Karen Horney tend to be very much in the background compared to Rogers, Freud, Jung, Erikson, Perls (and ironically it was Perls' wife who did the bulk of the work on his theory, something rarely acknowledged). And if you were to look along your shelves of counselling books, again you will see predominately male writers – John Norcross, Mick Cooper, John McLeod, John Rowan, Pete Sanders, Brian Thorne. Even in a profession that sees itself as very aware and places great emphasis on difference and diversity, diversity is very poorly represented and instead we see white western men dominating the scene. The reasons for this are many and complex but I do think as a profession it is something we need to keep in our awareness.

REFLECTION

Stop and think about your experience of counselling so far. Think of your training group, your placement and any therapy you may have had. Does any of this fit or is your experience different?

Q So we have recognised the historical lack of D&D within the counselling profession, but why is it so important?

A Many individuals who wish to access counselling, do not come from the groups that dominate the counselling profession. And if we are not able to keep a clear focus on this, and if we are not able to see the difference between ourselves and our clients then it is going to be difficult to get alongside them. However even when we can see the differences, or become aware of them, we may then begin to make assumptions of what those differences mean, and this can obviously get in the way of really understanding our clients' lived experience. Of course, where we do not see difference, but see sameness, this can be even more treacherous. It is even easier to fall into all kinds of assumptions around our client if they are very similar to us.

Another important factor to be aware of is the societal implications of what it may mean for your client to be seen as 'different'. For someone who is seen as different by society, they may have experienced all kinds of prejudice. However, this is another assumption we need to be careful of. In a discussion amongst black students it was very clear that their lived experience of racism was in itself very different (personal conversation). For some students it really was no big deal and had never been an issue they particularly came up against; for others, however, it was an ongoing issue within their day-to-day living.

Q Is there anything to say that difference does impact on the successful outcomes of therapy?

A The best place to answer this question is look at Mick Cooper's *Essential Research Findings: The Facts are Friendly*. Briefly, there is no suggestion that clients from any group do less well than any other group when it comes to measuring outcomes.

> Clients from marginalised social groups show some preference for working with therapists from similar groupings, and there is evidence that such matching may be associated with more positive outcomes but, in many instances the therapists' attitudes and values may be of greater importance. (Cooper, 2008: 96)

Essentially what this is saying, is that whilst some marginalised groups feel they will work better with someone from their own social group, the outcomes don't suggest that this is relevant. What is most relevant is that the therapist has a similar value structure, even when they may not be from the same social grouping.

At the end of the day, the most important factor within therapy is the ability to build a relationship – if this relationship is there, as has been stated elsewhere, then the healing work can take place. And what the research shows is that if both individuals are willing to meet the other and engage, then outcomes are good. And there is little to suggest that age, race or gender have any significant impact.

Q But what if my client has judgements about me?

A A very good point – so far we have very much focused on the differences between the client and the therapist, and how the therapist should handle that. However, we have only briefly touched on the subject of the prejudices of the clients who may walk into the room and not want to engage with you because by their perception your skin is the wrong colour, you are the wrong gender, or the wrong age, etc. So how might you handle that? The reality is that for some students this may not be unlikely in their agency placements. As we have said before, counselling is not represented well by all sectors of British society and if you are trying your hardest to work with a client who is in some way different but they are unable or unwilling to engage, there is little to do other than confront it head on and explore what the options might be. It may be that once it is acknowledged, the client is happy to give the work a go, but it maybe that they say 'No' and we have to find a way to be ok with that. And this might be easier for those who are less exposed to the 'isms' than those who experience it frequently in their lives. When a client does not want to work with us because of the colour of our skin, or because of our race, or our religion, etc., it's really important to have good supervision to explore how we handled the situation but also how it has impacted on us and our own therapy can become very important as part of this. If we have been exposed to any form of prejudice in our life, whether it's because of skin colour, or race, or accent, or gender, we are likely to be more easily triggered in the therapy room, so it's important we explore these areas within our own therapy. And if we have never experienced it, then we need to explore what that feels like and how that impacts on our day-to-day lives and how it might impact on our work with client groups who are different from us in the future. Which brings us back to the acknowledgement of our own role in the society we live in.

Q As you talk about where we have been exposed to difference, I am just thinking about being a woman in our society which is still patriarchal and male dominated. And if women dominate counselling as clients and practitioners then the majority of those in the profession have been exposed to some form of prejudice.

A Thank you for acknowledging this. Yes – this is important because whilst with the recent '#MeToo' movement this has been very much in the news, I believe it's something that is so deeply ingrained in our society that many of us, whatever our gender, are not always as aware of it as we could be. And maybe when it comes to difference the biggest thing to remember is to be always questioning ourselves and challenging ourselves around what we perceive as 'normal'. And that what is 'normal' may impact negatively on certain groups in our society.

SUMMARY

- Diversity is complex and covers a wide range of different areas.
- Diversity can impact significantly on our work with clients.
- Self-awareness is of particular importance when working with diversity and an awareness of our own prejudices and assumptions.
- Diversity issues exist within the counselling profession and also need acknowledgement.

4
A User-Centred Approach

This chapter looks at the process of making an agreement between you and your client on how you will work together and what you will work on, ensuring that your client stays at the centre of this work.

Q User-centred doesn't sound very nice to me though – why is it called that?

A It does sound a bit odd but that is because different agencies and lines of work call the people who come to see them by different words – they might be patients, clients, customers, patrons, 'friends', etc., so the term 'users' covers them all. User-centred then means keeping them, the users, at the centre of the process.

CLIENT NEEDS AND EXPECTATIONS

Q I'm used to doing role plays in class where I ask the 'client' what they want out of the session – isn't this the same?

A There are lots of similarities, but remember that the big difference now is that you will be working with real clients in an agency setting. Real clients don't have a scenario or brief to work to; they are bringing their own personal issues and concerns and emotions. Often they are in distress, not thinking clearly, and might be quite confused as to what it is that they actually want. If it is the first time they have seen a counsellor they might not even know what a counsellor can do – their expectations might be quite unrealistic.

Q Oh, yes I see what you mean. Actually I did think the counsellor would tell me what to do to get out of the emotional mess I was in at the time. I was surprised and rather annoyed that they weren't going to do that and that I had to do a lot of the work. It was a shock because I was blaming other people and didn't realise that I would have to look so closely at myself and my part in it.

REFLECTION

Take a moment to reflect on what you knew about counsellors before you either saw a counsellor for the first time, or before you started doing your counselling training. You might have imagined that they would wave a magic wand and solve all your problems, because that is what many people think.

A That's right, so you can see that there are two things here – there is exploring what the client is expecting, then there is matching that up with what you can offer within the limits of your agency and your own competence.

So the first thing is to give your client the opportunity to discuss their understanding of counselling and say what it is that they require or expect.

Q How do I do that?

A This is where your use of the core conditions and reference to your ethical framework comes in. It is important to start building a therapeutic relationship from the moment you first speak with them on the telephone or when they walk through the door. If the client feels safe and well held they will begin to open up and tell you what they are expecting from counselling. So it is vital not to judge, to be empathic.

REFLECTION

You could ask them if they have any previous experience of counselling, and, if so, how did they find that, what worked and what didn't. Or simply ask them what it is that they are expecting from the counselling sessions with you.

How else might you open up a discussion on what they are expecting? Write down some ideas and practise them in your training group.

Q You mentioned reference to my ethical framework. How does this fit in?

A We discussed in the first chapter that a big part of working ethically with a client is about respecting their autonomy, that is, letting them take the lead, not pursuing your own agenda or pushing your own ideas onto them. It would be easy to listen to a bit of the client's story and assume you know what is going to be best for them and steer them in that direction. When a client is feeling distressed and confused they can be very vulnerable and susceptible to another person's ideas. They might be used to what they see as someone in authority telling them what to do, they might want to please the counsellor, they might think that you are the powerful one and you know best so they have to do what you say.

Q I can't really know best though can I because I don't know them, and I'm a trainee so I'm still learning.

A Exactly, so you can see why it is so important to work with the client to explore what it is that they are expecting and what they want, so that together you can work towards this.

Sometimes the client's story is very convoluted and involved, with several different issues interrelated, and lots of people referred to. So this is where your skills of paraphrasing, focusing and keeping the session contained all come in. It is useful to summarise part way through the session and certainly at the end to check that you are getting the story and the feelings accurate and to determine the main thrust that the client wants to work on. If there are a number of issues and your agency limits the amount of sessions then it might be helpful to ask the client what is of most importance to them right now, or what they think might feasibly be achieved in the time available. This helps them to identify their main concerns, prioritise those concerns and focus on their own agenda.

Q So is it alright to be quite specific and tell them what I can't do?

A Yes, it is. For example some people get confused with debt counselling and it is perfectly OK to explain that any help with finances is not your role. Or they may think counselling is like Citizens Advice – so again it might be helpful to explain you are not there to solve housing problems or to advise on legal disputes, etc.

What is just as important though is to be very clear about what you can offer.

REFLECTION

So think carefully about what it is you can offer a client. It is very important that you are absolutely sure what you are offering, in terms of your own limits of competence and training, and within any boundaries set by your agency.

NB it is not sufficient to say something vague like 'This is a safe space for you to explore your concerns'. Consider what is wrong with this statement.

Q Oh, I thought saying this is a safe space was quite a nice thing to say. Isn't that a good idea then?

A Well, it is not necessarily a bad thing, but counselling is much more than that. Now that you have moved up a level to be an agency counsellor you are using your counselling skills and theory to offer therapeutic work, that is, an opportunity for a client to explore recurring patterns and themes in their relationships, to look at the influence of their personal history and family of origin, to explore aspects of themselves that they might not have thought about before.

Q I see, so it is not now just a safe space for someone to let off steam where I use my listening and responding skills; I am actually working with them to uncover maybe hidden or unexplored areas of their lives.

A That's right, which is why you need to find out their expectations and needs first. The client will have some reason, however vague, for coming into counselling, so it is helpful to extrapolate that. They will also have some idea about how they want to feel, or where they want to get to at the end of the sessions, but you might have to work quite hard to focus them and narrow it down to something which can be achieved in the time available.

Q You mean have a goal?

A Well, different theoretical modalities will have a different view on how prescriptive this might be, but it is helpful to have a direction to aim for, to both know where you are headed.

REFLECTION

There's a saying that goes something like, 'If you don't know where you're going you'll end up somewhere else.' What does that mean to you, and how do you think this relates to the counselling process?

It is so easy sometimes to go round in circles with clients if you haven't agreed early on what it is that you are going to work on. Having a 'clarity of purpose' is another way of putting it.

Q As part of being user-centred, shall I tell the client what my theoretical approach is?

ACTIVITY

Explore in your training group and from your reading, the different ways in which contracting and agreements are viewed by some of the different theoretical modalities.
Make sure you understand how you are expected to negotiate agreements from within the theoretical approach you are learning and within the expectations of your agency.

A That depends a bit on whether they already know what the counselling process is all about – perhaps if they have had any counselling before, then they might be aware of different approaches. They might even have sought out you or the agency because of the theoretical approach used. But many people do not know about the different modalities and if you say Gestalt, or TA or Person Centred or whatever, they will probably look bewildered. So it is more helpful to just say a little bit about how you work. This might include a little bit about your beliefs around how people grow and achieve their full potential, or how they might change their thoughts and feelings, and that you do not have a magic wand and won't be telling them what to do. If your approach includes giving them 'homework', that is, things to do between sessions then do tell them that from the outset.

Q My agency has a written contract that they give out during the initial assessment interview, how does this fit in?

A It is quite common for agencies to do this. Usually this covers all the boundaries that we discussed earlier on – things like confidentiality, missed sessions, fees and so on. It can be very helpful to have these written down as distressed clients may not remember everything that is said to them, so having something in writing to take away and look at calmly is a good idea. They may be asked to sign it to say that they agree to the 'terms and conditions'.

However this, and the referral note that you may get, may not really address what it is that they want to work on. They may have had their assessment quite a while ago, things may have changed in their life, and they may not have told the person doing the initial screening everything that was worrying them. So it is still vital that you as the counsellor make an agreement with the client for the actual therapeutic work you will do together.

EXERCISE

There is a difference between what might be called the business agreement and the therapeutic agreement. Make two columns – each with one of these headings and note down what might come under the business agreement, that is, things which are not generally up for negotiation, and those which are of a therapeutic nature.

Q Going back to agendas, my tutor talks about the 'unspoken agenda' but I don't really know what that is.

A It is great if clients start the first session by saying exactly what their concerns are and exactly what it is they want from the sessions. Their agenda is clear and 'spoken'. However, that doesn't always happen. It could be that they spend quite some time talking around the main issue. This could be because:

- They don't yet trust you enough to tell you their deepest concerns
- They feel they have to fill you in on all the background first
- They are not fully aware themselves of what the main issue is

Thus their agenda is not quite what they might have said it was at their assessment, or when you first asked them, hence it is 'unspoken'.

Q So how do I get to the unspoken part?

A This is where you have to draw on all your counselling skills by offering an emotional warmth and safety so that the client can trust you, showing in your words, tone of voice and non-verbal communication that you are open to whatever they might bring without judging them. You will be using your listening skills and experience of people to pick up on what it is the client is not saying. This is sometimes called 'the music behind the words'. If you are not sure what they are meaning then it is good to be congruent and say so and ask them for clarification. This of course may take longer than the first session as clients may be reluctant to trust someone they have just met.

REFLECTION

Think of someone in your life (past or current) who you really trust and would tell anything to – even those most uncomfortable thoughts and feelings.
What is it that that person offers you that makes it safe for you to unburden yourself?

Q So that is what I need to offer to a client?

A Yes, your aim is to emulate those conditions of warmth and safety and enable your client to tell you their unspoken agenda. They could be hiding strong feelings such as embarrassment, shame, guilt or anger.

Q So once I know what it is that they really want, then I can make an agreement to work on those things with them?

A Yes, providing that what they are asking is within the limits of your competence and within the limits of what your agency offers. If it is outside of your training and competence you might have to discuss referring them somewhere else, or if it seems like it could take 20 sessions and your agency has a strict 6–8 session policy, then you would need to discuss it with your supervisor and with the agency manager.

So keep checking back with your client, ensure that what you can offer them fits with their needs and expectations. Keep the client at the heart of what you do.

CASE SCENARIOS

Consider how you would begin to make an initial agreement with the clients in the scenarios below. Think about what they are expecting and what you can offer – how do these match up, what do you think the unspoken agenda might be, how can you go about exploring and negotiating an agreement with each client?

Scenario 1

I am about to get divorced. I feel so very anxious all the time. I'm worried about losing the house, about childcare for my youngest, not being able to afford a holiday, having to give up the car and hundreds of other things. My eldest is crying because she can't have a new phone. I don't really want any of that 'touchy feely' stuff but just want help to sort through all these financial issues. I'm not sleeping well and my GP recommended I come to see you, so what can you do for me?

Scenario 2

It's a very emotional time, I don't want this impending divorce and feel it is being forced on me. We've been together for 12 years. A friend had 20 sessions with a counsellor and it turned their life around, so even though my doctor has said that you, the counsellor at the surgery, can only offer six sessions I do think that because I'm in such a state I must be a special case. So can I have as many sessions as I want? It would be quite helpful if my wife/husband came with me for some or all of the sessions too.

Scenario 3

I'm about to start divorce proceedings against my partner of five years. It hasn't been working for a while and I'm quite glad to be getting out of the marriage. However, as time goes by I find myself suddenly getting upset and being overwhelmed by sadness for the loss of what had seemed such a promising life together. I don't really want to go into the whole background story but just want to know what to do when these feelings take over. I'm just looking for answers/tools/techniques to help me through these difficult times, especially when I'm at work.

THE ROLE OF CLIENT FACTORS

As we have discovered, clients come into counselling with a variety of needs and expectations, and if we are to stay with their agenda and enable them to be heard and progress in the way they want to, then there are a number of other things to be mindful of. Clients bring other variables called client factors and if we as counsellors are to be truly 'user-centred' then we have to consider these too if the agreement for the therapeutic process is to be effective and lead to a satisfactory outcome for them.

Q Client factors, what are these?

A In his book *Essential Research Findings in Counselling and Psychotherapy – The Facts are Friendly* (2008) Mick Cooper suggests that change during counselling/psychotherapy is largely due to the client themselves and their personal characteristics rather than the actual counsellor, the conditions th\e counsellor creates, the relationship they establish or what they do. These characteristics he calls client factors.

Not only are there observed characteristics such as age, gender, sexual orientation, class and ethnicity, but there are inferred characteristics, factors which can't be seen as such but are attitudes which are implicit in the makeup of an individual client and have a big influence on what they gain out of counselling.

Q Can you tell me more about these inferred factors as this sounds intriguing to me?

A The main inferred factors are:

- Motivation and involvement
- Outcome expectation

- Process expectations
- Predilections

Q OK, this all seems a bit confusing, can you explain?

A Well let's take each one in turn and relate it to your client work.

Motivation and involvement

Ben is a young man who has been 'sent' for counselling by a probation order. He is not the least bit interested in the process of counselling, doesn't believe in talking to strangers about himself and finds it almost impossible to name his feelings. He will not want to involve himself in the process, will not be motivated to change his feelings or behaviour and is just interested in paying lip service whilst attending the sessions so that he can say he has done it.

In contrast, take Emma, a young woman who is addicted to misuse of substances and social services are threatening to take her baby into care if she cannot get clean and demonstrate that she can be a good mother. She is desperate to keep her baby, but just as much she really wants to come to terms with problems in her past and start a new life. This is the reason she chooses to come to counselling. She is likely to be highly motivated and to engage well with therapy, ensuring a successful outcome.

Q Yes, I can see then that the more motivated a client is to make some kind of change then the more likely they are to be involved and take an active part in the counselling process. They perhaps already know what it is they want to achieve so it would be easier to make an agreement for the work and help them to get to where they want to be. So what about the next one?

Outcome expectation

This depends on how much belief clients have that counselling is going to work for them. Those who have faith from the beginning that this is going to be a life-changing process are more likely to succeed than those who are sceptical. It is thought that for some clients just embarking on counselling engenders hope where hope has been lacking. It is a bit like the self-fulfilling prophecy, or a placebo effect.

Q If they think it is going to work, then it most likely is. So, how does this differ from process expectations?

Process expectations

Research shows that clients who have realistic expectations about what is going to happen during counselling, what their part in it is and what they could gain from it, do in fact get the best outcomes.

Q Ah, so clients who do think that the counsellor is going to wave a magic wand are going to be disappointed and have an unsatisfactory outcome?

A They will be disappointed if they are not realistic about what the counselling process can offer, and if they do not understand that they have to take an active part, and quite often that means uncovering and experiencing painful feelings.

Q No pain, no gain uh?

A Something like that, yes.

Q But not all theoretical approaches require the client to do 'homework' between the sessions do they?

A No, not at all, but taking an active part means different things – it can mean engaging fully in the process in the room by listening carefully, asking questions and struggling to understand their part in their relationships or family history. It might mean beginning to respond to family, work colleagues and friends in a different way, reading or just quietly reflecting on or processing the session during the week.

So hopefully you are beginning to see how very important it is for you to get a picture of what your client expects from counselling and for you to be very clear about what you can offer and how you work. Also to explain what part the client is going to have to play in this work.

Q Yes, it is all beginning to fit together now. So what does the other factor – 'predilections' mean?

Predilections

This is to do with what clients believe to be the cause of their distress. If they receive help that is congruent with their beliefs then the outcome is more likely to be successful. For example a client who has visited their GP for sleeping tablets to help them get a good night's sleep but is advised to go for counselling, is less likely to engage and be successful because what they see as the root of their problem is medical or chemical not psychological.

Q So I could explain what I can offer, but what then?

A It is important to be congruent. If they are determined that all they want is to take tablets and have someone advise them how to get a good night's sleep then you have to explain that you do not give advice or work in a directive way and you can't give medical help. Your role is to work at an emotional level and explore the underlying reasons for their lack of rest. If they are unwilling to engage at this level then it may be necessary to refer the client on or back to their GP.

Q Can you give another example of predilections?

A Yes, let's think back to Ben above. He is on a probation order and thinks it is very unlucky and very unfair that he got arrested for road rage against another driver. He thinks it is the other driver's fault for pulling up too quickly at a junction and causing Ben to run into the back of him. The other driver got out of his car and shouted at Ben who then retaliated. Ben can't accept that he has anger issues which are part of his grieving for his Dad who died six months ago.

Q I can understand that, I think Ben might be quite difficult for me to work with. Are there any more of these client factors?

A Yes, there are some others – personality disorders, attachment styles, perfectionism, stage of change, social support.

ACTIVITY

Find out what each of these five factors means, and how they may have a bearing on how you initially agree the therapeutic work that you will do with a client.

CASE SCENARIO

Going back to Emma – she believes that the cause of her addiction stems from abuse she received from her stepfather when she was a teenager. Her father had left when she was five. When the abuse started her mother just wasn't able to support her and she moved out of home in a hurry. Whilst sleeping rough on the streets she got in with a rough crowd and started drinking heavily. This led to drug misuse. Desperate for some attention she became friendly with an older man and had two children with him (these are now in care). Unfortunately he was often violent towards her and there was a possibility that the children might be harmed. He had mental health problems and took his own life six months ago. Emma has since had a baby daughter and her drug use has escalated. She is not allowed to have her two older children back with her until she has proved that she is capable of looking after them, and it is doubtful if she can keep the baby with her. She has been in and out of drug treatment in the past, but this is her last chance.

Which of the above client factors do you think might come into play when considering making the initial agreement for the work with Emma?

Q So are you saying that so much of what happens in the counselling process is to do with the clients themselves that if I'm a rubbish counsellor and my clients finish after just a few sessions, or go away saying that counselling doesn't work then it won't all be my fault?

A On the other hand though, there is a lot of evidence to suggest that the relationship between counsellor and client is all important, so despite the above factors and irrespective of the theoretical approach, if a client feels safe, experiences consistent unconditional positive regard, and is put at the centre of the process then they are likely to flourish.

NEGOTIATING A SHARED AGREEMENT FOR THE COUNSELLING WORK

Q So what does 'negotiate' actually mean?

A It means each party listening to, respecting and taking account of the wishes of the other party. Each party should be allowed to have an equal input in the discussions and to have a say in the outcome.

Q So, in counselling terms?

A This means that you the counsellor must enable your client to express their needs and expectations and that you must make it very clear what you can offer and if you are able to meet their expectations within any possible limitations of your agency.

Q So, this is the 'shared' part?

A Yes, exactly.

EXERCISE

Imagine you are witnessing the following scene at your local market on a Saturday morning:

> Morning all, lovely day – best fruit and veg in town, picked fresh this morning, roll up, roll up, what can I do you for?
>
> CAN I HAVE A BAG OF POTATOES PLEASE – HALF A KILO?
>
> No problem, here you go. Who's next?
>
> SOME PORK CHOPS PLEASE.
>
> Does this look like a meat counter, what does it say up there (pointing up) – fruit and veg, the meat stall is round the corner, second on the left love.
>
> THREE LEMONS PLEASE.
>
> Oh I'm so sorry, not often I have to say this, but my supplier let me down this morning, no lemons, but I can do limes – if you want something citrusy they work just as well.
>
> WHAT ARE THOSE TOMATOES AT THE BACK, LABELLED IMPERFECT?
>
> They are just past their best so I can do a whole bag full for 50p, but I don't want you coming back next week saying they were squashy, that's why they're labelled imperfect.
>
> I'M IN A HURRY AND CAN'T STOP NOW, WHAT DAYS ARE YOU HERE?
>
> Every Saturday, all day 8 til 4.
>
> CAN I HAVE A LATTE TO GO PLEASE?
>
> You certainly can love, but not from me, that's the stall next door.
>
> MUSHROOMS PLEASE – THE SPECIAL OFFER, BUT I WANT 6.
>
> Well the special offer is 4 for a £, so you can have 4 or 8, but not 6. Maybe someone else will share a bag with you.
>
> I'D LIKE A PLASTIC SHOPPING BAG PLEASE TO PUT THIS LOT IN.
>
> Only brown paper bags here I'm afraid – you have to bring your own if you want to use anything else.

Q That sounds just like the stallholder outside my town hall on a Saturday, but what's it got to do with counselling?

A If you look closely you'll notice that the stallholder is very specific about what he can offer. He is clear about what time he operates, that he can sell potatoes but not pork chops or a latte. He can offer tomatoes and mushrooms, but with conditions. He can provide only paper bags. He can suggest an alternative to lemons.

Q Yes-s-s so you mean he is a bit like the counsellor – 'setting out his stall' – being clear about what he can sell and the limitations?

A Yes, and the customers are saying what they want, though some are a bit confused, just like clients, and if they are expecting something that he can't provide like pork chops or latte he is very clear that he does not offer those things. The sign over the stall, the labelling on his products and his responses all make it clear what he can offer, the customers then have an informed choice as to whether they wish to accept what is on offer or look further afield.

As this is a market stall the transaction is over very quickly – agreement is reached and a sale takes place very quickly, or the customer walks away and goes elsewhere. In counselling, teasing out the client's expectations and negotiating a shared agreement for the work together can of course take longer. Clients are not so clear about what it is they want and are often in a much more emotional state than they are likely to be when buying fruit and veg. The stallholder is jokier and much blunter than you the counsellor would be with a client, but nevertheless the principle of being clear and informative is the same.

Remember, in order to negotiate the agreement you have to first of all find out what the client's understanding of counselling is, and what they are expecting. Then together you can agree the way forward.

ETHICAL AND MORAL CONSIDERATIONS

Q We keep going back to ethics don't we?

A Yes, you will find that you need to draw on your ethical framework for guidance a lot of the time when counselling.

Q So how do ethics come into making a shared agreement?

A Remember that the work that we do as counsellors must be user-centred. Thinking of the business agreement first of all there are a number of ways in which it might be easy for a counsellor to follow their own agenda and manipulate a vulnerable client. Reflect on the following:

REFLECTION

- The agency has a sliding scale of payments and you know that the client has just received a large redundancy pay out. You could lead the client into paying the highest fee.
- The same client could be persuaded that they need far more sessions than is strictly necessary, so that the agency gains financially.
- You are so keen to accumulate the 100 client hours for your course that you outline the client's distress and ask your supervisor for permission to extend the sessions by another six.
- The agreement has been for an hour a week, but you regularly stop the session 15 or 20 minutes short saying that you recognise the client is tired and has had enough for one day.
- A client has missed one of the six sessions agreed without giving notice, but you ignore this and add on another one to make up the six.
- A client attends for the first session, you realise he has complex issues that you can work with, but you don't like him so you discourage him from signing the agreement and suggest he might like to see someone else in the agency.

Q I can see now that there might be ways in which the boundaries could be pushed or manipulated and the counsellor has to be sure to remain ethical and keep the client's interests at heart. What about ethical concerns around the therapeutic agreement though?

A We discussed earlier that the client has to be allowed to have autonomy. It is not the role of the counsellor to push or lead the client into areas they are not ready to look at. As we said it is not ethical for the counsellor to suggest working on particular concerns just because that happens to be their speciality, or they think that area of the client's life would be easy to fix, or have just learnt about it on their course!

Equally it is not ethical for counsellors to avoid painful areas of the client's life either because they think it might be too upsetting for the client, it might be too upsetting for them, or they think they would not know how to deal with the consequences of going there.

REFLECTION

Going back to the case of Emma above – you recognise that her unspoken agenda is around attachment issues – her father left when she was small and her mother

> was never really there for her. This rings bells with your own personal history and it is still very painful for you, so rather than raising this as something she might like to work on, you avoid it and concentrate on her addiction issues.
> What might be the consequences – morally, ethically and practically of avoiding Emma's difficult feelings?
> Remember to think about whose agenda is at work – is it the counsellor's or the client's (spoken or unspoken)?

Q My training course talks about contracts rather than agreements – what's the difference?

A Counsellors do tend to use the terms 'contract' and 'agreement' interchangeably. The *Oxford English Dictionary* (2016) says a contract is, 'A written or spoken agreement, especially one concerning employment, sales, or tenancy, that is intended to be enforceable by law'.

A counselling contract can be written or spoken, or both, in that the business side might be written and signed by both parties, but the therapeutic work is generally agreed verbally. Not every contract will be legally enforceable though, so it might feel more comfortable to call it a formal agreement. An agency might bind a client to an agreement to pay fees for missed sessions for example, but would find it more difficult to uphold a therapeutic agreement.

Q So I can see why I have to be really clear with my client what it is they are agreeing to work on, and what I can offer. What could they do if they thought I hadn't kept to our agreement?

A You are accountable to your agency and to your professional body (the holder of your ethical framework). Your client could complain about you to the agency and/or they could follow the complaints policy from your ethical framework. The business agreement is fairly clear cut, but the therapeutic agreement is less black and white and might be difficult to prove either way unless you had acted very unethically and very unprofessionally.

Q I'm going to be so careful to work with my client and pin them down to an agreement as to what they want to work on.

A It is good to be mindful of the worst consequences, however it is equally important not to be too dogmatic about the direction of the therapeutic work, as unfortunately counselling is not an exact science and is often open to interpretation and the counselling process can be a shifting landscape.

Q What else do I need to be mindful of?

A You might have heard of something called 'informed consent'.

Q I've heard of that but I'm not sure what it is – can you explain?

A It is all well and good to fully involve your client in making the agreement, but that is assuming your client is able to completely understand and take on board what it is you are offering.

Q You mean if I'm not being clear enough?

A Not necessarily – there might be other reasons why your client cannot understand and therefore give informed consent, for example, their age (a child or young person), impairment by drugs or alcohol, a learning disability, mental health problems, medical conditions like Alzheimer's. A client needs to have what is called 'capacity' to make their own informed decisions. Part of the reason for having an initial assessment in the agency is to screen out potential clients who would not be able to fully engage with the process.

ACTIVITY

Explore what your ethical framework says about 'contracting'. Find out what the procedure is in your agency regarding capacity and informed consent (how does the latter tie in with Gillick competence if working with children and young people?).

FOCUSING, REVIEWING AND RE-CONTRACTING

Q I thought we talked about focusing earlier on in this chapter?

A Yes, we did, but focusing doesn't just happen once, or just in the first session – it can take place at various intervals in the counselling process and/or throughout any or all of the individual sessions.

Q So, it could be called refocusing then?

A Yes, it could. It also might be called reviewing or recontracting.

Q So, why is it necessary to refocus? Surely if I've agreed with my client what we are going to work on then that's what we continue to work on.

A That is true to a large extent – however, there are a number of variable factors:

- the client's circumstances may change
- the client's feelings may change
- the client's relationships may change
- the client may disclose something that wasn't apparent at the initial contracting stage
- the client may not have told the whole story until they could trust you
- they might suffer a big life change like a bereavement or a redundancy
- the client's beliefs and values may alter due to the counselling they are doing
- they might just change their mind about what they want to work on

EXERCISE

Broadly speaking the focus of a client's work may alter due to:

- Emotional
- Practical
- Relational
- Behavioural or
- Spiritual changes.

Identify which of these would describe the factors next to the bullet points above.

So, you have to be flexible and be prepared to change the focus – always in negotiation with the client of course, and remaining user-centred. This is partly why, as we said above, it is hard sometimes to pin down a therapeutic contract, because the focus could shift from session to session, or even within a session.

Q Why even within a session?

A As clients talk about themselves and hear what they are really saying they might go deeper than they thought they would and decide to focus in a different area, or they might realise that what they came in with is no longer so important now they have got it off their chest, or different feelings come up and they want to go with those.

Q That sounds like when I use my paraphrasing and summarising skills during the session, and at the end, to make sure we are both still on track.

A Yes, you would use those skills and if it feels like the focus has shifted then in order to remain user-centred you must check with the client where they are at. It might help to think of it as 'retuning'.

Q So when should I review or renegotiate?

A You can see that it might be useful at the end of each session as part of good practice. However it is common to let the client know as part of the initial agreement that you will be reviewing more formally at the end of a certain session. This depends a bit on how many sessions your agency is offering – with six sessions it would be usual to review at the end of session four or five.

Q Does this take long?

A If the client is still on track with what you both agreed initially it will be a very quick process, perhaps just a few minutes. But if there have been lots of changes for the client since the first session and they want to change tack somewhat then it could take longer.

Q What might the pitfalls be?

A Beware of opening up painful areas that you might not have time to work on adequately if you are bound by a specific number of sessions like six. Be explicit with your client as to what you might do together in the time available.

It could feel like starting over again and uncovering your client's needs and expectations. So remember everything we said about being user-centred with the initial agreement – think about whose agenda it is to refocus, again listen for the unspoken agenda, do not move or blur the boundaries of the original agreement if you think there is no good reason to do so, or your client is manipulating you. Ensure that your client fully participates in any reviewing and renegotiation of the agreement.

I know you are going to say 'ethics again' but it is really helpful to refer to your ethical framework for guidelines on good practice around regular reviewing.

Q I feel a bit worried that my client could be manipulating me and I'm not aware of it. That could be really uncomfortable.

A Yes, and that's the key – if it feels uncomfortable then that is a sign that something is not quite right. This is when using clinical supervision is invaluable. Your supervisor will most likely be able to pick up on your discomfort even if you haven't told them exactly how you feel. Even if you just say 'something doesn't feel right' then your supervisor will explore with you what is going on. They will gently challenge you about refocusing – why do it, when to do it, whose agenda it is and how to keep the process user-centred.

CLIENT PROCESS AND THE COUNSELLOR'S AGENDA FOR CHANGE

Here briefly we will explore how the client's agenda and the counsellor's own agenda may get mixed up. We will consider how our perception of change and the client's personal needs may not always line up perfectly.

Q This book has already contained some focus on change, and I've been reading about a lot of techniques and approaches that promote change. I really want to help my clients change. How do I know what the best techniques are?

A Why do you want your clients to change?

Q That's what they're there for isn't it?

A Quite a big generalisation, 'That's what THEY'RE there for'.

Q But clients do come to counselling to change … surely.

A OK. When you refer to your client's changing, what do you mean by that?

Q A change that improves their lives. A change that makes life better, easier. For example, a client in a violent relationship would leave the relationship or someone with an eating disorder would stop whatever behaviour causes them pain or distress. An alcoholic would stop drinking. Positive changes.

A I agree, anything that improves life, making it better, easier, is a good thing. However, how do you know that the client in a violent relationship wants to leave? How do you know the alcoholic wants to stop drinking and the person with an eating disorder wants to end their dysfunctional relationship with food?

Q It's obvious, isn't it?

A No I don't think it is obvious and I don't think that what you want for your clients is necessarily what they want for themselves.

The client in a violent relationship might want the violence to stop but doesn't want to end the relationship. The relationship dynamics may be very complex and the client may be repeating old self-defeating patterns, there could be PTSD and a repeat of historic abuse. It could be living in the same dynamic as parents or care givers who were in similar violent relationships. We don't know anything about what the client wants and needs, or what change (if any) they want until we form a relationship with them and listen.

Q I would find it really hard to sit with someone who was in an abusive relationship.

A Interesting you chose that issue out of the others as the one you would struggle to work with.

Q I don't know how I could stay quiet, knowing they would probably leave the session and go back to hell.

A Hell? A lot of assumptions are being made about this 'fictitious' client … they need to leave their partner, they're living in hell …

Q I struggle to understand why I shouldn't try and help my client get out of a horrible situation. Surely, by doing nothing, I'm colluding with the violence. If I know something is happening, I think I have a responsibility to act.

A Of course, if there is a serious risk of harm, the limits of confidentiality will need to be revisited and perhaps some action taken. You seem to be talking about something different to that. From what you are saying, you feel a responsibility to direct your client to leave a violent relationship.

Q Yes to keep them safe.

A What if your client is the violent one?

Q Oh I hadn't thought of that!!

A We know nothing about this client apart from being in a violent relationship but you have added some 'fantasies' or 'phantasies' perhaps.

Q What on earth is a phantasy?

A It is an unconscious fantasy, something we aren't aware of consciously.

Q So you think I'm embellishing the situation?

A I think that this might have hit on a personal nerve that has triggered an unconscious emotional response, yes.

Q Give it to me straight, why don't you! Ok you got me – my sister was in a violent relationship but she wasn't the one that was violent. Perhaps that is why I feel quite involved in this sort of area.

A So you have personal experience of someone you love being abused.

Q Yes and I thought I was aware that I needed to keep my own feelings contained and not project them onto my clients.

A You have awareness, but …

Q My sister was in an awful relationship with a brute. I hated him, he treated her like dirt but she couldn't see it. Even when he hit her, she made excuses, blamed herself. I couldn't get through to her. She stayed for years and I watched her grow old and grey far too early. Ironically, he walked out on her for someone else. She went through hell and still couldn't leave him.

A Maybe your hope for your sister to be free from abuse, could lead you to directing a client suffering abuse to change. But this might not be what those particular clients want to change.

Q I see now. The change must be my client's choice, not mine.

A Absolutely. But you have raised an interesting question around 'Change'. Do clients come to counselling to change?

Q I'm not so sure now. Isn't that usually what they want?

A I guess most clients want change to occur but the nature of the change is up to them. What a counsellor can do is help the client to explore the situation and find out what change is possible.

Often the change that we want just isn't within our power. We want people to change, to heal, to love us, to approve of us. We might want some people to jump off a cliff or get out of our life.

Change can simply be a change in perception, how we see things. Acceptance would be a change if resistance was a problem.

It is important to remember, that wanting to change is not enough to actually change.

Q I think you are back to talking in riddles.

A Here's a riddle:

There are five frogs sitting on a log. Three frogs decide to jump in. How many frogs are left on the log?

Q Two.

A No. The three frogs only decided to jump in. They made the decision to jump. Making a decision is very different to taking action. The decision to make a change is a huge step but without action it means very little. Therefore, there are still five frogs on the log.

I think that brings us back to your original question but with a different focus.

If the client wants to make realistic and achievable changes, there are techniques that can help us understand the nature of change and what can help or hinder the therapeutic process.

Let's take the example you mentioned regarding an alcoholic client. You assumed that the client wanted to change and the change would be to stop drinking. What might happen if you directed the client to stop drinking and set goals to do so?

Q I understand that the decision must come from the client. If I set goals for the client to stop or cut back on drinking, then I am putting huge pressure on them and also a pressure to lie.

A To lie?

Q Well if I have set goals and made suggestions that the client hasn't kept to, I imagine there would be a big temptation just to come to the session and say they'd stop drinking or cut down, rather than admit they failed to meet the goals I'd set for them.

A Yes and if the client feels they have to lie to meet the counsellor's expectations, the therapeutic relationship is severely affected.

Q Also, it would probably stop us exploring what else was going on for the client, what alcohol gave them, what life did not give them, etc. It would stop me getting to know my client as an individual, stop me understanding their lifestyle, prevent me learning about their relationship with alcohol, their relationships in general.

A Also the alcohol use could be self-medicating which would suggest underlying issues that need to be understood. If the counsellor coerced the client to stop drinking, they could be stealing the only way of coping the client has and taking that away could cause great harm.

Agreed. It can take a long time to make a 'change'. It can help us as counsellors, to explore about our own change process and how we approach and implement (or not) change. We can reflect on what motivates us to change and what hinders the process.

Q I make decisions very quickly but only because I hate being uncertain. I'd rather do anything than do nothing.

A That can be very hard for a counsellor.

Q Yes, I struggle with just being with the client and letting the process and their story unfold, holding the space while they tell their story and explore their feelings.

A Sounds like you are in a bit of a hurry.

Q I am impatient but I want my clients to do well and improve their lives. I'm aware that I might only have a short time with my clients and we may have to get there quite quickly.

A It feels that a number of different issues are involved here. Up until now, we have spoken about two agendas, the counsellor's agenda and the client's agenda. As counsellors, we know and work hard to keep our own agenda out of the room and instead focus entirely on the client's agenda.

Could there be any other agendas present?

Q I know my agenda is present sometimes, even though I really try not to let it.

Sometimes it's about my personal life and history and how I relate personally to people but there are other agendas I think …

… my client's family and friends would have an agenda and I guess the risk is my client might be wanting to please or placate them and be focused on their agenda and what they want.

Sometimes a GP or Health care professional can have an agenda that the client follows a certain lifestyle and the client might be following that.

A Exactly, and there may be other agendas too:

Counselling agencies or organisations can have financial and statistical targets to meet which can also be an agenda if not carefully managed. They may also restrict the number of sessions a counsellor can work with a client for, thus increasing the sense of needing to change in a short time.

The judicial system, the police and courts can set an agenda that a client may agree to because the consequence of not agreeing is too high.

Q Wow, it's a miracle we ever get to the client's real agenda.

A Very true and perhaps simply finding out what the client's actual agenda is, is one of the greatest motivations for change there is.

Q I began by asking about what I could do to help my client change and instead I got a list of things that I need to change. I wasn't expecting that!

A It's always about the relationship and within the relationship there are two people. Both people need safety, respect and willingness to be there. So, it is about change for the client and the counsellor

And

It's **not** about change for the client or the counsellor.

Q Of course, how silly of me not to think of that in the first place!

SUMMARY

In order to maintain a user-centred approach when working with your clients you need to:

- Uncover what your client expects and needs from you the counsellor and the counselling process.
- Be clear with your client about what you can offer them.
- Be mindful of your own and the agency's limitations.
- Agree a client-led focus for the work.
- Explore hidden agendas, both your own and your client's.
- Understand the role of client factors in your counselling work.
- Regularly review (and if appropriate) refocus the work.

5
Working with Self-Awareness

> I am inclined to think that in my writing perhaps I have stressed too much the three basic conditions (congruence, unconditional positive regard and empathic understanding). Perhaps it is something around the edges of those conditions that is really the most important element of therapy – when my self is very clearly, obviously present. (Wosket, 1999, taken from Baldwin, 2000)

The need for a highly developed level of self-awareness is one of the factors that distinguishes counselling from many other professions. It has come up repeatedly in earlier chapters, and will come up again in future chapters no doubt. It is a vital and important factor in all areas of counselling. In this chapter we are going to explore why it is of such relevance and also look at how it can be developed throughout training, and continue to be developed through your professional life.

Q Self-awareness comes up repeatedly in my training, in the text books I read, and now throughout this book. Can you tell me why it is such a big deal?

A Self-awareness is an essential component in our work as counsellors. Our ability to critically self-reflect and to know ourselves intimately will be crucial to how effectively we are able to work with clients. It is also significant in keeping our clients safe – if we are unable to critically reflect on our work and to recognise what is happening in the room, we are unable to effectively monitor the work we are doing and develop an effective internal supervisor. It is also important in keeping ourselves safe. Vicarious trauma, compassion fatigue and burn out are sadly too common in the profession and without the ability to monitor ourselves we run the risk of falling into this trap.

Q Ok. So it sounds like safety is a big factor in this – the safety of both the client and myself. Can you say a little more about that?

A If I am unable to fully monitor my own reactions to different things, to be aware of what is my material in the room and what is my client's, then it can begin to become unsafe.

Let me give some examples: I am working with a client and half way through the session I become aware I feel very anxious and slightly breathless. I check with myself on why this is happening – has the client said anything that could provoke that level of anxiety in myself? No there is nothing that they have disclosed that is outside my comfort zone in working with them. Is what I am feeling the client's – are they feeling anxious and has their breathing become shallow? No – in fact they seem to have become more relaxed and they are laughing at themselves about what they have said. I feel a little confused but park it for now and refocus on the client. As the client pushes their hair out of the way, I realise the gesture reminds me of someone I used to know, someone who I didn't like and bullied me when I was at school. As I become aware of the connection, the feeling of anxiety begins to fade and my breathing becomes deeper.

This is an example of transference – where someone we meet reminds us of someone from the past with whom we have unfinished business. If I had not been able to recognise what was happening, then I may have acted out with this client – maybe I would have acted in subservient manner, avoiding challenging them when appropriate because of the anxiety I was feeling, and making the assumption it was the client 'making' me anxious and that they may react badly to any challenge. Or I may have become overly challenging and angry, which could have been damaging to the client. Or I may have dreaded every session after that, having bad dreams and anxiety, and unable to recognise that there was something that needed to be resolved through personal therapy. Without personal awareness and an understanding of myself and my own history, that situation could have been very easily misinterpreted with unsafe results for both myself and my client.

Q That makes sense. So where do I begin?

A Much of counselling training is built around developing self-awareness. This is done in a number of ways and good trainers will encourage students to use every opportunity available, both within the training environment and outside of the classroom. Everything that happens in our lives can be used to deepen our understanding of ourselves. And whilst this does not mean to say we have to be on alert 24/7, it can be useful to constantly keep an eye on ourselves and our responses to different people and different situations. The human psyche is a fascinating and enormous subject and our learning about ourselves never stops. This is because we are continually adapting to the environment around us which constantly changes, along with adapting to the different people who enter our lives, however briefly. Each event in our lives can be used to enhance our self-awareness. If this seems daunting, it can be useful to think of it as an exciting adventure where we get to meet the person we really are, to recognise where our conditioning influences us, and then recognising that we can begin to make choices of how to be in the world, and to make changes should we choose to do so, along with helping us to understand what the blocks might be to making those changes

Q So there is a feel good factor in this? Sometimes it feels so daunting!

A Part of increasing self-awareness is about accepting who we really are and that is a pretty good place to be, in that it allows us to feel comfortable in our own skin, wherever we are. It's really about becoming awake to ourselves and our responses. Most individuals drift through life paying little attention to themselves and their environment, or never stopping to think about why they may respond to a particular event or person in a specific way. If we move into training to be a counsellor we are asked to step out of that way of life and to become awake to ourselves. One of the bonuses of this process is finding that our confidence and self-esteem become much stronger, and we are less influenced by the opinions of the others. However, it can also mean that we begin to recognise how our behaviour has been impacted by events in our lives, and how our behaviour has been modified as a response to those events. We then have the choice of whether we carry on as we are or we begin to make changes in line with how our life is now, so we are not reacting from a place in the past. Can you see how this mirrors the work we do with clients? Self-awareness is certainly not always comfortable but it can be incredibly empowering and liberating!

Q It sounds like it's giving to ourselves what it is we attempt to do with our clients. I can see how that could be really useful in working with clients. I can imagine that at times though that could feel quite challenging.

A Yes, it is exactly that and yes it can be quite challenging. One of the ethical principles in the BACP is self-respect. This means we need to look after ourselves and to know our limitations. So a good place to begin can be to look at how we resource ourselves. This mirrors our work with many clients, where the beginning of the work can be around discussing where else our clients have support available outside of the session and what it is they do to take care of themselves.

EXERCISE

Think about what you see as your own resources – if you are tired and stressed, what do you do to take care of yourself? Make a list. This might include friends and

(Continued)

> relatives that you can talk to, or you know will make you feel better. Or it might be pets, or sports. It could be something like watching your favourite movie, or listening to some music. Or there might be a safe place you go to either physically, or just in your own mind. Our spirituality or religion can be another resource, as can spending time in nature. When you have your list, look through and think about how many of these are healthy. If some of your resources are not healthy – maybe you reach for a large glass of wine every time it all gets too much, or over work or over exercise, or go shopping when you can't really afford it, all to avoid thinking or feeling about the problems at hand, then it can be worthwhile to think about what alternatives you could build into your schedule to keep yourself safe and healthy. Are there things missing from your life right now that you would like to introduce to help you take good care of yourself?

Many in the helping professions are really good at taking care of others, but less so themselves, so it can be useful to think about what you might say to someone you cared about in a similar situation, or even to a client.

If you are in counselling training, your training group might now be a resource, along with your supervisor, your tutors, your agency placement, your therapist. If this is the case add them to your list. If they do not feel like a resource – particularly your supervisor and your therapist – then it might be worth considering why not and what needs to change so they become something to draw on in times of need.

Q That is a really interesting thing to have to think about and something I have never considered although tutors have said to us about needing to look after ourselves and to look at our own self-care.

A Having resources and recognising what they are, can be really important in undertaking this work. Training puts lots of demands on us – alongside all the other demands of our normal everyday lives we have to find the time and the money and the energy to meet all the extra demands of training. And once we finish training, the work itself can be demanding. It took some time for me to realise just how exhausting sitting listening can be – after all, 'all' we are doing is sitting in a chair listening! But the reality is each client takes 100% of our focus and our attention for each hour of work. And many of the things we hear can be shocking and disturbing and just downright sad. It can also be very stressful dealing with a very depressed client who may be suicidal or with a child protection issue, even if we are experienced therapists, let alone when you are training and have never had to deal with these issues before. Even when we have worked with a client for a while, we still do not always know what is going to walk into the room with them when they come for their session. As stated above, burnout, vicarious trauma, and compassion fatigue, are all common in the counselling profession, so beginning to recognise how you resource yourself is very important.

Q I am really beginning to see just how important this part of the training is – I had never thought about it in terms of my own safety and self-care but it really is quite difficult juggling all the different aspects of counselling training, and quite exhausting at times. I do love it, but sometimes I do wonder if I have bitten off more than I can chew!

A I think that is not an uncommon feeling at various times for many trainees. It can be useful to consider why you are drawn to this work. Many individuals who enter the helping professions, do so because that is the role they have played in their own families, and for many the call to the work is, on some level, an attempt to heal their own wounding. Many trainees come into training after their own experience of counselling and how it helped them and feel they in turn would like to give something back. Many individuals also enter the counselling profession (and this is true of other helping professions) because in focusing on the problems of others, we do not have to focus on ourselves, and we also can feel better about ourselves if we are the helper, in TA terms, we are ok, whilst the other isn't. That puts us in a position of power, and if we need to be in that role, that is not healthy for ourselves or our clients. None of these reasons are the wrong reasons to come into counselling, but it is important to recognise why we want to take up this role, and what it means to us. In owning that, we can then monitor ourselves and be aware when it begins to creep into the work in a way that may not be in our best interests, and certainly not in the best interests of the clients.

Q I was always the caretaker in my own family, making sure everyone was ok. And often the peacemaker too. Dad had quite a temper, so I used to keep an eye on him to make sure he was not going to lose it! I had counselling years later because of everything that happened at that time, and found it so useful, I thought I would like to help people who had been through a similar thing.

A I wonder how you carry on playing out those roles now and how they could help or hinder your role as a counsellor in the future. It can be useful to reflect on these kind of factors.

REFLECTION

So why do you want to be a counsellor? Write a list of the things that attract you to the profession. Some of the reasons may be:

- You want to help people
- Your friends have told you that you are a good listener
- You have always been fascinated by other people's lives and stories
- You had a great experience of counselling which really helped you and you feel you could do that too
- You are looking for a way of making money that puts you in charge of your life and allows you to work from home around other commitments
- It will enhance your current job role (teaching, nursing, social worker, etc.)

It may be many or all of these reasons, or none of them and there may be some that are completely different from these. It doesn't matter – it's just important to be really honest with yourself. Once you have worked out why you are in training, think about what your answer could mean in relation to your work, for example, if you want to help people, does that mean that you see yourself as stronger/more able than those you may want to help, and what will it mean to you if they no longer need your help? (There can be a danger here, that if we need to perceive ourselves as stronger/better than our clients in some way, we have an investment in keeping them less so.)

This is an area that is not always fully explored in counselling training, and yet it is fundamental to our work. It can indicate where our investments are in relation to our clients and can also indicate something about our relationships outside the therapeutic space.

Q I remember in the chapter on the therapeutic relationship there was an emphasis on understanding relationships outside of the client work, and seeing how that might influence the work inside the therapeutic space.

A Yes. This can also be explored in the class room. Some courses offer personal development groups where group process can be explored including your reactions to other members of the group, and how they behave in the group, and the things that they say. But if you are attending a course where that doesn't happen, you can still give some consideration to how you feel about certain people – who is it in the group that pushes your buttons? Who do you find difficult to relate to in the group? Where are your assumptions and prejudices in the group and where have there been surprises? All of this is really useful information about how you may react to your clients, but also in understanding yourself. Applying theory to yourself as you relate to people, both in training and out of training, can be really useful. If you work with a therapist who is trained in the same theory that you are studying, it can be useful to explore with them your understanding of how theory fits you.

REFLECTION

Take a few minutes to just sit quietly and imagine yourself in your training group. Imagine yourself looking round at the other members of the group – who in the group did you instantly like or dislike, if anyone? Are there people there who you tend to avoid and if so why? What assumptions have you made about the different individuals in your group – and how accurate have those assumptions been and where have been the surprises? Are there people in the group who remind you of someone else, or someone from your past?

Now think about your tutor/s – what are your expectations of them, and where do those expectations come from? What are your feelings towards your tutor? Do you like them, admire them, fear them? All of these or something else? When have you felt like that before and with whom? (It can be useful here to consider your earlier experiences of education and to think about what expectations from those experiences you carry with you now in relation to the counselling training, and whether they are appropriate to your current situation).

Q I have never really understood the point of process groups and personal development groups. Can you explain more about these?

A The training group is a great place for learning. And this is usually the focus of both process groups and personal development groups. Process groups focus on the interactions that take place within the group and what is coming up for the members of the group. It could be something like student A feels that student B takes up too much time in check in and is aware of feeling resentful. The process group can be really useful in exploring what is happening – it could be that student A never got much attention from a parent because one of their siblings was always the favourite.

As I said earlier the training group can be where all kinds of buttons get pushed and many can be to do with our experience of our own family, or about people who have been influential in the past. Personal development groups may also address the group dynamics and issues that arise within the training group, but in many personal development groups, it's whatever anyone wants to bring to the group which could be about their client work, their agency placement, something they are struggling with in their personal lives. It could be any of these things or all of them. What really matters in these groups is our courage to be honest, and to own our own feelings rather than projecting them onto other members of the group and blaming them for how we feel. This can be really useful in also monitoring our own responses to situations – do we want to make jokes to relieve the tension, be the peace-maker when members of the group are angry or just get out of the room when someone is angry and never come back? It's not unusual for clients to express anger in the therapy room – how will you deal with it in that situation if you can't in a safely held space with your peers? If you say something that's maybe a little provocative, do you then want to check everyone is ok. A good personal development group or process group will help you explore your own responses in these situations.

Q I hadn't thought of it in those terms, but now you say that I have noticed that I tend to look out for members of the group who don't seem very happy or comfortable in the group and want to make it ok for them. We had some new members join the group at the beginning of the course who didn't know their way around and I was one of the first to offer to show them where they could get coffee, etc. That's what I have always done in my family – make sure everyone is taken care of and ok.

A It's great that you have so quickly made that connection. Process groups and personal development groups are both places where these different aspects can be explored in a safe place. It also gives us an opportunity to hear how other people perceive us which is something that very rarely happens outside of the training. This is not always comfortable but there can be valuable learning in it and it also mirrors what can happen in the therapy room. We may have to share with our clients aspects of their personality that we can see which are less than positive and that can be uncomfortable. This is echoed in the work we may have to do with fellow trainees, and clients may get angry with us at times, as can our fellow trainees. If the group is well run, and everyone feels safe, this can be one of the most productive parts of training.

Q Sometimes I have noticed some strange unspoken feelings in the group and I can see it would be a good place to talk about what is really happening. I've also heard members of the group bitching about one of the tutors – could we talk about that there too?

> surprises for you in your understanding of your own self? How might this impact on your work with clients? And what about your personal history, how would you apply theory to understanding your own history?

Q I am beginning to get a real sense now of just how complex all of this is and how multi-faceted. I am beginning to understand why this needs to be an ongoing process.

A Carl Rogers described Person Centred Therapy as a way of being. Certainly in training, but for many therapists even once they have qualified, the self-reflection on our reactions to different situations and different individuals never stops. It is always something we can be doing throughout our professional life. We don't stop growing when we finish training, and our life circumstances can change, life carries on, and it will throw up new challenges. All of this impacts on us, so we need to carry on monitoring ourselves throughout our career and to recognise when we need to be checking out with our supervisors how our life in the outside world may be impacting on our professional work with clients. It also involves recognising when it could be appropriate to enter back into personal therapy, which again can be an ongoing resource throughout our professional life.

Q I find myself becoming quite irritated by all the pressure to do personal therapy. I'm feeling pretty together in my own life and don't understand why my tutor insists on personal therapy, and why we have to do process groups. I know some of the other students may need it but I really don't. It feels such a waste of time!

A I know this is something many students feel a resistance towards. However, it is as important to the training process as any time spent in the classroom. Firstly, there is the experience of being a client yourself, which will help you have some understanding of what that may be like for your future clients. Secondly, I think it would be very rare to meet anyone who was completely 'sorted'! Actually one of the best times to enter therapy is when we are in a good place in our own lives. When we are in crisis we are dealing with the crisis and our therapy is likely to be focused on that. However, when we are in a good place, we can really look at ourselves and how we function in the world, and if things in our life are pretty good, we have the resources in place to really look at areas in ourselves that may feel too scary when we are in crisis. And maybe a really good place to begin for you would be to explore why you feel irritated by the pressure to go into therapy and to explore what it means for you to feel 'sorted'.

Q So you think my irritation may be indicative of my own resistance?

A Possibly, but that would be for you to work out with your therapist. It's also important to remember that accessing the unconscious can be a slow process, and these are the areas that can cause the most damage in the therapeutic space – this can be material that is far out of sight and even when it gets acted out in the therapy space, we still struggle to see it or to identify it. We all have our blind spots, and however much work we do on ourselves alone, without someone to reflect back to us what they are seeing or hearing, we may miss some important understandings of what makes us tick! And although many people assume that in therapy the emphasis is on those less pleasant aspects of our personality, it is not unusual in our culture for individuals to be unaware of some of their more positive aspects too. If our conditioning has been that we must not blow our own trumpet – a very English way of being – we may struggle to fully acknowledge just how wonderful or amazing we are too!

Q It sounds like there are some good bits to getting to know myself much better.

A Yes – there are many real bonuses! Working as a counsellor really needs us to have deep level of understanding of ourselves. And it's worth remembering that many therapists believe we can only take our clients as deep as we have gone. We as the therapist need to know there are ways out of the depths because we have walked that path, and part of our role is to hold that knowing for our clients.

EXERCISE

Let's go back to your timeline again. Think about your life so far. What are the big events that you know have affected you either positively or negatively? What aspects of yourself do you struggle with? Are there areas where you feel you sabotage yourself or where you feel disappointed with yourself? Are there relationships which have not worked out, and where you still feel angry or upset, or just puzzled and confused? How would you like your life to be different? What stops you making the changes you would like to make? Who have been the most important people in your life and how did you or do you react to them? Are you someone who looks for approval, or do you not care too much what people think? Why do you think you are like this? These are all areas where you can begin to reflect on yourself.

Q You said something earlier about this process at times being scary – why would it be scary?

A Looking at all aspects of ourselves, both the good and the bad, can mean having to be very truthful with ourselves. Sometimes that can be very uncomfortable – owning our own motivations for something, recognising how our relationships have maybe impacted on us, and are impacting on us, and then looking at whether that needs to change and if so what those changes might be. The more we are resistant to therapy, the more likely it is there is something that is going to be a little uncomfortable once we start our process. Many counselling courses come with a health warning – because the training has the capacity to touch us in such a deep way and affect our way of existing in the world, it can throw up many challenges that are not always comfortable!

Something termed 'therapist factors' have also been shown to be a significant factor in successful therapeutic outcomes – which again outlines the importance of the area of self-awareness within the work we do.

Q Oh yes, you mentioned therapist factors briefly in Chapter 1. What do you mean by 'therapist factors'?

A These are the qualities present in an individual that contribute towards their way of working as a therapist. Some areas have been shown to have little significance – age and gender seem to be unimportant although it has been suggested that female therapists tend to have slightly better outcomes than their male peers. But what is shown is that it is relational factors that are most influential. This means it's our ability to be fully present in the room with our client, and to do that, to be able to be accepting and get alongside them, we have to leave as much of our baggage or our stuff out of the room as possible so it doesn't get in the way. The more we have processed our own past the less likely we are to be triggered in the therapeutic space.

> A recent meta-analysis of nine studies found a significant positive relationship between therapists' wellbeing and clients' outcomes, albeit a relatively small one. (Cooper, 2008: 83)
>
> A small number of correlational studies have suggested that experience of personal therapy are positively related to the therapists' levels of warmth, empathy, genuiness, as well as their awareness of countertransference. (Macran and Shapiro, 1998).

I think this also illustrates what I have said elsewhere, that it can be important to re-enter therapy at different times in our lives and to monitor our own psychological health. But also to put into place as many things as possible that will keep us psychologically healthy – those resources we spoke about earlier.

Q So how do I go about finding a good therapist?

A We will cover this in greater detail in Part II of the book. However, sometimes training centres have a list of recommended therapists in your area. If not, it can be a really useful learning for the future to begin to explore how you do find someone as your future clients will have to go through the same process. Recommendations are always a good place to start – asking family or friends if you know someone who has had therapy previously. Then there is always the internet or the local press. Most training centres recommend you see someone who works with the same theoretical approach you are training in – this can help you gain an understanding of how your theoretical approach works outside the classroom. Of course always check the therapist's level of training and experience – counselling is not currently a regulated profession so anyone out there can set themselves up as a counsellor and it's important that you work with someone who is safe and works ethically and is accountable to a professional body if things go wrong. If you know you have specific issues that need addressing, then it can be useful to look for someone who has experience in that area. After that, it is finding someone who you feel you can work with and feel comfortable with. The internet is also a good place to begin looking and professional bodies such as the BACP have a listing of approved therapists.

Personal therapy has many layers of learning. Working with an experienced therapist who models your theoretical approach and good practice can be enlightening And then of course there is the growing understanding of yourself.

Q How much personal therapy should I have?

A This depends on your training centre and sometimes on your theoretical model. Different centres set different minimum requirements. Sometimes tutors may ask you to do more than the minimum if they feel it would be particularly beneficial to you, and also your supervisor may suggest you enter therapy to address specific issues that they feel are hindering how effectively you are able to work with certain clients, or if they feel you are unsafe.

Q What do you mean by unsafe? That sounds very dramatic!

A In this situation it could mean that you are unable to separate out your material from your clients – that on some specific issues there is confusion around the client's agenda and your own and you are unable to be impartial. It could also be that some of your own material stops you allowing the client to explore all the areas they need to. If we find ourselves changing the direction of the therapy every time it moves near a certain subject then we need to be able to see that we are doing that, and then be able to reflect on why.

Q How would I know that?

A This is where the importance of good supervision becomes crucial. Your relationship with your supervisor would hopefully be one where you can be open and honest, and will give them the opportunity to accurately monitor your work and to reflect on the process with each individual client. (This is covered in more depth in the chapter on supervision.) Supervision is important throughout any therapist's working life, but even more so when you are in training.

Q I would imagine supervision is another place where I can explore my understanding of myself?

A Within limits this is a possibility. However, supervision is about your work with clients and less focused on you and your own history, as much as your reactions to the client and your process within the work. However, this is obviously also good learning and can lead you to exploring other areas of yourself.

Q So we have talked about personal therapy, application of theory to myself and my relationships and my history, personal development groups and process groups. Does developing self-awareness only happen within the context of counselling?

A Another useful tool to expanding our self-awareness can be journaling. Many training courses encourage their students to write a regular self-reflective journal and this can be really useful in exploring our understanding, and to help us spot reoccurring themes and patterns. This is something that many people do anyway, and has been a useful resource for them before they ever came into counselling and may be something that carries on long after training finishes, but there are other sources too.

In reality there are a large number of different possibilities in the way we access personal development. Any good bookshop will have a selection of personal development books along with self-help books. Some of these are very good and can be helpful in encouraging us to think about ourselves and explore different aspects of ourselves. Sometimes there are groups in your local area. Examples of these can be groups around gender and gender issues, spiritual and religious groups (most religions and types of spirituality encourage personal growth and self-awareness as an essential part of good practice), groups using drama, dance, music, art and writing to express aspects of yourself … Actually the list is endless and we can use any event or experience to observe ourselves and monitor our reactions and then analyse these factors based on our growing understanding of theory. The rewards of personal development can be immense and it can really help us become more confident within ourselves, more assertive, and just to be more comfortable in the world.

Q You said earlier about supervision and how supervisors can point out certain aspects that we maybe need to look at – can you say more about this?

Clients sometimes provide our best learning. The work in the therapy room can not only involve looking at the client's shadow, but it can be useful in triggering our own shadow and disowned aspects of ourselves. Maybe we have convinced ourselves that we have no prejudices about someone whose skin is a different colour then find ourselves working with someone who is from such a group, or someone who really does have prejudices and has no problem stating them out loud. Either situation may provoke responses in ourselves that may not be quite what fits in with the preconception that we have no prejudices!

As I said earlier, it's not unknown for trainee counsellors to be given a health warning on entering counselling training! The nature of the training with such emphasis on personal development, and our own healing, means that we invariably change as people. This can be quite challenging for the people around us who may not always appreciate the new person who emerges. Also as we grow and change and begin to understand our relationships, we might want to make changes about how they function. We may begin to see that relationships with which we are involved have become dysfunctional and either need to change or to end. This can be quite difficult not just for ourselves but also for those around us. And to be willing to engage fully with this whole process can be quite demanding. Often trainee counsellors become very enthusiastic about using their new skills and knowledge at every opportunity, which can be both annoying and uncomfortable to the people around them if this is done without invitation. Or even sometimes with invitation! It can be really useful to think about where your own boundaries need to be outside of the counselling room. By this I mean thinking about how you would like to be with friends and family members. Remember, it is seen as highly unethical to act as a counsellor to our own family and friends.

REFLECTION

Think about your friends and family and work colleagues. Make a list of the main people in your life who are most significant to you right now. Then think about different scenarios that could arise where you may find yourself called upon because of the learning and skills you are gaining. An example could be that your best friend finds out their partner is having an affair. As a friend no doubt you would have listened and sympathised, but now you are a friend who has a basket of other skills to call upon. To what extent are you willing to fall into that role with your friend and what might be the consequences for you, for her and for your friendship? At this point it can be worth thinking about your reasons for wanting to be a counsellor and also what it is that makes counselling different from just being someone's friend.

> There are very few of us I would imagine who would not want to step forward and offer support and sympathy to a friend in these circumstances. And it could be really useful and appropriate to use some really good listening skills. However, it would be easy in this situation to inadvertently open someone up more than we intended or is appropriate when we are not in the role of counsellor. And in this situation we are not able to be impartial as we would be with a client. Also what are the expectations we are creating for our friend in this situation?

Q One of the things I have noticed is that some people talk to me more and tell me all kinds of personal things and other people I know act quite suspicious around me and ask if I am 'therapising' them. How do I manage being a counsellor when I'm not working – people seem to act quite strange about it!?

A I have heard many students over the years say how they found themselves in uncomfortable situations with someone they have never met before, pouring out their life story on the train one day. I have reminded them that if they know how to encourage someone to open up, they also know how to give the non-verbal signals to close them down. This is not about being cruel or unkind but it is about taking care of ourselves. We have to learn to switch off and not be the counsellor in every situation that arises. Nor do our kids or our partners want us to be their counsellor – in fact most therapists I know who have kids frequently get told off if they go into that role! It can, however, be very uncomfortable and difficult to manage the feelings that come up when we want to help those we love and they won't let us … and this is where self-monitoring and self-awareness yet again become so important.

Q In class recently we were looking at some theories of child development and I began to realise how I had got some things wrong in bringing up my own kids. I felt really anxious for quite a while afterwards. Is this normal?

A One of the more difficult areas within training, is that as we learn more about the different theories of human development, it can impact on those who are parents and sometimes this can be quite disturbing. Within all theories there is an emphasis on how childhood impacts on the people we become, and particularly how parents, and usually the mother, influence development. This can create quite a lot of anxiety for anyone parenting, or for those who have recently parented, along with guilt, at not having got things right. This is another reason why personal therapy can be so useful. It provides a space where we can express our concerns with someone who understands, and explore any anxieties that come up.

A final point relating to this, Babette Rothschild wrote a book on supporting those who work in the helping professions in dealing with secondary trauma and burnout. In it, she states:

> It will come as no surprise that it is a good idea for a psychotherapist to be familiar with her own life history. The better you know yourself, the greater the chance you will be able to maintain clear thinking when you are provoked by a client or a client's material. All therapists come face-to-face with their own personal issues at times during work with clients. Sometimes a therapist's own experience can be used to enhance the client's therapy. At other times it can interfere. The only way to ensure your ability to tell the difference is to know yourself – present and past – as well as possible. Accomplishing that may involve private soul-searching or it may mean having hours of your own therapy. Being intimately familiar with your past will make it more likely that you will maintain clear thinking and easily distinguish your feelings and issues from your client's. Of course, having the opportunity to resolve problems that linger from your past can also be a bonus for your daily life. At the least, awareness of issues and problems not yet resolved will help to keep your thinking clear when your feelings become provoked in sensitive areas. (Rothschild, 2006: 171)

Enjoy this part of the journey!

SUMMARY

- Self-awareness is needed in all aspects of the therapeutic work.
- Self-awareness is significantly linked to client safety and the safety and wellbeing of the therapist.
- The importance of developing resources to support the work of being a therapist.
- There are a number of different ways of developing self-awareness but personal therapy, good supervision and supportive training are all very significant.

CBT, Psychodynamic, Gestalt, Brief Therapy and TA. The Person-Centred Approach tends to be largely non-directive so techniques as such do not play as big a part – there is more emphasis on the safe, therapeutic environment, which is where the core conditions come in.

Q I think I understand the difference now, but what about 'empathy'? Where does that fit in?

A Good point, and there is some debate about this, but if you look back at the definition above then empathy is not something that a counsellor does or applies to a client, but is more a quality which is embodied in the counsellor, and offered to the client. It is not a skill in the same way as the examples we have listed. Rogers called it a core condition because he believed that it is one of the conditions necessary for client change and growth.

COHERENT USE OF THEORETICAL APPROACH

Q What if I want to work with more than one theory? I like different bits of all of the ones I've looked at.

A There has been a lot of discussion around working 'integratively' or 'eclectically' and the implications of working in this way. Concerns have been raised about how possible it is to learn more than one theory in any depth in the time constraints of most training programmes. Where different theories have not been taught in any depth, newly qualified therapists can end up working without an adequate road map and understanding of the work that they are doing. What then tends to happen is that counsellors have a pick and mix approach when working which frequently lacks any cohesion or understanding of the deeper levels of work.

So this is an area that needs to be approached with a great deal of caution. Studying too many approaches might mean that you become confused, because they have different origins, come from different philosophies, and use different skills and techniques.

However, it is also recognised that not all theories suit all people and a therapist who has a good understanding of different theories is in a better position to address the diversity of their clients.

Q Did we confuse too many approaches last year then?

A No, not necessarily, it sounds as if you had a person-centred core, and used some other humanistic approaches – Gestalt, and also looked at TA, which can fit in quite well together if used appropriately. However, Psychodynamic and CBT come from completely different philosophical ideologies and don't fit so well with the others.

Q Woah, you are losing me now – philosophical what?

A Ok, let's go back a bit and look at where theories come from.

EXERCISE

Each theory was made up by someone having observed human behaviour and formulating a set of ideas or ideals about human personality and development. Think about your person-centred core theory. What are the philosophical beliefs about human behaviour, development and change which underlie this theory?

Q I know about the core conditions – empathy, unconditional positive regard and congruence – is that what you mean?

A No, it isn't – we'll come to these in a minute. Take a step back again and think about why counsellors employ the core conditions, what are they trying to achieve in order to help their client?

Q Oh, I see, we watched the Rogers/Gloria DVD last year and at the beginning he talks about people self-actualising and achieving their full potential, is that what you mean?

A Yes, you are on the right lines now. Rogers believed that the human personality is essentially positive, seeking growth and development, and is driven towards moving forward and achieving their full potential whatever that might be. He described this instinct as the drive towards being a 'fully functioning' individual, and the movement towards achieving full potential he called 'actualisation'. This is his philosophy or ideology – what can be called the core concepts of person-centred theory. He believed that we are each unique individuals who have an innate sense of what is best for us. We all have the capacity within us to find our own answers, to heal ourselves and to naturally move forward and achieve our full potential, but sometimes life events, past or present, get in the way and we lose sight of this capability. This is when we might need some help from a counsellor.

Q I get it now, is this where the core conditions come in?

A Yes, Rogers thought that if the counsellor could provide the right conditions within a safe and non-threatening relationship, then the client would feel held, understood and supported and begin to change by moving through the self-healing and actualising process themselves. Three of these core helping conditions are what you suggested above – empathy, unconditional positive regard (being non-judgemental) and being genuine. Rogers actually came up with six 'necessary and sufficient conditions' – you might want to remind yourself what these are.

> **EXERCISE**
>
> Write down what your understanding is of the difference between theoretical core concepts and core helping conditions.

Q It's coming back to me now, we also learnt about self-concept, organismic self and conditions of worth. How do these fit in?

A These form part of Rogers' concept of 'self'. In contrast to Freud who believed in stages of development, Rogers believed that a person's development was influenced by their interaction with other people and their perceptions of what other people think of them and expect from them. This 'self-concept' as it is called begins in very early childhood and stems from wanting to please parents or care givers – because they are the important people in a child's life. In an environment of lots of criticism and little love then a negative self-concept or self-image develops, can go on being reinforced in future relationships, and can remain into adulthood with consequent low esteem, little confidence and lack of self-worth. If we have been brought up where we get a hug only when we do the washing up, pass our exams, dress nicely, etc. rather than being praised just for who we are, then it feels conditional, that is, we have conditions put on our worth as a human being – called 'conditions of worth' by Rogers.

Deep inside ourselves though there is still an inner part which is more authentic and does not think, feel and behave according to what we deem others to want of us – this is the real self or organismic self. This is the part which Rogers believes sometimes needs some help to emerge and be fully functioning.

Q I think I get it now, so if as a counsellor I provide the right environment and offer the core helping conditions through my relationship with my client, I can enable them to change and to be self-actualising?

A Yes, that is exactly right. However, there is another area that you need to think about. Even though it might sound quite straightforward, it isn't always easy just to provide the right environment or offer the core conditions and hope that the client absorbs them. A client–counsellor relationship is two way and it can be hard work to ensure that your client is getting what you want them to get out of the sessions.

> **REFLECTION**
>
> Taking empathy for example. How would you show empathy towards your client, how would they know that you are being empathic, how would you know that they are feeling the empathy you offer?

UNDERSTANDING THE COUNSELLING PROCESS

Mostly, clients come into counselling because they want something to change, they might not know what it is that they want to change, or they might be very clear about this, and it is the counsellor's job to use appropriate skills and theory to enable change.

The CPCAB model (2015) identifies three dimensions of client problems (see the Introduction for more details).

Q Is this another theoretical model then?

A No, this is a framework under which any theoretical approach can be practised.

Q So what are these three dimensions?

A The first one is called the internal dimension – that is about what is going on inside the client, their thoughts and feelings about themselves. Sometimes referred to as the structure of personality or the structure of self.

Q So going back to Rogers, when he talks about parts of the self being in conflict – the self concept versus the organismic self say, this could be described as the internal dimension?

A Yes, that is right. And the other theories have their own versions of this too – for example, TA describes the Parent, Adult, Child, whilst Psychodynamic defines the id, ego and superego, and CBT works with the conflicts between rational and irrational thoughts.

So you can see that if you switch theories and discuss Parent, Adult, Child in one moment and then start referring to id or to self-concept a little later, it would be very confusing and not at all coherent. So it is good now to start to consider your own philosophy about how people change, and use the theory which has the best fit so that you can always remain coherent.

Q If that is the first dimension, then what are the other dimensions?

A Another one is the relational dimension. This explores patterns of relating – the ways in which the client behaves, communicates and relates to other people who are in their lives. Clients often seek counselling because they feel that the ways in which they relate to others are not working, and in fact may be damaging or destructive. These patterns have again usually started in childhood and continued into adulthood even though they are now outdated and do not serve them well. Counselling recognises that clients cannot change other people, but they can change themselves by relating differently and thus 'invite' others around them to change.

Q So when we studied TA we talked about 'transactions' – communications between people, or between parts of the self, so would this come under the second dimension?

A Yes, that's right.

Then the third dimension is the developmental dimension. This explores the client's issues in the context of their personal history and current life stage, for example, were they neglected as a child, are they in adolescence now, just retiring, starting a family? Erikson's psychosocial stages of development fit well with this dimension, as does Freud's psychosexual stages. Clients cannot change their past, but they can learn to understand it better and to work on viewing it in a more positive, less damaging way.

Each theoretical approach works with these aspects of the client (or dimensions) in its own way because each approach views human development and change in a different way.

EXERCISE

Which dimension would each of the following fit with:

- Childhood sexual abuse
- Always flying off the handle when feeling criticised
- Very black and white thinking
- Never feeling good enough
- Always thinking the worst is going to happen

Q Clients don't know the difference though do they in these approaches? So does it matter?

A Generally no, clients don't know the difference between the theoretical approaches and you might want to argue that surely it doesn't matter what you do as long as you have a good relationship with your client and they are moving forward.

In some cases this might be true, but as a trainee you should not make the mistake of picking and choosing tools and techniques that don't belong to the same umbrella approach. It might be tempting to use the empty chair technique with a client just because you have been introduced to it in your training group that day, but remember that as a trainee you must always be able to explain to your tutors in case presentations, case studies, learning reviews, etc. why you have used a particular intervention or technique and how it fits into your personal philosophy of human development and change.

REFLECTION

Interestingly, Mick Cooper says that 'In general there are only small differences in the effectiveness of different bona fide therapies'.

In addition, in his book *Essential Research Findings in Counselling and Psychotherapy: The Facts are Friendly* (2008: 156) he makes the following statements:

> Positive outcomes are associated with a collaborative, caring, empathic, skilled way of relating.
> Clients' levels of involvement in therapy and their capacity to make use of the therapeutic relationship are among the strongest predictors of outcomes.
> Therapists' ways of relating to their clients are more important to the outcomes of therapy than their personal demographic or professional characteristics.
> There is particularly strong evidence that cognitive behavioural therapies are effective in treating a wide range of psychological difficulties.
> Therapeutic techniques can be a useful part of the counselling and psychotherapy process.

Examine each of these statements in turn and evaluate their relevance to you and your client practice.

Q So if I say I am a person-centred counsellor and yet I believe that we can all unlearn everything we have learnt, but suddenly ask my client to take part in a word association exercise, then I would not be being coherent in my approach?

A Exactly! It would be very confusing for your client if you were to swap between fundamental concepts about human behaviour in the same session, or even series of sessions. In the extreme you might be listening attentively and gently reflecting back feelings at the beginning, then facilitating the miracle question later on, then challenging negative automatic thoughts at another point.

Q This feels a lot to think about. Are there other ways of working with differing theories?

A Yes. In light of all of the factors mentioned above Mick Cooper and John McLeod have developed what they term a 'pluralistic framework for counselling and psychotherapy'. The emphasis here is that there is no one truth when it comes to dealing with psychological distress, and for any one person at different times in their lives, elements of a number of approaches may be applicable. Cooper and McLeod also state:

> Pluralism in counselling and psychotherapy reflects the increasing degree of cultural diversity in clients and therapists, and the importance of developing therapeutic practice that embraces the multiplicity of beliefs that exist regarding healing and change. (Cooper and McLeod, 2007: 139)

Pluralism works with the latest research findings which state all therapeutic approaches are equally effective and stress both therapist and client factors as having the most relevance in successful outcomes, rather than any emphasis on a particular theory or theories.

EXERCISE

- Consider your understanding of different theoretical approaches. Which of these sits most comfortably with you?
- Do you feel more knowledgeable and experienced in one particular theory and what are the areas of weakness either in your understanding of that theory or the other theories you are familiar with?
- How well do you think you could work with theories at this stage in your development?
- Is one theory more dominant in your understanding, or if you have begun client work, are you aware of using one theory more than any other? (It may be that your training is in only one theoretical approach and you have no experience of any others – if that is the case what do you feel is missing, if anything, that may be useful to address?)

TO INTEGRATE OR NOT TO INTEGRATE?

Q You mentioned something about working integratively or eclectically a while back. Can you explain more about these terms?

A Working with an integrative approach means that you weave together a number of approaches into a coherent whole by integrating another theoretical model, or models, into your core approach. This can be done within a framework which has been developed with this idea in mind – one of the most well-known being Petruska Clarkson's Therapeutic Relationship Framework (see Clarkson, 2003). If you are using a framework you need to understand the principles of that framework and decide which theories you intend to use within it and which will enhance the principles of the framework.

So for example, one of the five relationships in Clarkson's model is the I–Thou relationship which fits very well with the person-centred approach. Another of the relationships is the transpersonal, where psychosynthesis would be a good fit. Both person-centred and psychosynthesis share similar philosophical ideologies which come under the humanistic umbrella, so these would integrate well. However, attempting to integrate CBT into the Person-Centred approach can be very jarring as the philosophy behind these approaches is very different.

Q That sounds like lots of learning. I feel I am only beginning to really understand my own person-centred core approach!

A Yes, I know, it might be a tall order right now, yet experienced counsellors on the other hand are more able to select and integrate appropriate tools from their repertoire when they have had years of working with all sorts of clients, a wide range of presenting issues, and have had frequent solid supervision.

Q And eclectic – what does that mean?

A In the eclectic approach you would again have a solid understanding of more than one theoretical approach and when a client comes for their initial assessment, you make a decision which of those theoretical approaches will be most appropriate to work with for that particular client. For example, if you are trained in CBT and psychodynamic approaches, and a client comes along who is only able to pay for short term therapy, and who just has one immediate problem to fix, say anxiety about leaving the house, then CBT may be the preferable option. However, for someone else who has no limitations on attending therapy, and is struggling to understand their relationship patterns, the psychodynamic approach may be much more appropriate.

However with a growing leaning towards what is known as 'the dodo effect' – from the dodo bird verdict in *Alice in Wonderland* where after judging a race around a lake the bird declares that 'everyone has won and so all must have prizes' (that is, no theory is better than any other) – along with an emphasis on the therapeutic relationship, there is a growing movement towards some level of integration. This is also due to the demands placed on qualified therapists when working in different settings.

An ability to adapt to short term work, plus the demands of the organisation in which you are working, may mean that the option of working to one particular theory may not always be an option.

REFLECTION

Thinking about the theory or theories you have learned about so far, where do you see there may be problems in working integratively or eclectically? What do you think would be the pros and cons of working in these ways and if you were to choose this way of working, what is it you would need to put into place to do this well? It might be worth doing some research into the arguments for and against these ways of working and thinking about how these arguments impact on your own ideas.

Q Sometimes it's not so much about theory or even skills, it's just that I feel inadequate with the knowledge I have around the issue that the client is bringing into the session.

A This is a good point. Outside of theory, gaining knowledge and understanding around specific issues can be very helpful, and with some areas absolutely necessary. Your theoretical approach can help you understand from one perspective but additional understanding can really help in working with clients who present with specific issues. This can be true with issues such as bereavement, substance misuse, domestic or sexual abuse, eating disorders and a whole host of other issues. The training is often not from a particular theoretical perspective, although it can be, but looks at patterns and trends in the behaviour of the individuals concerned, along with deepening understanding of how to work in the therapeutic space with any individuals who present with these issues. Quite often this will involve bringing together different theoretical understandings and techniques.

Q That sounds like integrative or pluralistic ways of working.

A It can be but it looks at the particular needs of clients in those specific situations. You would still need to integrate the specialist knowledge and techniques into your own particular way of working, which will have evolved out of your theoretical approach in training. And of course, it must always be adapted to suit the particular needs of your client. Two clients who have the same presenting issue may respond very differently and may need very different support within the sessions.

Q Isn't that one of the benefits of working with more than one theoretical approach?

A Absolutely. Having different ways of understanding a problem, and different ways of working with individuals can only be a good thing, as long as those ways of working are well grounded in your understanding. And also they don't jar too much with your general way of working. It can be shocking for a client and damaging to the relationship if your style of working suddenly changes!

Q It sounds like there are no rights and wrongs here.

A I think it's more complex than 'right' or 'wrong'. The most important basis is understanding why you do what you do and how that is likely to enhance your understanding of the person in front of you. What is also important is that each theory in some way reflects the person who developed that theory and their philosophy which arose out of their own life experiences. What can also be useful, and again is shown through research and the dodo effect is that all theories have validity and all are different ways of seeing human development.

So if you like, we could see someone as a prism with many facets, and if we turn the prism and look through our psychodynamic glasses we may see something slightly different than if we looked at them through our person-centred glasses. However, to come back to the base line, all of this is irrelevant if the therapeutic relationship isn't well established.

Q It almost sounds like I don't need to understand theory!

A Well that isn't true either and actually can be quite dangerous. Theory is the map that shows us the way through the territory – if you haven't got an adequate map, and if you can't read the map and understand the symbols, both you and your client may get very lost. And that isn't good for anyone!

Q I remember at the first group supervision, there was this counsellor who used lots of language I was unfamiliar with and sounded so clever … it was really quite intimidating but I felt very envious of her knowledge. She sounded very sophisticated and intelligent.

A This is why it can be useful to familiarise yourself with the different language used in different theoretical approaches. It doesn't mean you have to understand it in any great depth, but really much of the language is just shorthand for understanding some concept. Even if you are at least familiar with the words, you will have some sense of following what is being talked about. But I would also add here never be frightened to ask!

Q I have noticed that different theoretical approaches are recommended for different issues – what if I'm not trained in a specific approach – does that mean I shouldn't work with the person?

A That would be something for you and your supervisor to discuss. However, although certain theoretical approaches are recommended for certain issues, it doesn't always mean that it's the only way to work but it may be that it has been shown to be the most effective according to research. However, sometimes having counselling, with whatever approach is available, is definitely better than having none at all. So it may be that your theoretical approach is not recognised as being as effective as another, but it does not necessarily mean that it is ineffective either! That brings us back to the dodo effect again and the importance of the therapeutic relationship.

Q I can see that – a friend of mine had therapy through a local agency, and although she had been told she should have CBT the agency did not offer that, only person-centred. However, she said how great it was just to have someone who really listened to her. So she still felt better. We were talking in class about the different influences on mental health and different ways of working – I find it quite scary to think of the responsibility and unsure how I would recognise something serious.

A This is where the importance of good support, both from your agency, who hopefully will be very careful about who they refer to you and will be making sure that you are not seeing anyone that you do not have the experience to work with, and also your supervisor. This is not just vitally important to the mental wellbeing of your client, but is also of vital importance to your own mental and emotional health. Working with individuals who are outside your levels of competence is not only highly unethical, but puts you at risk of vicarious trauma and burnout – which is not something you would want to be faced with at any time in your career but particularly when you are only just getting going!

Q It can feel a long time sometimes between seeing my supervisor when I have questions.

A A good supervisor will be available to support you with queries in between the appointments – obviously within reason. This is why it is important to gain experience during training where you have the support of your tutors and your peers and the supervision groups within the training course.

Q I hadn't thought of it in those terms. I often feel anxious about seeing clients when I am not yet qualified.

A Counselling is a job where you constantly learn by practising – it is not a coincidence that therapists refer to their '*practice*'!

DEVELOPING A PERSONAL WAY OF WORKING

Q So will I get to choose my particular theoretical approach? I quite like the idea of some, but not others.

A The approach that you follow with your clients will initially depend on what you are being taught in your training centre.

Something we have touched on elsewhere is the importance of choosing a training where the philosophy behind the theoretical approach offered, matches your own personal philosophy, that is, you will likely find that you feel most comfortable when the theory being studied mirrors your own beliefs and values about human beings and the nature of change – another example of coherence. It would be hard to work genuinely and congruently with CBT tools and skills for example if you do not think that this approach carries value for you as a person and fits in with your own beliefs about how people can change.

However, in reality this is often very difficult for trainees. Firstly they often do not have the understanding to be aware of the importance of this, and even if they do, they may not have the background knowledge to make a valuation. Alongside this, for many learners, there is little choice of training facilities within their local area and they might just opt for the nearest or cheapest centre.

With that in mind, it may be that you find yourself training in a theoretical approach that doesn't sit comfortably with your own philosophy. This can be quite challenging and there are no quick fix solutions. If you are undertaking a training where you are offered more than one theory, this is a little easier as at least you have another or more theories to consider and work with.

EXERCISE

From the understanding you have gained so far, both through training and through working with clients, if that is something you have begun to do, list what you feel you have learned about the accuracy of your theoretical approach or your approaches. Where do you feel they do not help you understand your client or work with them?

REFLECTION

Let's think more about developing your personal way of working. From your learning so far, in the classroom, from reading, from any work with clients or from your own personal therapy, what do you think is the most important thing you can offer your client?

Here are some ideas – tools and techniques, kindness, compassion, listening and bearing witness, understanding, psycho education. Or is there something else – maybe relaxation techniques – or do you think they are all equally important?

What kind of therapist would you like to be? How do you picture yourself? As all wise and knowledgeable, or as someone gentle, kind and compassionate, or someone who has been through the mill and is really there with your client – or maybe a mix of all three! And how does the theory or theories you have studied fit with this image of how you see yourself as a therapist?

ACTIVITY

From what you have learnt in your training so far, and from reading and research, explore the differences in philosophical ideas (core concepts), beliefs about human development, and the associated skills and techniques of each of the main theoretical approaches. As part of your professional practice (and possibly when seeking accreditation or registration with a professional body) you must be able to explain, verbally and in writing, which theoretical approach informs your client work, and why you work in this way.

Q So when we were doing skills practice last year my tutor would sometimes stop the session and ask me, the counsellor, why I had used say reflection at that point, or why had I asked a closed question, or whatever – so I guess he was testing out if I could link my skills to my theoretical approach?

A Indeed, your core theoretical approach and the philosophical concepts it holds inform the counselling conditions that you hope to set up, and in turn inform the counselling skills that you will employ. It is really good practice when you have recorded a class session to listen back and analyse each intervention in terms of the skills used and how they relate to the theory which informs them.

EXERCISE

Let's just go back to the case of Emma who we last came across in Chapter 4. The counsellor has recognised that Emma has attachment issues – her father left the family when she was little, and her mother has never been there for her emotionally. Emma says 'My Mum was always out, drinking, sleeping around, partying, not caring what I was up to. I had to go shopping for food, cook, do the laundry, everything really, but actually that made me stand on my own two feet and I had to grow up fast.'

Here are two different responses:

a. So you think that your Mum's attitude helped you to grow up fast?

b. What I'm hearing is that although your Mum's attitude helped you to grow up fast, what you really missed was her being there for you.

What skills are being used in each example, which theoretical approach do you think they each might come from and how do these interventions aid the counselling process?

Q So I like the person-centred approach and find that it fits in well with my own beliefs about people and how they develop and change, but one of the things I am noticing is that the agency in which I do my placement asks that we use tools from CBT with our clients. Sometimes this feels overly directive and doesn't sit comfortably with me. It also means I get confused sometimes when I am doing skills sessions in the classroom and realise I've picked up 'bad' habits!

A Yes, I understand that. It can be very difficult for many trainees whose agency placement demands something different than the training establishment. But that is also something to raise with tutors and to ask for help with – it can be worth thinking about how you can use those tools in a person-centred way. Sometimes it can be as simple as the language we use and making sure we are still staying with the client's agenda rather than the agency's!

As mentioned above, the nature of the client problems in any specific agency might determine which approach is most suitable, for example it is quite common when working with addictions to use a more directive approach such as CBT or solution-focused therapy, but in bereavement work it is more appropriate to use the person-centred approach.

However, if the preferred approach of your agency placement does not fit in with your own personal beliefs about human development and therapeutic change then it might not be the right placement for you. Discuss this with your tutors, your peers, the placement manager and your supervisor.

You may find that after qualifying and when you have been practising for a while you then want to specialise in another theory or way of working such as Trauma Therapy, counselling children and young people or couples counselling.

APPROACHES TO UNDERSTANDING COMMON AND SEVERE MENTAL HEALTH PROBLEMS

Q One of the things we talked about in class was the high incidence of mental health problems and where they originate from. I don't think I had fully realised just how many people struggle with their mental health at some point in their lives and many in the class have shared their experience of their own or their family members' problems.

A The latest figures suggest one in four people will struggle at some time in their lives with their mental health which is a high figure. However, if we step back and look at the way many of us live our lives it's hardly surprising. Many, many people face incredible pressures and stresses within their daily lives and high expectations both from society and from themselves and their families. I think you only have to turn on the news to see how it's no wonder it's so difficult for so many people. And that is not even beginning to touch on the bigger issues where people have suffered trauma or abuse, or where they struggle with dreadful living conditions and poverty, or loneliness, or disability or racism.

REFLECTION

Think of three other people you know. The statistics suggest that one of those will be struggling or will have struggled with some level of mental ill health – and it might be you.

(Continued)

> What is your experience of mental ill health either personally or amongst the people you know? What were your thoughts at the time? Were you surprised by that person having mental health problems, or did you feel you could see a reason for it? What was it that most helped them (or you) at the time?

Q We had a discussion on the contributory factors – whether its biological or whether it's a result of societal factors or whether it's both.

A It can be worth thinking about your theoretical approach and how that views mental ill health and distress and from that perspective how your theory would deal with the issues raised.

Q When we have talked about person-centred theory in relation to this we have focused on not labelling people, and yet in my agency when I get a referral the client has often been labelled as depressed or anxious. It can be quite difficult to get away from that.

A Depression and anxiety are often referred to as the common colds of mental health, but both vary in severity enormously and in the effect they have on individuals. Sometimes these terms can be useful as a form of shorthand, and sometimes it's the client who uses the terms to explain how they are feeling. Or it could be that their doctor has suggested depression or offered anti-depressants. In reality we always need to sit down and just listen to our client's experience of whatever it is they are describing. So often I have worked with clients who have been told they are depressed, but then when I hear what has happened to them, it turns out they are having a healthy emotional response to events in their lives which are incredibly sad. Unfortunately we live in a society where sadness is often treated as an illness rather than a healthy response to certain life events which is why the labels are always unclear.

Q I volunteer in a bereavement agency and it is shocking how many clients have been offered anti-depressants when they were grieving.

A We all suffer loss, and transitions, which in themselves are a form of loss, and are one of the biggest reasons people come into counselling. In all of the above situations, even when positive there is a loss of some kind. And we are not always very good at recognising the loss in these situations and the need to grieve. We sometimes have a quick fix attitude as a society and unfortunately that means when someone loses someone they love, there is an expectation they will get over it quickly and if they don't there is something wrong with them.

So here we are with a society that puts pressure on us all to be amazing and successful and happy – and then when we can't cope or are sad for any length of time, we are told there must be something wrong with us, which then makes us more sad or more anxious. It's a horrid ongoing cycle for all involved. However, within all of this there are also some very serious categories of mental health problems and there are ongoing discussions on the factors which contribute towards mental ill health.

Q I think it's the big things that worry me – how will I know if someone is psychotic for example?

A As I said earlier, this is where your supervisor becomes very important and you need to be able to check with them and your tutors when any concerns come up about someone's behaviour. And it may be that you have to refer the client on because it's outside your level of competency.

Q I would feel awful though if I had to do that and tell a client they were too ill for me to work with. How would I do that?

A With the help of your supervisor and agency guidance – and it can feel uncomfortable to have to refer someone on, particularly when we have begun to form a relationship with them and we know they have been rejected before because of their mental health issues. But never the less, we always, always have to work to the client's best interests, and although it may be uncomfortable initially, in the long run it is for their benefit and if it is done well and done gently, then the client can understand that aspect.

Q You mentioned earlier about the different influences on people's mental health – that in itself seems to be a big area.

A It is, and ever changing. The British Psychological Society has recently released a large body of research which they call *The Power Threat Meaning Framework* (Johnstone and Boyle, 2018). This suggests that all mental and emotional distress is a direct result of events that have taken place in the client's life, and the client in turn has developed ways of making meaning and coping with those events. And whilst sometimes those ways of coping can appear dysfunctional, they argue that on some level they make sense if we can listen to the client's story. In many ways this rejects the medical model of mental health, and recognises the validity of counselling in helping people to make sense of their experiences and to bear witness to their story.

Q You mentioned earlier something about categories of client problems? What does that mean?

A Yes, broadly speaking the nature of the problems or concerns that clients present with can be categorised into three main levels – what the CPCAB model defines as service levels. The service levels define or categorise client problems and therefore client need, and also the training and expertise required by the counsellor to work safely and effectively at each level.

Q Can you explain what these service levels are?

A They are given the letters A, B and C.

Service Level A

Service Level A includes everyday or common life problems, things which happen to most people at some time in their life. These are usually current problems, happening now or in the very recent past, and are quite specific and containable such as loss of a job, breakup of a relationship, death of a partner, 'empty nest' syndrome. This level would be characterised by a client saying, 'Generally I'm OK but I'd like help with this particular problem.'

Q So in other words the problems are not deep seated needing psychological help?

A Not at all, often these problems can be addressed successfully with the help of family or friends. But sometimes an external person can give a different perspective which can be very helpful. The problems would not normally be affecting the state of someone's mental health so a trained and skilled helper or a counsellor having done a Level 2 or 3 course would be well suited to helping someone with these concerns. Remember though that the client's problem must be seen in the context of the three dimensions listed above.

Service Level B

Service Level B includes clients experiencing common mental health problems. Their problem is not so much to do with what happens to them, but more about what is going on inside of them. So not just a life event, though a life event may have triggered off the problem, but more to do with the client's psychological state, rather than situational, that is, anxiety, depression. This level would be characterised by a client saying 'I'm still feeling depressed even though it is two years since my partner left me. I felt like this when my mother died a long time ago'. So this is a recurring or repeated pattern and is explicit in that the problem is known and fairly easily identifiable. A first year Diploma student using formally contracted therapeutic work would be able to work with such a client and enable them to build up their resilience.

Sometimes these problems can develop into the next stage where the cause is implicit, not so easily identifiable. A client might be saying 'I keep sinking into a depressed state whenever there is a life event associated with loss.' More in-depth therapeutic work would be required to explore and work through these repeated difficulties, more exploration of the roots of their difficulties, and maybe some forgotten or 'no go' areas of their past. A second year Diploma student, with the support of their agency placement and good supervision would be able to work with such a client.

Q So what you have said here is still all about common mental health problems, but what about more serious ones like schizophrenia, bi-polar, disassociation, PTSD?

A These would fall into the next category:

Service Level C

Service Level C includes those clients who would be described as experiencing severe and complex mental health problems. The root cause will be in the foundations of their being, and go back to early childhood experiences. A client might be saying 'I feel so bad all the time, my problems are affecting my whole life and I can't hold down a job or make meaningful relationships.' Such clients usually need support from a range of services at the same time, including psychiatric help (and medication) and may have spells in residential care. Only specifically trained counsellors or psychotherapists should work with this category.

Q These categories of client work sound quite cut and dried don't they?

A Yes they might do but of course in reality clients don't present in quite such a neatly packaged way; their problems are often mixed up and overlapping with each other. Also it is very common for a client to present with one thing, but then deeper psychological needs are uncovered as the counsellor–client relationship deepens and the client feels safe enough to disclose more of themselves.

For each of these service levels it is important that you understand how your chosen theoretical approach conceptualises mental health problems and the treatment of them.

It is also important as a trainee that you keep up to date with current research on theoretical perspectives as thinking does change. For example bereavement work was originally based around stages of grief such as shock, numbness, anger, bargaining and acceptance. Later on there was a movement towards 'tasks of mourning' – a series of things to work at in order to get through the grieving process. However, today the more contemporary thinking is not so much about going through a step by step linear process, but to spend time exploring the meaning of the deceased to the person who is grieving, valuing the dead person and continuing to keep the bonds that were important when they were alive (as first purported by Klass et al., 1996).

> **REFLECTION**
>
> Going back to Emma, how would your chosen core theory inform the way you would work with Emma if she was your client? Consider the philosophical concepts of the theory, the skills and techniques you might use. What do you think Emma needs from counselling, and which other theories might you wish to draw on?

Q That's very useful. I'm motivated now to do some more reading around my theoretical approach.

SUMMARY

In order to be able to use counselling skills and theory effectively and safely with your clients you need to:

- Have a thorough understanding of one core theoretical approach.
- Use that theory to inform your client work, and apply the associated skills, interventions or techniques coherently.
- Consider carefully what and how you might integrate into your core approach.
- Understand the difference between integration, eclecticism and pluralism.
- Understand the nature and levels of client problems and mental health issues.

7
Working Self-Reflectively

This chapter looks at monitoring and evaluating your own progress, both personally and professionally, by using self-awareness, self-reflection and supervision to maintain high standards of work with your clients.

Q Oh yes, we looked at supervision last year because I can remember thinking that it meant that someone else would be in the room with me making sure I treated my client properly and that I worked ethically and safely. That's not the case is it?

A No, hopefully you now understand that no one else would be in the room, otherwise that would compromise the client's confidentiality. It is precisely because no one else is in the room to monitor the work though, that there have to be other measures in place to ensure safe and effective practice. This is where self-reflection, self-assessment and supervision come in.

EVALUATION OF OWN PROGRESS AND NEEDS

Q After I've done enough training though, and have been accepted in a placement surely I can be trusted to work safely and effectively.

A Well it is not so much about trust as about your own development, keeping pace with your learning and progress, in and out of the client room, and understanding where you might have gaps in knowledge, skills, experience and most importantly self-awareness.

REFLECTION

Take a moment to reflect on what kinds of things could go wrong if you did not continue to look at yourself and your part in the counselling process, and your own learning and development needs.

TIP

Take a look at your ethical framework. It might be timely to revisit some of the significant words such as respect, integrity, accountability, courage, humility. These, and others, can be severely tested in the heat of the moment or in difficult situations with clients, particularly if we do not stay alert and self-aware.

Q Oh, yes I see what you mean. I suppose I could kid myself that everything was fine but I might be missing opportunities to work more effectively. Or I might think I was working soundly but not notice that I had taken away my client's autonomy for example.

A Exactly, because counselling is about working through relationship and using ourselves in that relationship and process, we could so easily as mentioned in an earlier chapter, take advantage of our client without meaning to, not pick up on cues because we are preoccupied with what is happening in our own world, not pay close enough attention to what is going on for them, not realise that a specific tool or theoretical model could be effective. We all have blind spots from time to time and we can all fail to take enough care of ourselves, fall ill and stop working competently.

On your training course you will be used to evaluating and assessing your self and your work, and having others review your progress and development.

EXERCISE

Jot down all the ways in which your progress and development are assessed and evaluated on your counselling course.

You might have thought of self-reflection through reflective journals or learning reviews, written self-reviews, group check in time, process groups, group training supervision. In addition your tutors and peers will also be evaluating and assessing your progress – informally through observation, and more formally through tutor written feedback comments on essays, case studies, learning reviews, etc., tutor feedback on skills (which may be written and/or verbal), peer feedback on skills, one to one or group tutorials.

Q Sometimes it feels like everything I do is being assessed – will I ever get used to it?

A You are training to do an important and professional job with clients who are often in a vulnerable state, so it is really vital that you are being assessed, observed and evaluated by others so that it can be determined whether you are fit to do that job safely to the very best of your ability, and for the best outcome for each client. However, part of the training is also about how well you can self-reflect and assess your own development.

As we said earlier a supervisor is not actually in the counselling room with you and never meets the client. So the supervisor only gets to know the client through you and what you tell them, and you might be tempted to give the impression that everything is going well, or you might truly believe that it is going very well, when really it is not. A skilled and experienced supervisor will be able to help you to acknowledge your strengths and any weaknesses in the work and help you to keep a balanced view, but the more self-reflection and self-assessment you can do the better.

Q So how do I go about doing that?

REFLECTION

You've just listed above a number of ways in which other people might be assessing you, some of it verbal, but most of it written down in the form of feedback comments. So the first thing to do is to collect all this feedback together and read it through reflectively.

Think about what it is saying about you, are there any broad themes, is there a common thread, what are your strengths and what are your weaknesses? Are the comments for your skills really good, but your written work seems to be poor on theory, are you skilled at contributing in group discussions but find it difficult to articulate your ideas in an essay? Are you up to date with all the work, or behind on some things, is your attendance up to the required level?

Be critical of yourself, and analytical, in an objective way as if you were reading about someone else – maybe get a buddy to help you. Then make a list of areas that you have identified as needing some attention.

Q This sounds like a massive exercise. Won't it take me ages?

A The first time you do it, it might take a while, so don't leave it too long – at the end of the first term might be about right, then termly. When you have done it once though, you are more likely to be continually on the lookout for all the positive feedback which reinforces your progress and shows that you are addressing those gaps. This is the beginning of good practice in monitoring your own progress and identifying your needs.

Q So when I've looked through all the comments and identified my strengths and weaknesses, what next?

A Then make a plan for how you will address the areas where there is a learning or developmental need. Write down the area to work on, and next to it write down what you are going to do about it, with a timescale; for example, if your skills are lacking, ensure that you take the role of counsellor every time there is a skills practice in class; if your knowledge of theory is scanty undertake to do some relevant reading by the next half term holiday; if you are finding it difficult to be open in process groups then it might be a good time to start personal therapy.

EXERCISE

You might find it helpful to do a SWOT (Strengths, Weaknesses, Opportunities and Threats) analysis.

Put these four headings on a sheet of paper.

From looking through all your feedback, list all the strengths and all the weaknesses that you have identified, then consider any opportunities these might give you. For example, if your knowledge of theory is good then maybe you could use that to your advantage by doing a presentation to the rest of your group. If your theory is not so good, then take the opportunity to ask your tutor for some relevant reading and give yourself a deadline for doing it.

Threats might be that the Christmas holiday is coming up and it is always such a busy family time that you know you won't get much work done – so be realistic, but also plan in some time, even if just an hour here or there where you can do some reading.

Go through this same process for every strength and weakness you have listed.

Now you have a plan. In your training centre this might be called an Individual Learning Plan, or be part of a CPD (Continuing Professional Development) programme.

Remember, that in the same way that others are giving you feedback to assist your learning, so you are doing the same every time you complete a skills observation sheet for a peer, or contribute to group training supervision, or give feedback on their case presentation. Knowing how to word your feedback constructively but not critically is also a part of the learning process, so that you are praising their strengths, and helping them to find out what might be useful for them to work on.

Q Sometimes my peers don't always agree with the feedback that I give – I don't think some of them are as self-aware as I am and it can get a bit awkward, what can I do about that?

A Sometimes it helps to defuse the situation by saying that it is just your view, your opinion, and they do not have to agree with it. Sometimes people find it hard to hear what they interpret as something critical, yet often when they have processed it they find there is something in it to be learnt. Make sure you stick to facts that you have observed, things that they can actually work on if they wish, not personal comments about the individual themselves.

You might have heard of this (alleged) exchange between Winston Churchill and another lady. She called the Prime Minister a drunk and he retorted with, 'My dear you are ugly, but tomorrow I shall be sober and you will still be ugly'.

Remember too that as your peers begin to work with clients in an agency setting they might be counselling in a slightly different way than you have been taught in class, perhaps because of the unique type of client issue, or because the approach is different. So allow yourself to be curious, rather than critical, about what it is they are saying or doing.

Q What about if I disagree with the comments my tutor has given though?

A This can be equally as difficult. Do your best though not to be defensive about it, don't start saying things like 'I only did that because …' or 'No I'm sure I didn't say that.' Just listen quietly, maybe ask for it in writing if it is verbal then read it quietly when you are away from class and reflect on which if any parts of it might be true. If you can honestly say that it is not right, then don't dwell on it, your tutor might have been having a bad day! Otherwise resolve to watch out for anyone else giving you similar feedback and learn from it.

If you are looking at written feedback on a piece of work you have taken home such as an essay or Learning Review and can't understand the comments or don't agree with them, then it is best to talk to the tutor who has assessed it as soon as you can. This might mean contacting them before the next class to make an appointment to meet. Before you meet, put aside some self-reflection time, and think carefully about what it is that is really concerning you, and what you want to happen – an explanation, a re-mark or whatever. Be very clear in explaining what the problem is, but again avoid becoming defensive – there may well be something you can learn from the feedback.

Q So, this has been all about my learning and development in my training, what about being able to reflect on and evaluate my counselling practice?

A Yes, you are right and this is where supervision comes in. Your tutors and peers will be able to give you feedback on your counselling competence in class, and help you to reflect on your own performance, and your peer role playing the client will be able to add their observations and feelings too, because they are also in training. In placement though your tutors and peers will not be there to give you this feedback. Your client, though you can ask them how the session has been for them, or review together how it is going, will not be able to feedback on your use of skills and theory in the same ways that tutors and peers can, so self-reflection and supervision become vital.

Q I've heard people talking about 'clinical supervision' – what does this mean?

A This is supervision for therapeutic work with counselling clients, as opposed to other kinds of work like mentoring, nursing, befriending, social work, etc. where a supervisor would mainly be helping you to manage your case load, juggle appointments, review the progress of each service user or patient and so on. But therapeutic or clinical supervision pays in-depth attention to what is going on for you in the relationship with your counselling clients, the patterns of behaviour that might emerge for both of you, the emotional impact on you as a person, and the care of your clients.

Q But I will be going to my own personal therapy to look at what is going on for me, so why do I need supervision as well?

A Personal therapy, or your own counselling is about you, how you are made up, your personal history and your patterns of relating – it helps you to self-reflect and to feel what it is like to be 'on the other side'. Your therapist though will only be interested in your client work incidentally, not primarily, whereas your supervisor's main aim is to look at you within the context of your client work. Their focus is on the safety and wellbeing of your client through you as the intermediary.

Besides, it is an ethical requirement to have regular and on-going supervision.

As we have explored above, you can learn to do a lot of exploration and processing on your own through reflection, through feedback from others in your class, from your tutors and so on, but no one else will actually be able to spend the necessary time talking with you just about your client work.

Q What do I look for in a good supervisor then?

A Finding a supervisor who suits you can be as tricky as finding a therapist. As a trainee you may not yet have got fully formed ideas of how you work with clients so you are probably not too sure of what you actually need in a supervisor.

See Part II Practice Issues on what to consider, how to find a supervisor and how to work out how much supervision you need. Here you will learn more about the importance of working with someone who you feel is in tune with you, your values and your counselling approach and the ways in which you reflect on your work. You should be able to be yourself, so if you find yourself hiding things, feeling criticised and not talking openly then the relationship will not be useful – so trust, openness and honesty are essential ingredients. A supervisor who has counsellor training in the same modality as you are studying can really help you to understand and apply the theoretical concepts you are learning. It might also be worth exploring the supervision model that the supervisor uses.

Q Supervision model? Don't tell me there are models of supervision like there are models of counselling!

A Yes, indeed there are.

Q Oh, no, I'm only just beginning to get my head around the different approaches to counselling – do I have to learn about a number of supervision models as well?

A Well, only in as much as it is useful to know that these models exist, maybe to explore with your supervisor which approach they use and why, and so that you can maybe understand more clearly how they are working with you.

Q OK, I get that, so what are these models then?

A We will have a look at three or four of them, just an overview, so you can read more about them yourself.

A developmental approach to supervision was first originated by Stoltenberg and Delworth (1987). It has since been adapted and developed by other theorists, yet all illustrate the various stages of development of a counsellor in supervision (based on understanding, skills, knowledge and experience):

- Level 1 – supervisees are generally entry-level trainees who are high in motivation, yet also high in anxiety, insecure about their role and ability, and fearful of evaluation or judgement. The task of the supervisor is to balance support with uncertainty and 'not knowing'. There can be high dependency on the supervisor and yet a reluctance to share. Some theorists call this stage the Novice stage or the self-centred stage.

- Level 2 – supervisees are at mid-level and experience fluctuating over or under confidence, motivation and despondency, often linking their own mood to their success (or not) with clients. They move between dependence on the supervisor and autonomy, sometimes feeling overwhelmed, and sometimes carried away with excitement. Emotional holding balanced by space to learn is necessary. This is sometimes called the Apprentice stage, or the client-centred stage.
- Level 3 – Here supervisees have increased self-confidence in their work and begin to move away from dependency on the supervisor. There tends to be more ease with sharing, more work at an emotional level and more in the way of challenge from the supervisor (than at Level 2). They are able to be more considerate of the client, and to adjust their interventions and approach to the needs of the client. This is sometimes called the Journeyman stage, or the process-centred stage.
- Level 4 supervisees are qualified and experienced practitioners, essentially secure, stable in motivation, have appropriate empathy tempered by objectivity, and use their whole therapeutic self in the counselling process. They may be moving into consultative supervision (that is, peer to peer or in a group of similarly experienced therapists). This is sometimes called the Master Craftsman or Expert stage or the process-in-context-centred stage.

REFLECTION

Read through the four levels or stages above and decide which one you fit into at the present time. You might want to check this out with your supervisor.
Which level would you like to be in at the end of your current training (or a two-year Diploma)?

Q I like this model – it is easy to understand, I don't feel quite so worried about supervision models now, and I can see very clearly which level I fit into. So what other models are there?

A Inskipp and Proctor (1993, 1995) developed a model based around 'tasks of supervision'. They described three main tasks or functions, namely normative, restorative and formative:

- Normative (also labelled 'managerial') provides the quality assurance and monitors standards – ensures the counsellor is working safely and ethically.

This is largely to do with boundary issues, legalities, procedures and record keeping.

- Restorative (also called supportive) allows space in the supervision sessions for exploration of the counsellor–client relationship and concerns the counsellor might have. The counsellor might need re-motivating and need lots of support. It is also the time for 'play' – playing with creativity, tools and techniques, using imagination.
- Formative (also called educational) enables further exploration of the client and the interventions or skills which the counsellor has been using. For trainees there might also be a deepening of knowledge and links with their theoretical approach. Self-awareness in terms of the counsellor's own reactions and responses to the client would also be part of this task.

Q So would I as a trainee have to work through each of these three tasks in turn?

A No, it is very different from the model above – these are not stages of development. These three tasks can all be used at any level, and the amount of attention each task is given in any one session depends on yes, to some degree the experience of the counsellor, but more on the nature of what the counsellor brings to any session.

Q Can you explain that?

A Let's think of an example – if the counsellor had a child protection issue with a client then the counsellor and supervisor might spend quite a lot of the session in the Normative function, but if the counsellor felt completely deflated after an uncomfortable session with a client, then they would most likely spend a lot of time in the Restorative function. Have a go with the examples below.

REFLECTION

Take each of the following in turn and think about which 'task' they could fall under (remember that the tasks can overlap) if you took them to supervision:

- A client is continually late for her sessions
- Your client is very angry and is barely containing it in the counselling room
- It has become apparent that a client's sister is a friend of yours
- You believe that your client would benefit from referral to a specialist therapist

(Continued)

- You are aware that you have slipped into the habit of asking too many closed questions
- A client has read about the Gestalt two chair technique and wants you to use it with him next time
- A male client revealed that he often looks at internet porn and you feel shocked
- Clients in your agency are allowed six sessions and a young man is pushing for more
- You are left with a deep sense of sadness after your client, a young woman, talked about the sudden death of her baby
- You want to practise a new technique you were taught at College today

Another well-known model is the Process Model, or six-eyed model, developed by Hawkins and Shohet (2012). This is different from the ones above as it is not about stages, steps, levels or tasks, but much more about what is actually going on between the client and counsellor, and between the counsellor (supervisee) and the supervisor – in other words the relationships and processes which are present, hence the name the Process Model.

This model advocates looking at the various processes and relationships from a number of different perspectives, or 'eyes'.

Q You are losing me now, what are these eyes?

A Hawkins and Shohet described six eyes (later this was adapted to eight, but we will keep it simple here) or six different ways to focus in supervision:

1. Reflection on the content of the session – how the client presented, what the client shared, what was the client's story. The focus is on the client.
2. Responses, interventions, techniques and strategies used by the counsellor – what he or she did or said and why, and exploration of alternatives. The focus is on the counsellor.
3. The relationship between the client and the counsellor – what was happening consciously and unconsciously between them in the session, what happened round the edges, and use of metaphor and images. The focus is on this relationship.
4. The internal process of the counsellor – what was going on for the counsellor in the session and what the counsellor has been left with – thoughts, emotions, bodily feelings and images. The focus is on the internal world of the counsellor.

5. The relationship between the counsellor and the supervisor – a close look at what is happening in the supervision room in the here and now as it might be that the counselling session is being played out or 'paralleled' in the supervision room, for example the counsellor may have picked up the client's anger and be behaving angrily towards their supervisor. The focus is on this relationship.
6. The internal process of the supervisor – what was going on for the supervisor in the supervision session and what he or she is left with – what thoughts, emotions, bodily feelings and images. The focus is on the internal world of the supervisor.

Q There are a lot of words here and it sounds a bit confusing, do you think a diagram might help?

A Hawkins and Shohet illustrated their model with a diagram called the double matrix – essentially a series of overlapping circles representing each area of focus or 'eye'. You might want to look it up to learn a bit more.

Q Yes, I will do that, because although it sounds a bit complicated, I can see that it really looks at the processes and the relationships and that fascinates me. Are there any more models?

A Yes, there are more, but we won't go into all of them at the moment – other than to mention one in particular which is often taught on training courses, and that is the Cyclical Model. Developed by Page and Woskett (1994), this is represented by five circles which when depicted in a circle themselves form the stages of supervision – namely Contract, Focus, Space, Bridge and Review. Each of these five circles has five segments which list the components of each stage. The five stages might be worked through in one supervision session, or over a number of sessions.

Q All these circles – I can see why it's called the 'cyclical' model! I think I need to have a closer look at these models, and I will certainly ask my supervisor what he/she uses. It seems to me that I will have to think carefully about what I want out of supervision, and all of the models above in one way or another focus on the relationship between client and counsellor.

A Most supervisors will not want to be burdened by too much 'story' or narrative; they will prefer to work with the process of what is happening between you and your client.

Q Oh, I get it, they don't want all the 'he said ...', then 'I said ...', then 'he replied ...'.

A No that's right, they want to hear about the nature of the relationship between you and your client and how you are using that relationship, aspects of yourself and your skills and theory to help the client. If you are struggling or feel stuck your supervisor will be able to listen, help you to reflect more deeply and suggest ways of moving forward. Sometimes just reframing a sentence, or using a different word, can give a different slant on the situation. Your supervisor will see the bigger picture rather than just the microcosm that you are in with the client.

Q So I should learn something about myself and my client work by the end of my supervision session?

A Invariably you will. Sometimes trainees are nervous about going to supervision for the first time because they think that they and their work with clients might be judged, and found wanting. A good supervisor will not be like that and supervision should be enjoyable, a place of safety, containment and development. It will soon become a habit or routine, an integral part of your good practice, and not some imposed add-on that you resent having to spend time and money on. It is part and parcel of your counselling work.

EXERCISE

On an A4 sheet of paper draw a circle in the middle to represent yourself, and label it 'trainee counsellor'. Now draw across the page another 15 circles randomly. Take each of the words listed below, think about where you hold or visualise that item in relation to yourself as a trainee and place each one in an appropriately placed circle relative to yourself, for example, if you believe that your training group is very important and 'close' to you just now, then you would put that in a circle very near your own circle. Continue like this throughout all the words, and lastly decide where 'Supervision' should be placed.

PERSONAL THERAPY, AGENCY PLACEMENT, ETHICAL FRAMEWORK, CLIENTS, TRAINING GROUP, PEERS, TUTORS, COURSE WORK, SOCIAL LIFE, FRIENDS AND FAMILY, WORK, THEORY, SKILLS, SELF-AWARENESS, SUPERVISION

Now look at the representation of your counselling world as a whole – do you want to move any of the items? How does it feel to move some of the items nearer to you, or place them further away, what does this mean? You might want to try this same exercise later on in your course and see if the emphasis has changed in any way.

Q Yes, I've got a better idea now of where supervision fits in. I'm quite relieved actually that there is someone else who can help me to self-reflect, to oversee my fitness to practise and take some responsibility for my client work.

So when I've had my supervision session I just carry on then with each client until the next month?

A At the end of your supervision session it might help to make a note of what you and your supervisor discussed, what you have learnt and/or decided as the way forward. It is not the same as therapy and you can take notes during the session if you want to. The important thing then is to continue to reflect – reflect on what you have learnt and take this learning back into the work with your client.

Q I am not sure what you mean by 'taking it back', can you explain?

A It is one thing to reflect on the counselling process with your supervisor, talk about your feelings, how the client is progressing, etc. but that is only part of the story. You will need to think about your part in the process, how your skills, thoughts, behaviours have impacted on the client–counsellor relationship. Your presence and use of self may have enhanced the relationship and process or may have impacted negatively – either way it is helpful to reflect on what you can actually do, say, or be, next time in order to maintain a good relationship and continue with effective work.

Q Is there a name for this?

A Sometimes it is called 'reflexivity' – that is the skill of actively reflecting on your part in the process and doing something about what you have learnt, which is different from passively reflecting where you might be doing some excellent reflection and processing, but if it all stays in your thoughts and in your head then nothing much is likely to change in the counselling room.

> **TIP**
>
> Remember that supervision is not personal therapy though and whilst your supervisor may be interested to know what is going on for you, this is only in so far as it impacts on your client work, and you will be advised to go to your own counselling if that is likely to be beneficial.

REFLECTION

Think about how you might demonstrate in your training group, to your tutors and peers, and to your supervisor, how your client work has been enhanced by the use of supervision.

DEVELOPING AN INTERNAL SUPERVISOR

Q I have heard about the internal supervisor, but what does it mean?

A As you become more confident and more experienced as a counsellor you will find that you automatically reflect on your work on your own and come to rely less and less on your supervisor. That is not to say you will not continue to need your supervisor, but between supervision sessions you are likely to do quite a lot of the processing for yourself.

Q How can I do that?

A Remember we talked about your awareness and developing a heightened sense of self-awareness? When you are more experienced and are not too burdened down with getting all the details of the contract right, remembering the skills, watching the time, listening and responding appropriately you will be able to sit back a little and allow your 'high alert' factor to kick in.

Then you will be able to make use of all your senses to pick up on a deeper meaning, to really hear what is not being said out loud, to make connections in what the client is saying. You may not wish to voice all of these at the time but to register them, explore their meaning for yourself and remember them to bring back into the sessions when appropriate. Out of the session when you reflect on the work you will find yourself working things out on your own, you may well 'hear' the voice of your supervisor making suggestions.

This is your internal supervisor at work.

Some people call these 'helicopter skills' – imagining yourself floating or flying just above the two of you in the counselling room, just slightly outside of yourself – what can you see or pick up on, almost as if you were a third person in the room. You can choose to stay hovering, and just absorb the atmosphere, or zoom in and examine something in more detail, then zoom out again, you can land on something to explore and fly off again. Developing these skills comes with practice and experience and proves you are truly becoming a competent counsellor.

EVALUATIVE TOOLS IN COUNSELLING WORK

Q We did something last year about 'outcome measures'. What are these and how do they fit in here?

A We have talked a lot about self-reflection, self-awareness, monitoring and overseeing. Supervision really helps with all of these, but rarely actually measures our client work in terms of knowing if the client really feels any better at the end of the sessions. How do we really know that what we are doing is meeting the client's needs?

Q I always ask my client though how they feel and we have regular reviews.

A And that is good practice, but is very subjective. The client may have moved on a lot, but can't see it, they may have become dependent on therapy and are afraid to say they feel better because you might end the counselling, they may want to say what they think you want to hear to please you.

On the other hand you might want to please your tutors, your agency and your supervisor by saying how much progress your clients are making but how can you really tell? Indeed you might want to tell your client that you think they are doing well – to bolster them up, to motivate them, to make yourself feel better.

Q I suppose it comes down to feelings.

A And feelings can be so subjective, for the reasons above.

In addition often it is beneficial to be able to demonstrate to other people that counselling is working. That might be the trustees or management committee of the agency, the NHS, or the fund holders who are keen to know that the money they are contributing is reaping rewards, that is, having a positive effect and that client needs are being met, that therapy is effective and that the service is being maintained or improved.

Q That is why it would be useful to have some kind of measuring device I suppose.

A Exactly – some kind of evaluative tool can be really useful, if not essential.

Q So that makes me think of client assessment which we looked at earlier in the book. Are the two linked?

A Yes, they are – it would be difficult to measure the outcome or end result if you hadn't gauged the starting point. So most tools are used at the beginning of therapy and then again at the end – to measure the progress of the client over a period of time. Some tools are even used at the beginning and end of every session.

Q Is this the same as 'evidence-based practice'?

A Yes, it is. You are probably assessed on your training course through evidence-based criterion referencing, that is, you collate evidence of your competence to meet a set of criteria. You probably started your course by completing something like an Initial Learning Statement, a review of your current skills, knowledge, thoughts and feelings, and ideas for where you want to get to by the end of the first year, say.

Q Is this the same as client assessment and evaluation?

A In many ways yes, you will be ascertaining your client's needs and where they want to get to, and then working with them accordingly. At the end of therapy you will review with them where they are and if their needs have been met, like on your course where you will hand in a completed portfolio where the work has been assessed against criteria to determine if you meet the standard for the qualification.

Q So what do these assessment and evaluation tools look like?

A They usually take the form of a series of targeted questions (often on computer, for example, www.coreims.co.uk) which are designed to reveal the emotional and physical health of the client by looking at symptoms which can limit wellbeing. Client answers are scored or scaled – an example might be 'On a scale of 1 to 10, if 10 is the best, how well are you sleeping at present?'

At the beginning of counselling the assessment of symptoms can help to diagnose levels of distress and enable the counsellor to carry out the most effective work – sometimes called treatment. At the end of counselling a significant or even small reduction in symptoms would show client improvement, so this is clearly then measured – often referred to as client outcome measures.

Q I'm not sure how happy I am about doing questionnaires with my client. Won't these 'tools' get in the way of the counselling?

A There are different schools of thought on this, and your theoretical approach can affect how you view them or what you choose to use. Assessment tools and outcome measures fit very well with the cognitive behavioural model, CBT, but maybe not so well with the Person-Centred Approach.

Q Is there just one tool then or lots?

A There are quite a few – look back to Chapter 1 for the names of some of the more commonly used ones – some are more suited to counselling rather than psychiatry or medical diagnosis.

REFLECTION

From the list of the evaluative tools you considered in Chapter 1, which one fits best with how you work as a professional counsellor, and with your client base?

Q I understand now about the range of tools available and why it can be so valuable to measure the progress of my clients. I think I will have to consider carefully how I introduce these tools though so that I do not discourage my client from entering into the process.

A Yes, that is a good idea as it is important that you feel comfortable with any tools you have to use, that you are familiar with how to use them, and can introduce them in a client-centred way.

SUMMARY

In order to work self-reflectively as a counselling professional you will need to:

- Take time to reflect on your development – both personally and professionally.
- Monitor and evaluate your own progress and needs.
- Develop your own 'internal supervisor'.
- Make full and effective use of clinical supervision.
- Understand a range of evaluative tools.

PART II
PRACTICE ISSUES

8
The Counselling Training Placement

FINDING A PLACEMENT

Completing placement hours is often the most exciting and nerve-wracking part of a trainee's experience. Here we look at some of the positives and pitfalls of gaining and maintaining a work placement in a counselling service agency.

Q The thought of working with real clients is pretty daunting and scary but on the other hand I can't wait to get on with it. I feel I have had lots of practice in class now what with role play and working with my peers … the next bit is to do the real thing, but how do I even start?

A It might be useful to start by considering what you would like to get from your placement work. Do you have a particular area of interest, or a client group you have always wanted to work with?

Q I'm not really fussy, I'd like to work with the widest group of clients possible. So I thought I'd just send out my CV to a few generic agencies locally and wait until they get back to me. Does that sound enough?

A Hmm, that sounds a bit random. It can be very hard to find a placement of any kind but it's worth spending a bit of time thinking about what you are looking for and why. That will help you tailor your approach to any specific agencies and help you explain why you want to work there and what you can offer.

ACTIVITY

Draw up two lists to describe what you are looking for in a placement. One list should identify your 'needs', these will be the key areas that you absolutely must have in place for a placement to be viable for you, e.g. within 20 miles of where you live, and on a public transport route. The other list should identify your 'wants', these will be the other aspects that in an ideal world you would hope would be provided by a placement, e.g. free in-house supervision from an experienced supervisor.

Consider all the practical and experiential aspects of a placement and really focus on what is important for you and for your training. When listing all your 'wants' don't be held back by what you think is possible or impossible – at this stage let your mind wander and create as full a picture as you can of what a great placement would look like for you.

Q But I'd like to ask why the tutors don't just find an agency for me to gain my client hours. After all, if you train as a nurse, or doctor or social worker the placement would be part of the training wouldn't it? I wouldn't have to go and find my own placement like I do here.

A I think that is a good question which is not that easy to answer. It is partly that counselling is not a statutorily regulated profession so there is less oversight of the training. But in reality it is more because counselling agencies often operate using a lot of volunteer help from trainees and so both parties gain from the arrangement. To put a positive slant on it … you will have more autonomy in choosing a placement that suits you and hopefully somewhere you will really enjoy working.

Q As I'll be giving my time for free I'm sure that any placement will just snap me up though. Surely it's just a case of contacting an agency and saying when I'm free to volunteer?

A Ahhh think about the sort of work you are offering to do … if you were an agency would you just allow every person to have access to your clients so easily? No probably not. Actually the placement market can be quite competitive and you will really need to show them that you are the best person for the 'job'.

REFLECTION

If you were running a counselling agency in the future, would you take on every volunteer who contacted you? If not, why not?

Q Yes I can see that makes sense, it all sounds really hard though. I have another idea! If I don't manage to find a placement, me and a couple of other students could just set up our own agency and advertise for clients and hire a room locally. You know, we could share the admin and so on. Or maybe we could put up a notice offering counselling in the college. There must be loads of people who would welcome a chance of free counselling.

A Whoa … slow down a minute, there are loads of things to think through here both ethical and practical. Let's start by thinking about what the placement is for and why it has to be an actual placement rather than just a way of getting clients or setting up in private practice?

Q Actually given how hard it is to find a placement it would really help me to understand why it has to be an agency placement. Surely if you have supervision of your client work isn't that enough?

A Ok let's look at what we mean by an agency and what it can offer:

A good agency will:

- Provide appropriate indemnity and liability insurance.
- Provide appropriate client assessment and referral procedures.
- Meet the health and safety obligations to client and counsellor.
- Work in accord with relevant legislation.
- Provide induction, training, mentoring and line management support to the trainee.
- Provide agency supervision, OR monitor supervision provided by independent supervisors who are not part of the agency.

Working as a volunteer in an agency setting to begin with means that you will have a higher level of support and an ethical structure in place to ensure that you and your clients are safe. Do you see how this is really different from just advertising for clients and setting up on your own?

Q Yes, I can see that now. So I would need to make sure that an agency has all of those things in place when I began and make sure that it will provide me with enough support?

A Yes, your tutor or training college should be able to help you work out the sort of questions you might want to ask. They may even have a written agreement or placement guidebook to help you establish the working contract between you and your agency.

Q Ok so now I have a better idea of what I want to look for, where do I start looking? Is it as simple as searching on the internet?

A Great idea – the internet is often a good place to start. There are many directories of counselling services and a web search in your local area will provide you with many results. You could also ask at your college or share ideas with your peers on your course and see what agencies they know of.

Q But surely they're my competition! Why would they share their ideas with me, or I with them?

A Because it's not a case of one placement fits all. They may have found somewhere offering a great placement, but it might be too far away and they don't drive, or the placement may want someone on weekdays and your peer can only do weekends. You won't know until you ask. Remember as you move on through your working life as a counsellor your peer network will be a great form of support and that might as well start now.

ACTIVITY

Make a long list of all the counselling services in your area. Include their contact details and ideally the name of someone who you can make contact with.

APPLYING FOR A PLACEMENT

So you now have a lovely long list of potential agencies and it has come to the time when you need to start to contact them. What sort of questions are going through your mind?

Q I'm really nervous about approaching agencies and making a bad first impression. It's really important to me to make the right sort of application. I've applied for jobs before and got them, is this really going to be so different?

A Actually that's a really good way to look at it. If you consider it to be like a regular job application and make the same level of effort you will be heading in the right direction.

Q So if I put together a decent application letter and a CV and send it off to a few agencies and then wait for an offer to come through would that be a good start?

A Well yes that's a good starting point but you might want to review some information on how to tailor a CV and a covering letter to each application. For example, what do you know about each agency and the sort of work that they do? What is their company ethos and what theoretical approach do they work with? How can you show this knowledge in your application and explain that you have the skills and commitment to offer them a valuable service?

> **EXERCISE**
>
> Note down all the ways you can think of to research a chosen agency to find out about the sort of work they do and how they are structured. This might be a good point again to make use of that developing network of people in the field, e.g. peers, tutors.

Q Ah yes I think I see what you mean. I need to show them that I really want to work for them in particular, not that I'm just another counselling student sending out blanket letters.

A Yes! Think about it paralleling the counselling relationship – you would want your client to feel individually valued and respected for who they are, not that they are on an impersonal conveyor belt. It is this prizing of their uniqueness that begins to build rapport. You would want to extend that same feeling into your first encounters with placements, so that they get a real sense of you and why you would be a good fit for their particular agency.

Q So I want to make sure that they know how special they are to me. How do I go about showing them that I'm special and they should choose me above all their other applicants?

A This is a great question and one that will help you in your initial approach to an agency and in any sort of interview. You could start by considering what you have to offer them that makes you stand head and shoulders above the crowd, and how you might phrase it so that your abilities are clear to them.

Q Hang on a moment there, did you say interview?! What sort of interview will I be expected to do? This really does now feel like a job application and I'm a bit scared. I always get nervous at interviews and I can't imagine what interviewing for a counselling role would be like.

EXERCISE

See if you can complete these starter sentences with your own information and ideas. They might be useful phrases to use in a CV or to explain in an interview.

I feel I am right for this role in your agency because …

I am skilled in the following theoretical approach …

And my understanding of how this supports clients is …

Through my years in work/study I have the following transferable skills that would be useful in your agency …

Through my counselling training I have received positive feedback about my ability to …

The personal qualities I bring to the role are …

I understand the importance of supervision and reflection to be …

I am willing to offer the following day/time commitment to a placement position …

A Well there is your first hint as to why it might be useful now to attend an interview. Just think of a couple of years' time when you want a paid job as a counsellor and how much more confident you will feel when it comes to an interview because you've already been successful at one when finding a placement. You can develop some really useful skills right now by going through this process.

In practice the style of applications and interviews can vary greatly between different placement agencies and some will be more challenging than others. Remember what we said about how agencies want to know you are going to work safely with their clients – if they are the sort of ethical agency that you'd like to work in then they should have a decent interview process. Think of it as a mark of their integrity and yours. Let's consider below some of the sort of interviews you may come across.

CASE SCENARIOS

Scenario A

Ben is invited to interview for a placement role at a local college. He receives an email invitation in response to completing an online application form for a vacancy on their website so until this moment he hasn't met anyone face-to-face or spoken on the phone. So far all he has is a place and a time but is unsure of the nature of the interview which has left him anxious, but he has prepared himself as best he can and tried to think of the sort of questions they may ask. When he arrives he is greeted by the receptionist who tells him to grab a seat in the waiting room. After a few minutes a woman appears and shakes his hand while introducing herself as Angie the senior agency counsellor. She guides him into a room where there are two other people sat in comfortable chairs around a coffee table. They introduce themselves as the manager of the agency and a placement counsellor.

They explain to Ben that they'd like him to feel comfortable and that this is an informal chat to get to know him and see if he is a 'good fit' as a trainee. The manager spends five minutes talking about the agency, how it was founded and the sort of client work they do and Ben is then invited to tell them about himself and what his interests are. They also ask him to explain what sort of counselling placement he is looking for and what he feels he would be able to offer. It feels very natural and although Ben is nervous he is happy talking about his skills and abilities. After about half an hour they thank Ben for his time and say they'll be in touch within the next week. Two days later Ben receives an email offering him a placement and asking when he can start.

Scenario B

Jackie responds to a poster handed round at her counselling diploma class which offers a date for an 'open interview' at a local counselling agency. She emails the centre with a CV and covering letter and they respond to thank her for the information and to invite her along to the group interview day that had been advertised. They ask her to bring an 'item' that represents her approach to counselling with her.

Jackie shows up on the date and is shown into a large, well lit room, with tea and coffee set out on a side table. There are about 20 other trainees in the room who are milling around chatting to each other. At the side of the room two people are sat with notepads watching the group and talking to each other. After 10 minutes they ask everyone to take a seat around the edges of the room.

The agency manager and volunteer coordinator introduce themselves and they explain that the day will be split up into three parts. After the first two parts some of the group will be told they are not successful and will be allowed to leave for the day. There is a sense of nervous excitement in the room.

Firstly the trainees are asked to introduce themselves to the room and explain the meaning of their 'item' and how it sums up their approach to counselling. Jackie has

(Continued)

brought a small wicker basket and explains how it holds her client's experiences while allowing them room to grow. It is also a natural material and shows how she feels supporting people comes naturally to her.

Secondly the interviewers ask the trainees to volunteer to be either a counsellor or client in a 'role play practice session' which will take place in a goldfish-bowl arrangement in the middle of the room. Those not participating will be asked to give feedback to the counsellor and client. Jackie volunteers to be the client role and is told to bring something to the session from her own life that the counsellor can work with in the session. Jackie feels daunted by this as she is unsure how much about herself she is comfortable sharing with this new group of people. Several rounds of counsellor–client practice sessions take place, and Jackie is aware that some people she observes are noticeably better than others. She doesn't get a chance to be the counsellor, but tries her best to give some good feedback.

After a short break, the group are divided into two groups and one group is told they are unsuccessful and can go home. Luckily Jackie is in the successful group, though she feels bad for those who collect their belongings and leave.

The final phase is a panel interview with the two staff members and Jackie in a separate room. Here she is asked a series of formal questions about her training and experience and the interviewers take notes throughout. Jackie is nervous but feels that she presents herself well and explains what she can offer. At the end of this Jackie is told she will receive a letter to tell her if she is being offered a placement and if not then she can ring them for feedback.

EXERCISE

Consider how you would feel in the above interview examples. Do you feel you would be prepared for both an unstructured informal interview, and a structured formal interview? What are the strengths and weaknesses of these types of interview, a) for the interviewee? b) for the agency?

Q Ok so now I see that interviews can take really different shapes and I might not fully know what sort of interview I'm stepping into beforehand. So I guess the best I can do is to understand what I'm looking for and what I can offer, and think about the words I want to use to explain about myself and what I am capable of so that they get a good picture of me?

A Yes exactly that. You are meeting them as a fellow professional and remember you are all there for the same reason; to provide an excellent service to clients. So get out there and start making some applications and put your best foot forward!

Q Help! I've been out there now for several weeks and I keep hitting a brick wall. Either agencies are saying that they aren't taking on volunteers at the moment, or I send them my application or talk to them on the phone and I keep getting turned down. What is wrong with me?

A Ok firstly let's eliminate the practical issues before we address the possibility of there being something 'wrong with you'.

It is possible that agencies only interview or take applications at certain times of the year, or they may have their hands full with their current placement volunteers at the moment. When they say this to you, consider asking when would be a good time to apply. Make a note of when they say and start to create a placement search planner.

Q A placement planner? What do you mean by this?

A Well remember earlier we looked at how you might make a list of places you could contact? Well you could start to create a table or a chart to map out who you have contacted and how, and whether they have responded. This will help you keep track. Shall I give you an example?

TABLE 8.1 Placement Search Tracking Grid

Agency Name	Contact Person	Contact Details	Phoned/Emailed/ Letter	Agency Response	Follow up?
Rivers Agency	Steve Pond	River View House, Tel No	Phoned on 07/11/19 spoke to Volunteer coordinator as Steve was off	Told to re-contact when they are taking on volunteers	Contact again in January
Central Counselling Service	Unknown	High Street, Tel No	Emailed the reception 12/10/19 Phoned on 20/10/19, left answerphone message	No response from either contact	Try ringing again in November, find a named contact person

Q Ahh I see. So if I track who I have contacted then I won't miss anyone out and if they take applications in a certain month then I can make a note of that and ensure I catch them at the right time. That makes sense to me and I will do that. But how does this help me work out if I'm doing something wrong?

A Good question. Depending on how detailed you make this tracking system you might find that it highlights some flaws in your process. For example in the chart above it is clear that for the Central Counselling Service you might need to find a named person to contact as it seems that your emails and phone messages are just falling into the ether, as no one is getting back to you. Or if you made a note of the times you rang them you might notice that you are always ringing later in the day and not getting an answer.

Q Yes, so what?

A Well check that against their opening times. Perhaps they only operate between 9am and 3pm and you're only ringing at 4pm. It seems like pretty basic stuff, but particularly when you are contacting a fair few agencies at first, these little details can get lost in the process and they might be the difference between the perfect placement and missing out.

Q I took on board all your ideas and suggestions and it turns out that placements are like busses … you wait ages for one and then three come along all at once!

A That's great, so now you have the chance to choose between a few and you can decide what the best fit is for you.

Q There are a few areas I'm unsure of about them though. Can I run them past you and you can tell me if they're suitable?

A Well yes you can, and I can tell you my opinion, but the final decision will come down to your training centre as they will need to work with you to make sure the placement meets the requirements of your qualification.

Q Ok so here is a breakdown of the three placements I've been offered:

> This *first* one operates a drop-in service in the city centre where people come in to get support. They have said that they have had placement counsellors before but they call us 'mentors' or 'befrienders'. When I asked them what the difference was they said that it's basically counselling but they try not to call it that as it can be off-putting to people to think they're coming for counselling. Do you think that will count towards my placement hours?
>
> The *second* one has their own pre-placement training course to ensure that we are all working at the same level, but I can't start until I have completed this and passed their assessment. They offer individual counselling sessions, but also do group-work with clients. If I did group-work sessions can I count those towards my placement hours?
>
> The *third* one has a set-up I've never come across before. They have a pair of counsellors working with every client. They are both in the room at the same

time and one leads and the other supports. They say I'd start off supporting and move into a leading role. They have said they will offer me extra training to be able to do this, but it's very different from what I've been taught and I'm not sure if I can count those hours towards my placement?

A Ok so this throws up a lot of questions for me. Many of which you will need to check out with your training centre but I can say what I think might be the key issues you need to consider. Let's start at the beginning:

With the *first* placement your issue may be that it is classed as a 'drop-in'. Most qualifications will require you to carry out formally contracted counselling sessions with the same clients over a period of time. If the only service they offer is an ad-hoc drop-in then you are unlikely to be carrying out actual contracted counselling and might only have single sessions with people. This might be why they are less comfortable with you using the title counsellor in this role.
Drop-in support is a really valid service and they are right that sometimes it can be a much easier first step for people to access a service like this when they are in need of help. However, it probably won't be something you could count towards your placement hours. However, if you are interested in the service they offer you could volunteer anyway to gain the extra experience.
With the *second* placement this sounds much more reasonable, as they obviously are serious about ensuring the competence of their volunteers. But of course you have to ask yourself if you have the time to dedicate to additional training at this point. Other good questions to ask could be whether you need to pay for the training, and if the placement is guaranteed if you were to successfully complete it.
Group-work is a different type of work to individual counselling and so this part might not count towards your placement hours. Group therapy itself has an entire theoretical foundation and a different set of technical skills to individual work and you would need to see if it maps onto your qualification in any way. This is definitely one to check out with your training centre. However, again it might be something you would want to learn about and volunteer to do alongside the individual counselling to add further strings to your bow.
Well the *third* one certainly is an unusual situation and I'd be interested to know the theoretical approach and reasoning behind having a pair of counsellors to each client. It would be something I would suggest finding a lot more about and then talking it through with your training centre. It might be useful to explore whether at this stage in your training you feel you are prepared for working with the dynamics that might be created by this set-up.

Q Great that has really helped me to make a decision. I think I will go with placement number two and offer to do the group-work as a way of gaining more experience at the same time as clocking up my individual counselling hours. Also gaining more training can't hurt me in the long run, it can only help my future prospects. I will make sure my training centre are happy with it and then agree a start date.

MAINTAINING A PLACEMENT

Ok so you've got your placement secured and will have completed an induction programme or been introduced to your role and colleagues informally. It is possible you might have completed some initial in-house training to get to this point, but now you are about to be allocated your first client. Is there anything on your mind at this stage that we can help you with?

> **REFLECTION**
>
> Consider waking up in the morning on the first day you will be actually counselling a real client. Today you will go into your placement and you will walk into a room with someone who has come to see just you and is looking for help. What sort of thoughts might be running through your mind? What might you be feeling? How can you process and be aware of these thoughts and feelings so that you are able to be fully present for your client?

Q Wow it all feels so real now. I have seen my first few clients this month and so far it seems to have gone well. This week however, I had my first 'DNA' which is the agency terminology for 'did not attend'. It was a bit of a surprise as the week before the client had seemed to engage well and I thought we were developing a therapeutic rapport. I'm going to explore what this feels like for me in my supervision this month, but what it did make me wonder was if I can still count that hour towards my placement time? I mean I was there at my agency waiting around, and it was a pre-booked session.

A Unfortunately not. You will only be able to count actual client contact time towards your placement hours as it is this experience which counts towards your qualification. It is a great idea to take this to supervision though, as clients missing sessions or sometimes not coming back again can be valuable in terms of exploring your response. For example, do you feel abandoned? Rejected? Annoyed? Bored? Resentful? How might these feelings impact on your future rapport with this client or others?

Q Well now I know that I can't count the hour I can see how I might begin to feel resentful over time. Especially if a client keeps doing this, I mean they're wasting my valuable time aren't they?!

A That is definitely something to take to explore in supervision. This is a great example of how the real world of counselling clients can raise issues we've never thought of before and how we need to use the support around us to help manage it ethically. In a later chapter we will look at the use of supervision in a placement agency and consider how this can best support our practice.

Q On a different subject I have a bit of confusion around one of my agency processes. The agency's senior counsellor meets each of my clients to do an initial assessment before they are allocated to a member of the counselling team. I have been told that they have a standard form that is completed and they then decide who the best match to them as a counsellor is. I guess what I'm trying to say is that this whole process feels a little odd to me for a few reasons. I am not involved in this process at all and I don't even know if I'm allowed to read these forms to see if they contain any information that might be useful to me. I'm also wondering what they are looking for when they 'match' someone to me, I mean is it that they look really easy to work with, or are they matching personalities up, I really don't know!

A Well this sounds like you have a real sense of uncertainty around the assessment and allocations process in your agency. I'm also getting the feeling that you feel a bit 'left out', or 'out of the loop' when it comes to how the clients end up being matched to you.

During your training you will often cover the theory and practice of client assessment and there are many models of assessment that agencies choose to implement. The CPCAB itself has an evidence-based model of helping work and counselling practice (see www.cpcab.co.uk/public_docs/cpcab_model) which includes what we call 'Service Levels'. In this we talk about the level of complexity that a client can present with, and the sort of help they are looking for, and we match this to a depth of counselling work and the level of training of the counsellor. It is possible that your agency are using something similar in their assessment and allocations process which helps them to determine if a client's presenting concerns are something that fit within the limits of your proficiency at this stage of your development.

Q Ok so I need to find out a bit more really don't I?

A Yes, perhaps you could ask them what assessment and allocations model they use and see if they'd like you to become more knowledgeable about it. If you show a keen interest then they might offer you an induction into that part of the agency.

In some services the counsellors will conduct the assessments themselves, whereas in others they might have dedicated assessment workers who gather initial client information and guide them towards the best type of counselling or helping work for them. You can compare it to the process of triage in a hospital where a patient is met by a member of staff who explores what is troubling them, assesses their level of need and directs them to the correct department.

Q Ok so I can always be sure that I'm only working with clients who aren't too difficult?

A Well that's the idea. Assessment and allocation are designed to ensure you work within the limits of your competency. However, sometimes deeper issues may come to light as the counselling progresses and you would need to seek the support and advice of your agency manager and your supervisor to ensure you weren't exceeding what you are capable of. In this case you might be supported to make a referral, or gain extra guidance on how to work with a slightly more complex client.

REFLECTION

Consider how you might feel if you began working with a client who had been assessed as appropriate for you. However, after a few weeks they begin to mention more complex issues like a past history of substance misuse and childhood abuse. You felt you had started to develop a good relationship with them, but now are concerned they might be too complex for someone at your level of training.

Q I've been at my placement just over a month now and I received an email from the agency manager with a list of dates for my diary. They want me to attend a monthly team meeting on a Monday afternoon and to go to some in-house training on equality and diversity, and data protection. I don't really have the time to do all of this in addition to my client hours, supervision and holding down my own job. Can I refuse to go?

A I totally understand. Balancing a home life, work life and the demands of professional counsellor training can be really difficult. Your agency may feel that these extra meetings and training are vital to your placement and you might miss out on some real opportunities if you are unable to go. On the other hand if you genuinely can't make it then you'll need to talk it through with your agency manager and negotiate what is possible.

EXERCISE

Make a list of all the aspects of your placement life. For example, client counselling hours, time to write up notes, meetings with other staff, group supervision, individual supervision, extra training. Note what time allowance you need to make to ensure you meet all these aspects.

Are you able to fit all of these into your lifestyle? Consider which ones are non-negotiable and whether you need to re-negotiate with your placement what you are able to commit to long term.

Q But my placement was so hard to find and I should be appreciative of anything they offer me. So shouldn't I just do anything they ask of me regardless of the time it takes?

A It certainly is a challenge to find a placement and by offering all of this to you they are taking the time to commit to you and your training, so keep that in mind at all times. However, you need to balance it with self-care. Remember that self-care and resilience are core aspects of many ethical frameworks for a very good reason. If you are tired, resentful and rushed in your own life then your client work can suffer.

Care of self as a practitioner

91. We will take responsibility for our own wellbeing as essential to sustaining good practice with our clients by:

a. taking precautions to protect our own physical safety
b. monitoring and maintaining our own psychological and physical health, particularly that we are sufficiently resilient and resourceful to undertake our work in ways that satisfy professional standards
c. seeking professional support and services as the need arises
d. keeping a healthy balance between our work and other aspects of life. (BACP, 2018)

Points b and d in the BACP *Ethical Framework for the Counselling Professions* quote above are particularly relevant here. It is vital to monitor your own health, both physical and psychological and make sure that you are not drowning in work and training, but also taking some time out for yourself and doing other things you enjoy in life.

Q Ok so it's really important that I take time to myself and make sure that I am capable of carrying out all the responsibilities I have signed up for. It seems that counselling ethics not only help us to take care of our clients but also of ourselves.

PLACEMENT PROBLEMS

Once students have secured a placement and have started to create a balance between their ongoing external pressures of workload and home life, it then becomes time to focus on building up client hours and developing practice. But the course of every placement may not always run smoothly. Here we will look at a couple of examples of what could go awry in the placement and consider how best to address these sorts of issues.

Q So I've started seeing clients in my agency and other than initial nerves I think I am getting along ok. I am aware of something that has come up though and would like to get some advice. I started out my contracting by explaining my boundaries and limits just like we had been taught, but when it gets to telling my clients that I am still a student I can feel myself being a little bit embarrassed and wanting to justify myself to them. I spoke to my agency manager about it and they have suggested that I just leave it out in case it puts my clients off.

A This can come up in some agencies and the reasoning behind it may vary. Firstly it's important to consider your own motivations and reservations about acknowledging your trainee status.

> **REFLECTION**
>
> What do you think about when I say you must let all your clients know that you are still in training?
>
> What do you imagine they might think of you?
>
> Why might it be easier for you to leave it out?
>
> Why is it important that you tell your clients about your level of training?

Q I know that I'd rather I was just trained, because I fear they might reject me because of it.

A Ethically it is important that you tell them for that very reason. A client has the right to choose, and if they feel you aren't the right counsellor for them (for any reason) then they should have the right to say so. It goes back to when we talked about 'informed consent' in Chapter 1.

Q Why might my placement manager want me to leave it out?

A They really shouldn't be suggesting that you avoid the question, or avoid being up front about it. But they may also want you to not be rejected by the client, either for your own self-confidence, or because it's a pain for the agency to find another counsellor, or they might have a vested interest in 'passing you off as qualified' so that they don't have to pay for so many qualified counsellors to work there. It's a minefield! Either way, it is definitely something that you should tell your clients. It is also likely a requirement not only of your course, but of your ethical body.

Q Ok, another question that has come up. I started off quite glad to just have a placement to begin with. But now I'm talking to my peers they all seem to be enjoying theirs a lot more than me. Some even get free supervision, and travel expenses paid. Is it ok for me to swap mid-course?

A It's not an absolute no, but you should carefully think through the pros and cons of any change. Sometimes having a gap between placements, or even the lag time it takes for you to be inducted into a new placement can have a significant impact on your ability to complete some of the assessment aspects of your course. So a change at the wrong point might be disastrous.

But the other side of the coin is that if your current placement has some serious issues, or on closer inspection you realise it might not help you meet your course requirements then it is prudent to seek a new placement as swiftly as possible.

Q So I should really think this through … Hmm actually my current placement is ok, I just thought others might be getting something I'm not. I need to check out whether I'm just having a 'grass is greener on the other side' sort of process going on.

A Sounds like you are on the right track and don't want to steer yourself wrong. It's a good thing that you keep critically engaging with your work.

Q Ok, so last placement question then I'll let you go.

My placement supervisor was great when I first met them, and though they use CBT most often and I am training in Person-Centred Counselling they said it would be ok because in her words 'PCC is what most counsellors start off doing as a base anyway'. But as time has gone on she keeps suggesting I introduce more techniques to my work, and advises on pieces of homework my clients could be doing. I'm finding it really jarring, as if she's implying that my approach alone isn't really enough. What do I do?

A Having a supervisor from a similar theoretical approach can be important, but not necessarily vital as long as there is a clear contracted understanding between you and they can support your chosen practice approach. It feels like in this case both your perceptions of how this would work needed more ironing out. Your approach is enough in itself, but when the person who is supporting you feels that it doesn't then they might lead you away from it simply due to their own perspective. Have a look at Chapter 9 in this book on placement supervision.

Q I must admit I'm quite interested to know about their approach and learn from them too – is that ok?

A Professional curiosity and further learning are always good. But just remember that you are being assessed for your course on the approach they are teaching you, and don't dilute that by trying to diversify so soon, or without proper support to integrate new approaches.

SUMMARY

- Focus your placement search on what is really important for you and for your training.
- Placement applications are a competitive business – make sure your application stands out for all the right reasons.
- Stay positive, and don't let refusals knock you down.
- Make sure any placement you apply for actually meets your course requirements.
- Use your placement induction wisely – get to grips with the requirements of the agency and ensure you know what is expected of you.

9
Placement Supervision

Supervision is a key ethical responsibility of both an experienced practising counsellor, and also a new trainee counsellor. Supervision, as you have seen in Chapter 7 on working self-reflectively, is one of the most important ways in which we review our client work, check that we are working effectively, consider how we might develop and improve, and also reflect on and explore our own personal experiences as a counsellor, and as a human being in connection with another human being. Rather than go back over the theory and purposes of supervision here, let's look at how it links to counselling placement work and the main factors you will need to consider when seeking placement supervision.

Q Once I start in placement I know I have to get myself a supervisor. I'm not really sure how I should go about it though – do you have any suggestions?

A Well a good place to start is to read through Chapter 7 of this book where we cover an introduction to supervision, a few models, and some underpinning skills of the supervisory relationship.

> **REFLECTION**
>
> From your experiences of group training supervision in class and from receiving feedback on skills practices from peers and tutors, consider what you personally would need in a supervisor, and write yourself a list.

When considering your supervision arrangements you will need to explore a few contributing factors to make sure that your needs are fully met. The main rule of thumb is that you need a supervisor who you will find supportive – you are not likely to work well with someone who you experience as overly critical. As a trainee you need to feel safe enough to admit your mistakes and ask for help – when you feel safe it is also good for your learning to be challenged sometimes.

Q Sounds good. Where do we start?

A There are often four factors at play in this decision:

- Your personal needs, wishes, preferred style of supervision.
- Your training course needs, that is, what is stated in your training handbook as the requirements in order to pass your course.
- Best ethical and professional practice.
- What is possible within your means and the means of your placement.

In an ideal world all of these areas would match up perfectly and create a flawless supervision process. But we may find that some of them are at odds, or need a little revision in order to make them fit.

Q Ah so I may need to compromise a bit?

A Perhaps marginally, but only in certain areas. For example, you can't compromise on the ethical side of things as you must absolutely ensure you protect your clients and yourself. Also if you want to pass your course you won't be able to compromise on the course requirements side of things. For example, if your course states you must have twice monthly supervision you can't have less than that and still pass, or you can't pretend to have had more than you have, as that becomes unethical.

Actually perhaps 'compromise' is the wrong word. Think of it more as ensuring that you have a full understanding of all the requirements at the outset, including reviewing what you need to get from the process. This way you can plan ahead and make any adjustments needed early on so that you meet both your personal needs, and achieve good ethical practice. It is likely that your supervisor will be required to complete at least one supervisor report for you whilst you are working together, so it is worth ascertaining from the beginning that they are happy to do this. This can be an integral part of your learning if approached collaboratively, rather than feeling like some add-on that your training centre has imposed.

Q That's clearer. So I need to draw up a list of what must definitely be in place, and work from there?

A Yes, let's look at what cannot be altered.

Firstly, in order to qualify it is likely that you will have a set amount of client hours to complete, and a corresponding number of supervision hours. It is often set out in a ratio, and might be specifically in line with guidance from an ethical body. You should make sure you know exactly how this ratio will pan out, particularly if you start to pick up more clients and the number of supervision hours you require increases.

Your course provider might also state whether you are permitted to accrue supervision hours through group supervision or if it must be one-on-one individual supervision.

Q What are the differences?

A Look at Tables 9.1 and 9.2 to see the differences:

TABLE 9.1 Individual supervision – meeting up with a supervisor one to one

Benefits	Drawbacks
• Developing an in-depth relationship with your supervisor • The supervisory relationship is informative in itself, interpersonal dynamics can be explored • Gaining personalised feedback and support around your particular areas of concern • Increased self-development through mapping out a personalised plan, and establishing goals	• Only one other person's perspective to draw upon • If interpersonal conflict occurs it may be hard to work through • The supervisee may not be able to see if their supervisor is not up to the task; nothing to compare it to • Often quite expensive

TABLE 9.2 Group supervision – meeting up with a group of peer supervisees, often other trainees and practitioners, led by a group supervisor

Benefits	Drawbacks
• Gain a wider breadth of perspective • Hear about other practice settings • Learn from others' experiences • Still gain input from a more skilled professional • Often cheaper	• The group supervisor must be skilled in facilitating this style of supervision to enable all participants to gain value • Can lose out on as much personalised input as gained in individual supervision • Can be affected by group members dropping out, or not participating well • Can be affected by broader group dynamics

Q It seems like both options have good and bad aspects. Perhaps I might get to do a bit of both?

A In terms of a range of experience you really can't beat trying out everything on offer. Some individual supervision, supplemented by group supervision would enable you to get the best of both worlds.

Q What if my agency supervision is in a group and the number of hours per month is not enough to satisfy my training centre, or my ethical framework?

A The usual model is of a minimum of one and a half hours of supervision per month. However, if you have group supervision with up to five in a group then you can count half of that time each time you meet. If there are five or over in the group then you must divide the meeting time by the number of people in the group.

So if you don't meet the requirements of your training course and/or ethical framework then you might need to make an additional arrangement either with another supervisor or individually with your group supervisor to top up the additional hours required. This multi arrangement would need to be carefully managed so that you are either not missing out any areas of your practice, or alternatively covering the same ground twice. Telephone supervision might be an option for the 'top up' time but do check with your training course and agency that this is acceptable. If you are lucky enough to have more than one placement and have supervision at each placement then you may well be fully covered by supervision requirements.

Q Some of the peers on my course were saying that their placement just told them that a senior member of staff would be their supervisor. Essentially they were just handed a free supervisor on a plate and they didn't need to consider any of these factors. While that seems like a really easy and simple way of getting a supervisor, some of them didn't seem all that happy about it. What could possibly go wrong?

A Ah, so yes it is an easy way of getting a supervisor, and if it goes well then it's an almost perfect option.

Q Almost?

A Well when you say, 'they didn't need to consider any of the factors we're talking about', I bet you that that isn't the case. It might be assumed that the placement has worked out all the kinks, and fully understands what is needed both ethically and academically. But it is dangerous to absolve yourself of the responsibility for checking that even this supervision meets your professional needs. In-house supervision can be a huge advantage, especially if it is provided for free, and the supervisors perhaps have a long standing relationship with the agency so they are familiar with the client group and the policies and procedures of the agency. But do ensure that they are not beholden to the agency in any way, that they are still independent. Also you still need to have a good working relationship with your supervisor – just because you don't have to search for a supervisor or you are not being charged, does not mean that you will automatically have a good relationship.

Let's look at a few examples below.

CASE SCENARIOS

Scenario 1

Kareem has started in his agency placement and feels very much at home. Although it is in a community support service for people with mental health diagnoses he has been reassured that his counselling caseload will be people who fit within his capabilities. He has been allocated an in-house supervisor and they have agreed to be available for clinical supervision once a week. When Kareem asked them about their experience supervising trainees they have said that as a clinical psychologist they have not supervised counselling trainees before, and although they are not a counsellor themselves they have a good understanding of the client group and will be able to support his client work.

What are the reasons why this arrangement might not be suitable?

Scenario 2

Jo, a diploma in counselling student, has managed to gain a placement in a local counselling agency. They are a small charity and have a team of four volunteer counsellors, and one overall line manager. Jo really liked the small, personal nature of the agency and agreed to begin as soon as her training centre said she was ok to start. When she came for her induction the line manager explained that she also does the supervision for all the volunteers there and would be both Jo's line manager and supervisor. They explain that they are qualified as a supervisor and they have a written contract that outlines how the roles of manager and supervisor are different so that every volunteer knows what 'role' she is in at any one time. Her supervisor explains that it's even beneficial as she can guide her practice from a practical agency angle and therapeutic angle at the same time. Jo agrees, but is worried that her training centre won't allow it.

What are the reasons why this arrangement might not be suitable?

Scenario 3

Yvonne has begun at her placement at a bereavement service. She has picked up a decent sized caseload of clients and sees three a week. Her placement supervisor is someone who is employed by the agency as a senior counsellor and supervisor for the trainees. However, after meeting her supervisor at her induction she has found her increasingly hard to get hold of. She seems to work on different days to when Yvonne volunteers, and has started to leave messages in her in-tray

(Continued)

rearranging their supervision sessions at the last minute. Yvonne's ratio of supervision to client hours has started to decline and she is scared of telling her tutor about it in case they make her drop some of her clients, or even worse leave the agency. So she has decided to keep plugging away and hope that it picks back up again, and hopes that no one notices the gap in supervision.

What are the reasons why this arrangement might not be suitable?

Q Wow those are some really extreme examples! What is the likelihood of that happening though?

A It can be more common than you think for initial misunderstandings to become bigger issues. Think of it like setting out a good counselling contract, so if you aren't clear about what you need, how can you assume that you will receive the right support from their side?

Q So from those examples, it would be important for me to check out these areas:

a. That my supervisor is actually qualified or at least experienced in delivering the sort of counselling supervision I need.
b. That there are no dual relationships or conflicts of interest between the role of a supervisor and other roles in the agency.
c. That my supervisor understands how important it is for me to maintain the right ratio of supervision.

A Yes, and even more so in the last example. If your supervisor is hard to get hold of at the best of times – for example, when appointments have been pre-booked – are you guaranteed to be able to access them when it really counts? For example, if there was a serious safeguarding issue with one of your clients, or you had made a mistake in your work and needed to ensure that you dealt with it appropriately.

Q So I'm better off getting my own supervisor then?

A Not necessarily, you just need to ensure that whether in-house, or external, that your supervision arrangements meet the needs of you and your clients. I really cannot over-state how important good supervision is to a developing trainee counsellor. See Tables 9.3 and 9.4 for the main advantages and disadvantages of in-house or external supervision:

TABLE 9.3 In-house supervision

Benefits	Drawbacks
• On hand to deal with day-to-day support needs • They understand the working context and may have greater insight • Often cheaper or free • May be able to take place on-site and within normal placement hours • Easier process of obtaining supervision, don't have to do a search or meet several in own time • Supervisor has been nominated by the agency as suitable and knowledgeable enough	• Supervisee might feel obliged to accept whatever arrangement is offered to them • May be more difficult to hold supervision boundaries if they work in the same environment • Supervisor may have their own opinions about the working context that could leak into supervision • May not be the 'ideal' supervisor, but might be more of a 'best fit' that the agency has to offer • Supervisee may not get the choice of who supervises them – less sense of autonomy • Difficult to challenge issues, or change supervisors if the relationship breaks down • Can feel pressure to not raise negative points about the agency itself

TABLE 9.4 External supervision

Benefits	Drawbacks
• Can make own choice about the person, and the style of supervision • Easier to maintain boundaries between placement expectations and supervisory support • Easier to raise interpersonal issues, negative points about the agency, or be honest about own flaws • Greater feeling of confidentiality and autonomy	• Supervisor may not understand the working context as well as someone in-house • Often more expensive and off-site • Supervisee needs to find the right person themselves and may have limited understanding of what they are looking for at the early stages of placement

Q So, if I have to find my own external supervisor how do I go about finding one?

A Your training course might have a list of supervisors in the locality that students have used in the past, so this is a good starting point. Also ask around, in your group, at your placement, through social media. You can look on the Counselling Professional websites, or in their monthly publications, also in local leaflets. Remember though that a recommendation from someone else does not automatically mean that that person might be right for you as you are a different person. It can be as hazardous as recommending a good restaurant to other people. A good supervisor should be able to offer you an introductory session for free to enable the two of you to explore how you relate to each other, how you might work together, compatibility of approaches, specialties that might match with your client group, for example, experience of working with children and young people, working with a CBT approach, working with addictions.

Whether you are going to use an in-house or external supervisor, it is your responsibility to find a supervisor and to ensure that you have supervision in place before you see your first client.

BEING A GOOD SUPERVISEE

It's easy to talk about how to get yourself a 'good' supervisor, and making sure that the needs of the supervisee are met. But it's important to balance this with a cautionary tale about making sure that you are a good supervisee also.

Q But of course I would be. It's in my best interests isn't it! I would make sure that I showed up when they booked me in, and did whatever they needed from me in order to make it work.

A Yes it absolutely is in your best interests. I'm interested in the slant that you have taken in your answer though, as it sounds like you're putting quite a lot of the onus on them to take charge, 'they booked (you) in', 'whatever they needed from (you)'. Bear in mind that it needs to be a shared relationship, and just as your supervisor will be using the skills of supervision, you will also need to use 'supervisee skills' to get the most out of it. Let's take a look at this extract from an interview with a supervisor:

> Well the first time I met Graeme I was impressed by the keen commitment he expressed about his upcoming placement at a local counselling agency. He was halfway through his first diploma year and had done his research about the supervisors in town and said he'd like to work with me. We agreed to meet fortnightly for an hour at a time at my offices, and established a good initial contract. I told him about my model of supervision and we discussed the levels of exploration that formed the supervisory relationship. I was certain at that point that he understood.

CASE SCENARIO

We started off a little 'clunky' with him giving me just a descriptive narrative of his client sessions, or raising issues he had with the set-up of his placement. I worked hard to help him reflect more on 'how' he was working with clients, and with his colleagues, rather than 'what' he was doing. However, it just went downhill from there. The more he spoke the more I felt myself being pulled into a dynamic where he wanted to tell me what he did with clients, so I could offer my approval, nothing more. It alternated between that and him seemingly wanting to draw me into a collusion about how poorly organised his placement was. When I used immediacy and brought this into the room he got defensive and said he was only voicing his concerns, and wasn't it my role to check he was working ethically anyway. I tried to share with him my concerns that he was seeking my approval and how I saw my role more as helping him to develop his own 'internal supervisor' so that he could self-reflect. He left that day really shut down and refusing to talk any further.

He missed his next session and a few days later I got a brief text saying 'I'll be there next time, but I'm not sure what I'm getting from supervision anymore. I'd like to talk about whether I need to come so often.'

He was late for the next session and was solely focused on working out how many hours per month he actually needed to meet his training requirements. I asked him if he felt he would be able to continue coming and work at a reflective level with me, with the aim being his personal and professional development. He said he'd like to carry on as we had been 'checking in about his work with clients' but wouldn't be talking about himself if that was ok with me. I said that didn't match my working style or in my opinion fulfil the purpose of supervision. He left that day saying he'd consider it – he never came back.

Q Well that's not going to be me. He sounds really blocked from being able to see his part in his relationships with his clients or others.

A There is clearly something going on there yes. My point is to highlight that a supervisor can only 'lead your horse to water' but you have to decide to drink. Preparation, openness, and a willingness to cast a critically evaluative eye over your own practice is absolutely key to the process.

Q Ok, so when I have found my supervisor, how does supervision actually work and how do I get ready for it?

A The idea is that you discuss or 'take' your client cases so that you can get support, advice, and confirmation that you are working safely and effectively with your client.

REFLECTION

Write down as many reasons as you can think of for attending supervision. If you have not started client work yet, then think about client scenarios that might be difficult for you and tease out what you would want to discuss with a supervisor. Look back at the case scenarios in Chapter 3 if you are stuck for ideas.

Most supervisors will want to know a little bit about how you are at the beginning of the session. This is to check your fitness to practise by ensuring that you are emotionally and physically healthy enough to be seeing clients. Alongside this they will also want to know how many clients you are working with at any one time in case you are overloaded.

It is helpful to share some basic facts about each client such as how many times you have seen them, what their presenting problem is, some information about them and their lives, and how you are working with them, plus of course any difficulties you might be having. As you might have had three or even four sessions with each client since your previous supervision, it is good to keep notes to remind yourself of significant things that you want to bring up in supervision, and to take these notes with you to supervision. Some supervisors will ask you to keep more structured notes than others.

Q So my supervisor will listen and tell me what to do next with my client?

A Not exactly. It is a collaborative process and is much more two-way than therapy. It provides a framework for your clinical practice by setting your work within an ethical and professional boundary. Your supervisor provides emotional support when you are feeling challenged, may suggest skills and tools associated with your modality, and will advise on issues of confidentiality, legalities, safeguarding. It is where you can admit to mistakes, explore them, learn from them and move on to become an even more effective practitioner.

You will also find that you use supervision to explore clients who might need to be referred elsewhere, for example, for specialist counselling such as PTSD, or for mental health problems which are beyond the scope of your competence. As a trainee you might think that you can work with anybody, and you might be so anxious to build up your client hours that you offer to take anybody who comes into the agency, but you do need to be realistic about what you can do, so do tell your supervisor if you feel that you might be getting out of your depth otherwise you could do more harm than good – again look back at your ethical framework for guidance.

As a trainee, you will be working under the umbrella of your agency and they will usually take clinical responsibility for your client work and be held liable for any malpractice – providing that you are abiding by their policies and procedures and by your ethical framework.

Your supervisor is responsible for monitoring you and your client's safety which means supporting you in keeping your client safe. This is why it is important that you discuss with your supervisor any concerns you might have, even if they seem very trivial, and especially if they are of a legal or safety nature. Your supervisor cannot advise you if they do not know what is going on.

ASSESSMENT AND CONTRACTING

Q So when I meet with my placement supervisor for the first time how will I be able to work out if we have a good match and can work together?

A Well, you have studied counselling, how would you do that with a client?

Q I'd start out by getting to know them a bit, asking what they want to get from the counselling and perhaps assessing their needs. I've learnt about how some agencies do this stage really formally using assessment tools and a written contract, and sometimes they do it in a more informal way. But that's counselling, supervision is different isn't it because we both totally know what we're there for and we'd both be aware of all that contracting stuff?

A As practising counsellors you would indeed both have a good knowledge of the supervisory process, and things like confidentiality – we hope anyway! But as to assessing your needs as a supervisee and agreeing a working contract together that would certainly be a great way to start up a supervisory relationship. There would be many areas that you might need to 'thrash out' at this early stage to ensure you are a good fit.

Let's consider what might be useful to cover in a supervision contract.

- How often you need to have supervision, where you can meet and when.
- Where you are doing your placement and with what sort of client group.
- Your current theoretical orientation.
- Your supervisor's model of supervision.
- Whether your college has any additional requirements, like a supervisor's report to be completed at the end of your placement hours.
- Whether you've had supervision before, and how you see this supervision going for you.
- An assessment/evaluation of your developmental level as a practitioner, e.g. where you feel your strengths and weaknesses are.
- How the supervisor could work with you to help you develop your practice.
- When and how you can get hold of your supervisor between sessions.

Q Wow so it can be as detailed as a counselling contract really?!

A Sometimes even more so. Because you both have a deeper understanding of the process than a client may at the start of therapy, you can really drill down into your personal and professional needs. And your supervisor can be very detailed in terms of their style of work, and how they offer supervision so that you can make sure the relationship is well established.

One thing that is useful to straighten out is confidentiality. As your supervisor holds some responsibility for your ethical practice, would you expect them to keep it confidential if you started to behave unethically in your placement practice? Could they tell the agency, or your college?

Q Well … I … Um … Oh I actually don't know that. I feel like I want to say 'no' because it's not one of the typical limitations to confidentiality, I'm not harming myself or a danger to others, it's not like I'm a terrorist! But at the same time I can see how that would probably be part of their job. Should they?

A It's an area of ethics and legality that you should explore with your supervisor. Potentially if you were behaving very unethically you could cause significant harm to a vulnerable adult or young person, which could bring it in under a legal limitation to confidentiality. However, it is more likely to be an ethical consideration, perhaps that you are working outside the limits of your competence or are having a personal crisis and perhaps should take a break from client work. In which case it might be very appropriate for your supervisor to discuss this with your college or line manager to ensure that both you and your clients were kept safe. Ideally this could be part of their supportive role with you, but your supervisor does share some clinical responsibility for your clients so even if you weren't in agreement they might still have to share any concerns. You can ask your supervisor to clarify their responsibilities and their lines of communication with your agency and your training centre. Take a look at your training centre's Handbook and/or at your awarding organisation's guidance on agency work and supervision. There is likely to be a tripartite agreement between your training provider, your agency placement and your supervisor. This means that each of them has the right to contact either, or both, of the other two if there are any causes for concern.

Q Well my college expects a report to be completed by the supervisor each term anyway, so I guess they'd be in direct contact through this. So isn't there an overlap of the confidentiality boundary in this respect?

A This is often the case, but it's important to discuss and both agree what is shared between the supervisor, the agency and the training provider. This often avoids any future upset.

REFLECTION

> I work in a counselling agency as a receptionist, it's what got me interested in becoming a counsellor to begin with. Now I've started my diploma they have said I could do my placement hours there too. My manager would also be my placement manager and one of the senior counsellors in the team would be my supervisor, I've known her for years and feel really comfortable with her.

What might you want to take into consideration if you are already working in an agency in a different role, and they offer you a placement also?

RECORD KEEPING

Whether as a trainee or a professional counsellor it is a good idea to keep a record of your supervision as this is really valuable if you are looking to progress to becoming an accredited counsellor at some point in the future. You may have a template for logging your client and supervision hours given to you by either your course tutors or your placement agency. You need to make sure that you understand how to keep a record, and that it meets your responsibilities under the General Data Protection Regulations (GDPR).

Q What do you mean by that?

A Well if you just keep a simple record of hours when you attended supervision, and your supervisor signs each sheet, then that's pretty simple. If however, you decide to start adding notes to each logged session about which clients you discuss, or reflective notes on what you learnt and how you could apply this to future sessions, then it starts to become more like client notes, and these should be kept confidential. If you ended up having to put these into a course portfolio, could you guarantee the confidentiality of this information?

At this point it might be useful for us to talk about record keeping in general and GDPR.

Q I have heard lots about this and it seems to cause a lot of problems. I absolutely believe in my clients' rights to privacy and confidentiality, but I'm worried about getting things right and meeting all my legal responsibilities.

A This is a confusing area, so your concerns are understandable. My first suggestion would be to check things out with your supervisor but the letters GDPR can be confusing for all of us.

First, GDPR, General Data Protection Regulation, is responsible for ensuring personal data and information is gathered, stored and used within strict guidelines to ensure an individual's privacy is respected.

The law itself can be very confusing and serious concerns and issues can be taken to experts in data protection for resolution. The ICO (Information Commissioner's Office) website is an excellent resource for information and guidance.

Q I've heard of the ICO, someone said we have to register with them. Is that true?

A Again, not a simple response. It would depend on the setting you work in, agency, workplace, private practice, etc.; how data is stored; what your role is – trainee, manager, supervisor, etc.

As a rule of thumb, all business including sole traders (counsellors in private practice), who process personal information electronically need to register (see ICO.org.uk).

Q Ahh, it's only things I keep electronically. So, if I only keep hand written notes I won't have to bother.

A As long as you don't process electronic data, you don't have to register in that way.

Q Well that's what I'll do then!!

A Just a minute. It's not just client notes we have to consider. Do you use a phone to speak to your clients or to text? Do you ever send or receive emails? All these things process data in some form.

Q I hadn't thought of that.

A As the Borg in *Star Trek* said, 'resistance is futile'.

Q Ok, what do I have to do?

A This isn't the place to go into the finer details and the law can change. Actually, as counsellors, we are ahead of the game because we already protect and respect our clients' privacy and confidentiality.

It is important, though, to be clear yourself about what data you do keep.

A table of data can help and can be updated regularly. It can contain information on:

- All data kept
- Where it came from

- Why it's kept
- How you store it

Q That would be good to do anyway. I am really careful with my clients' personal details but I have got emails not stored carefully that I need to think about.

A The most important thing is to give your clients a clear privacy statement, so that they know why, what and how their information is used and stored including for how long.

Q Not so complicated after all.

A We have discussed the basics. You will need to ensure you comply with the law and protect your clients and you may need further advice and information to do that.

SUMMARY

- When finding a placement supervisor consider both your professional and your personal needs for support.
- Plan ahead and take responsibility for your supervision needs – you can't assume that someone else will do this for you.
- Take time to develop your skills as a supervisee. You will get more from the supervision process if you fully commit to it.
- Assessment and mutual agreement are just as important in supervision as they are in counselling.
- Ensure you fully understand where your responsibility lies when keeping confidential records of your supervision and counselling sessions.

10
Agency Requirements

> Ask not what your country can do for you, but what you can do for your country!
>
> (John F. Kennedy)

In this case we are asking not only what your agency can do for you, but also how to find out what requirements your agency has so that you can be sure you can do everything you need to for them. Briefly in the chapter on finding a placement we mentioned what to look for in a good counselling agency placement. We will revisit this here as well as looking at what requirements the agency may have of their trainee counsellors. A good fit between trainee and agency is important, as is ensuring that all parties are clear and up front about what the whole placement will entail.

WHAT DO I NEED FROM AN AGENCY?

Q Ok so what really do we mean by an agency? When I have been asking around about where counselling takes place I heard about school and college counselling. Can I go to my son's school and offer my services to counsel their students?

A Well this has a few variables you would need to check out. Firstly your training provider may have some specific considerations they need to be in place, so your first port of call should be to check with them. But the two things that spring to mind here relate to the client group, and the agency set-up.

It is important to make sure that you are equipped to work with the chosen client group at your agency. If your training course equips you to work with adults and yet the school setting would mean your client group were young children then it is unlikely that this would be a suitable placement. The skills you need to work with children and young people vary from those used with adults and without proper training and support it would be unethical to assume that you would have the necessary competence. Your course may also require some, or all, of your counselling hours to take place with adults.

Secondly, the set-up of the agency setting is vital. If the school or college already had an established student counselling service, with an infrastructure that included counselling rooms, policies that relate to therapeutic work, supervisors and other counsellors on site also doing what you would be doing, then this might be a good placement.

Q But what if they just are aware that their students need some counselling, and would like to set up a counselling service? They are an established business and surely have rooms and policies in place for a range of things. Surely I'd be doing real good in the world by helping them get this off the ground?

A While it might be a worthy endeavour, are you really the best person to set up a service from scratch? Is that really ethical? There are many skilled counsellors out there in the world who would be better placed to do this than an untested trainee.

A good rule of thumb is to ask yourself; 'Who at this agency does the job role I'd like to be in one day? Who will I be learning best practice from?' If the answer is 'No-one' then it's not a suitable counselling placement.

Q Good point. It sounds like there are a lot of things to consider. Where do I get all this information from?

A Your training provider should be able to provide you with a list of requirements, or a placement handbook. Many have three-way agency agreements that need to be completed by the three parties (training provider, agency manager, trainee counsellor) which will help ensure that everything is suitable and above board. This is your chance to get the placement opportunity of a lifetime, so avoid cutting corners.

WHAT MIGHT MY AGENCY NEED FROM ME?

Q I found what looks like a really good counselling agency placement. But they have their own programme of pre-placement training that they want me to go on. It includes lots of safeguarding information, health and safety, and aspects of the approach to client work that they use. I have told them that I'm already doing my diploma and have been assessed as ready to enter placement but they say I have to do this training on top. It's ridiculous, I have to pay for it, it's extra time out of my week, and there's no guarantee that I will pass their course and even get the placement at the end. I think they're out of order for even asking. What shall I do?

A Ok first off, you might think about where that anger is coming from. Put this into perspective; they're not asking YOU to do their training, they are asking trainees who want to have a placement with them to do this training. It's not personal, it's simply the high standards they set for their trainees, and as you say they are a really good placement so it is probably that they are so popular they have the prerogative to set their standards very high. No one is at fault here; it might simply be that what is required doesn't match what you can give.

Q I see that. It just feels like I'm doing my course just fine, but agencies all want all these extra bits from us that we don't know about. What else might an agency need that I haven't thought of?

A I'll give you an overview of what often comes up. But you would need to look into these in more detail and check them out in relation to your setting:

- Agency commitment contracts – you might be asked to sign up to a minimum number of hours a week, or a commitment period that extends beyond the minimum hours you need to achieve.
- Team meetings – in addition to accumulating your counselling hours, you may also be required to attend in-house meetings or other work events.
- Indemnity and liability insurance – while many agencies will have their own insurance, they may also require you to take out your own insurance in case of lawsuits, libel or slander.
- Student membership of a professional association – it may be that as a student you have already joined a professional membership association such as the British Association of Counselling and Psychotherapy (BACP), National Counselling Society (NCS) or Association of Christian Counsellors (ACC). There are many different associations who support the counselling profession and your chosen agency may require their trainees to become members of a particular association.
- Disclosure and Barring Service (DBS) checks – when working with young people or vulnerable adults it is likely that employers will expect an employee or volunteer to pass a DBS check. The DBS carries out the functions previously undertaken by the Criminal Records Bureau (CRB) and the Independent Safeguarding Authority (ISA) (see www.gov.uk/government/organisations/disclosure-and-barring-service/about).
- Travel and supervision costs – an agency may provide a subsistence rate, fund your travel and pay for your supervision while you are volunteering for them. However, due to the limited funding available in talking therapies this is getting rarer. When adding up your ability to afford your training, it is wise to take all possible cost requirements into consideration.

Q Wow that sounds like an awful lot to remember and get sorted out. I'm a bit daunted.

A It is probably one of the most complex practical aspects of your training. But don't worry too much. It is your first time doing this, but I doubt it is your training provider's first time, and most established agencies have experience inducting trainees into their placements. Use the knowledge and experience of those around you to guide you, and make sure you take the time to ask all the questions you need.

SUMMARY

- Ascertain that your agency meets the practical and academic requirements of your training course.
- You would be wise to add up the potential costs of all aspects of your agency work before committing to a placement.

11
Personal Therapy Requirements

WHY ENGAGE IN PERSONAL THERAPY?

> The degree to which I can create relationships, which facilitate the growth of others as separate persons, is a measure of the growth I have achieved in myself. (Rogers, 1961)

This key quotation from Carl Rogers typifies the belief system that underpins this chapter. The majority of practitioner level training programmes for counsellors include an expectation that the student will undertake some form of personal therapy during the course. The quantity and style of therapy varies significantly between training providers, but students often have a range of questions both practical and philosophical about this requirement. Here we will hope to answer some of those questions.

Q I am just about to start my diploma course at the local college and the student handbook says that I have to attend a minimum of ten hours of personal therapy during the course. I can understand this to some degree, but can you explain to me the reasons behind this requirement? Surely it should be up to me if I go to see a counsellor or not?

A This is one of the most often asked questions about the personal therapy requirement – the 'Why?' And the answer is multi-faceted. Let's sum up the main reasons and then break them down.

- It's useful to experience it from the client chair

As a developing counsellor yourself it can be extremely useful to sit in the client chair for real. Although you will have done this in your early stages of training in skills practice sessions, nothing quite compares to the real thing. Doing so will help you understand what it is like for your future clients approaching you and beginning to trust a stranger with their innermost feelings and experiences. While your circumstances for entering counselling will be different to theirs, it is the willingness to 'be the client' that starts to open you up to their perspective.

- Therapy helps us grow as individuals

Nosce Te Ipsum – 'Know Thyself'. Therapy helps us grow as individuals. Although we may feel at this point of time that there is 'nothing wrong with us', it is important to acknowledge that in terms of personal growth and self-understanding we are never 'done', that is, we are never the completed project. In humanistic psychology there is the concept of 'self-actualisation' and while it can be seen as the self-awareness ideal it is simultaneously understood as something that is never completed; we are in an ongoing process of actualisation. Therefore, there is always room for more self-understanding, and this is a great time in your practitioner development to engage therapeutically with yourself.

- You owe it to your future clients

Carl Rogers believed that our personal growth is reflected in the personal growth of our clients and that our clients can be limited by our own emotional limitations as a therapist. It is often said that our clients can only go as far as we are willing to go ourselves. Therefore, we owe it to our future clients to know ourselves as well as we can, so that we do not unknowingly restrict them from growing in their self-knowledge. This is quite a complex area and we will explore this a little more in a moment.

- Learn from your therapist

While I am not advocating going to therapy solely as an academic learning experience, it would be difficult to ignore the possibility that seeing a real therapist at work would be educational. Your main focus should be on self-development, but you will likely also be aware of the therapist's style, what they do or don't include in their contracting with you, how they explain their therapeutic approach, and this can be valuable to hear on the receiving end.

- You need to believe it works!

It is all well and good learning about therapy from a trainee standpoint, and you will probably find by now that you have chosen a training course that advocates a theoretical style that most aligns with your personal beliefs about therapeutic change. However, to be on the receiving end of this form of therapy and actually feel it making a difference to your own life is a whole new ballgame.

Q Ok I hear all of those points but there are still some things you said that I'd like to challenge.

A Go right ahead, this is part of the process. You absolutely should critically engage with these ideas, ask questions, challenge and reflect. All of this will help you explore your reasons for going into counselling and how best you could utilise it.

Q Ok, first off what if I have been a client in the past? Part of what brought me into wanting to be a counsellor in the first place was that I had some difficult times in my teens and went to see a counsellor back then. So I have already sat in the client chair once, why should I have to do it again?

A Great question! So you've already sat in the client chair, and as you then chose to become a counsellor I would presume it already instilled in you a belief that it works. So this in part covers the first and last points above. But imagine how it might be a different experience for you at this point in your life. More years under your belt, a greater understanding of what counselling is all about, and all the new experiences you've had since then. Not to mention the personal insights that may have emerged during your counselling training so far. Imagine how much use you could make of more therapy at this time, the things you could learn and experience!

Q I see where you are coming from. So what you are saying is that although counselling early on in my life helped me get from A to B in terms of self-awareness, I am now further down the line as a human being, and this next period of it could help me get from D to E. And this greater awareness could be even more useful to me and to my future clients.

A Yes exactly that. I suppose it might be useful to look at it from the other side of the equation – would you turn down a client who came to see you simply because they had had therapy before? Probably not. You'd understand that they wanted to explore something present in their lives now and you'd hope to help them do that.

Q Yes, absolutely. I can feel myself starting to shift when looking at this. I think I had been focusing on it being a course requirement and perhaps a burden, whereas it feels more now like it is something that would be a benefit to me and I can see it as an opportunity.

A Yes. It is one of those times in life when you will be actively encouraged by your course tutors and your counsellor to fully focus on yourself and spend time on your own development. Sadly, that is something that isn't always forthcoming in modern society.

Q Perhaps that's where my resistance is coming from. It feels rather self-indulgent to dedicate all this time, money, and focus on just my own wellbeing. Isn't that crazy considering the field of work I want to be in!

A Not at all. It is something that counselling trainees often experience. Those of us who are drawn towards the caring professions are often givers, who focus on helping others sometimes at the expense of their own wellbeing, often feeling guilty if they spend time on themselves. As I'm saying this I'm even thinking that if that is something you recognise in yourself it might be exactly what you could look at in your counselling! Obviously, I'm not being prescriptive here, but it's a good example of the sort of personal insights that arise through counselling training that would be vital to look at before we work in the field. Think about how that sort of self-sacrificing tendency might play out in your counselling relationships with clients, how easily you might get burnt out.

WHY NOT ENGAGE WITH PERSONAL THERAPY?

We've started to tease out above the reasons why practitioner level training courses often include a requirement for trainees to attend personal therapy. It is interesting to note that this requirement is often not welcomed by trainees, and tutors often experience resistance like the situation above.

Let's briefly look at some of the reasons why trainees might not be willing to take up their own therapy:

- Expense
- Time commitment
- Resistant to look at themselves
- Scared they will uncover something painful
- Fear of sharing something personal that may show them in a negative light
- Guilty about spending the time on self-care/development

(Continued)

- Perceive therapy as being for individuals who have 'something wrong with them'
- Commitment to the idea of being the 'well expert' rather than the 'vulnerable client'
- Worried that they (or the counsellor) will realise they have too many personal issues to be a good counsellor
- Resentment that it is a requirement of the course, rather than a personal choice

Just like the reasons for engaging in therapy are all valid and worth reflecting on, these reasons why trainees may be resistant are also valid and worth exploring. If you as a trainee are finding it hard to sum up the motivation to start personal therapy it would be useful to consider why this may be. The following reflections might be useful.

REFLECTION

- What do I believe to be the reasons why my training provider sets this requirement?
- When I decided to do this level of training do I feel I was fully informed about this requirement?
- What do I feel I might be able to benefit from going to personal therapy?
- What are the reasons I might not want to go to personal therapy?
- Is there anything deeper underlying these reasons?
- How might I overcome my reasons for not going to personal therapy?
- What actions do I need to take?

FINDING A THERAPIST

Q Ok so now I've decided that going for some counselling wouldn't be the worst thing in the world, there are quite a few practical issues swimming around in my head. I really need to think through how I begin this process. Where do I begin?

A Well a good place to start is to 'window shop' and do a bit of research into what is available in your area. There are many resources available to help you find a good local counsellor and using a range of them could help you work out what you are really looking for.

There is a plethora of online directories with listings of therapists, many professional associations will hold listings for their members, registrants and accredited therapists, and many therapists will have their own website or social media pages that give you a sense of who they are and what they offer.

Q What sort of things should I be looking for?

A Finding the right counsellor for you is a very personal thing, and it isn't a one size fits all situation – which is quite lucky for those going into the field, as there is less pressure to be everybody's cup of tea. While some things are important like their qualifications, their professional association status, their work background and practitioner experience, what it often comes down to is whether it feels right or not.

Q Ok so I need to think about who I, personally, would feel comfortable being counselled by?

A Yes, and no. Yes you need to think about what you would like from counselling, and what type of counsellor might allow you the space to do that. But when I say 'No' I am referring to your use of the word 'comfortable', because yes you should feel able to open up and relaxed enough to do the exploration you need, but sometimes when clients seek out primarily a sense of comfort they miss the opportunity to be challenged by the process.

Q I'm not sure I understand.

CASE SCENARIOS

Let's look at the following two interview clips with students who have gone for their own counselling and see what they said when asked how and why they chose the counsellor they did:

Annabelle

I've been going to see my counsellor for about five months now, she's so lovely. I found her on the internet on a big directory. In her picture she looked really smiley, about my age, also a woman and though she had decent qualifications there wasn't a huge long scary list of them like some of the other counsellors had. I thought I don't want someone who is too intellectual and can run rings around me. I'm just starting out and I don't want to feel overwhelmed by someone too 'much', you know?

(Continued)

When I started seeing her I instantly felt relaxed, we just chatted about why I was there and my home life and course. I go to see her once a fortnight and I update her on how things are going. It feels supportive and she knows lots about me now and I'm really finding it helpful to check in with someone regularly so I can feel I'm on the right path.

Rachael

When I started out looking for a counsellor it took me ages, I went through the online searches then looked at their own websites. Some of them weren't properly accredited by a professional body so I ruled them out as I wanted to find someone really committed to their work. It was also important to find someone with the same theoretical orientation as me, so that I can feel what it feels like on the receiving end.

Well eventually I went to see a few for the first session, and though they were nice it just didn't feel like I would get enough out of it. I then found Hugh. He mainly works with the same theory as me but with a bit of integrative stuff in there too, and instantly I felt energised by our opening session. I've been going for four months and I really feel like I'm exploring some deep rooted stuff from my life. There's no wiggle room for me avoiding 'my stuff' when I'm in there, he's not directive but I feel he can see into me when I'm hiding things from him (and hiding them from myself really). I end my sessions exhausted and exhilarated, and I've discovered what can really happen in counselling when both people are in it together.

Q Well now I'm even more confused! Which one is better? The first one sounds so comfortable and like it would help me make my way through my qualification but I feel like I should be saying the second one is better as it feels like they got a lot more out of it in terms of self-exploration. But I feel a bit scared of the second one; I'm not sure if I'm ready for that.

A It's good that you're questioning this for yourself. As I said earlier, it's not a case of one size fits all and what works for one person may not for another. When going for counselling it's important to consider your motivations, what you want to get out of it and how ready you are. A good counsellor will work at your pace, but it should feel different to just a friendly chat. Remember, that engaging in counselling is part of developing yourself as a counsellor and as a person.

REFLECTION

How important is it to have a therapist who works from the same theoretical approach as you?

This question is often posed, particularly by students in regards to their personal therapy requirement. Some training courses will insist that you attend counselling with someone who uses the theory that students are being taught. There are important reasons for this, but it might be useful to consider how you feel about this yourself.

What do you feel might be the benefits or downsides to your therapist having the same theoretical orientation as yourself?

Q Ok so I have thought a bit more about my reasons for going to counselling. Are there any other practical issues I haven't thought of?

A Well of course you need to think about how much you are willing to pay per session, how often you are able to attend and when, how far you're willing to travel, and when you are ready to start. It's important to remember that if you're going to commit to this for the whole process you will need to prepare a little bit in advance. This might mean setting aside an amount of money, clearing a consistent spot in your diary and organising your travel arrangements accordingly.

Q Well I can't afford much money or time, so I'm thinking of finding the cheapest person nearby and maybe seeing them once every month or so. Do you think that will be ok?

A Though it's not always the case, you may find that counsellors will offer a reduced rate for students who are attending for their personal therapy requirement. That might ease the financial burden a bit, but ideally choose your counsellor based on who is the most suited to you, rather than the most suited to your bank balance. Some students who have gone for the cheapest option find that they end up feeling they got exactly what they paid for – not much.

In terms of how often you will need to go, well that can be negotiated between you and the counsellor you choose to contact. Many will expect you to attend more frequently than once every couple of months. If cost is an issue consider waiting to begin until you have a little money set by to see you through, rather than dragging it out, or ceasing midway through a process just because you have run out of money.

Q Ok, I understand that. My course requires me to attend ten sessions and I think I have enough to cover that so I'm ready to start any day now. Anything else I need to consider?

A Hmm … ok so you're not going to like me saying this … but … Do you really think ten sessions will be enough?

Q What do you mean?! Do I look like I need years of therapy or something?

A No, no that's not it at all! I simply mean that training providers will often designate a minimum amount of hours required to pass your course. But a minimum is exactly that, a minimum. It might be that they set the amount quite low so as to not disadvantage students on a very low income, but perhaps if you have the ability to do more then this gives you the opportunity to do that.

Q I might be able to, but I don't really know now. I feel like I'd like to 'dip my toe in the water' first and see how it feels.

A That seems really sensible and even sounds like something you could bring up when meeting with a new counsellor. You could check out if they are able to offer ten sessions, with the possibility of adding more if you feel that things are going well.

MEETING WITH A THERAPIST

Q Ok so I bit the bullet! I looked on a load of websites and read a ton of counsellor profiles. I eventually found one I liked the look of, so I gave them a call and booked in an initial meeting. I was really happy as they offer a free first session so that I can see if I feel comfortable and ask any questions I need. It all feels really real now, and I'm aware that later on today I'm going to be sat in a client chair for real and telling someone that I want to be their client. Is it normal to feel a bit scared?

A Feeling scared is fine. It might be useful to think through what it is you're scared of.

Q I've got all nervous now it's actually coming up to the moment when it all gets real. I'm aware as I say that that I've said 'real' a few times now.

A That seems significant.

Q I guess up until now when I've been doing skills practice sessions in class and I've been the client it has felt a bit 'faked', like it mattered more to the 'counsellor' for the session to go well, rather than to me as the 'client'. Does that make sense?

A So what I'm hearing is that when you've been in classroom sessions as the client it has felt more like you are playing the *role* of a client to enable your course peer to practise their skills. So the purpose of the session was for them, rather than for you. And this shift in purpose made it feel less real to you, even if you were genuinely talking about something happening in your life.

Q Yes that is it exactly. We've always had it drilled into us by the tutor that we are 'playing the client' and we have to bring something real to allow the 'counsellor' to practise on us. So it was always very controlled, and focused on it being an educational exercise.

But now it will be focused on me, and only on me. There is no formal educational purpose to serve, just me and my self-awareness. That is why it feels so different … and so scary. What if I'm no good at being a real client? What if I clam up when all the focus is on me? What if I slip back into pretending to be the useful classroom client again? What if I do with my counsellor what I do with my peers, which is to secretly analyse their skills and abilities as they are counselling me?!

A Wow … well these are all great questions!

Q You're not going to answer them for me are you?

A I don't think I have a definitive answer to them for you. You may very well do some or all of the things you mentioned above. But what feels really important is that you are asking yourself these questions. This level of awareness of your own process is really promising. It feels like if the relationship were right between you and your counsellor that you could explore some of these things with them. That level of transparency might really help you both agree how you're going to work together.

EXAMPLE

This interview excerpt from a counsellor working in the field highlights some of the trials and tribulations of counselling a counselling student. It might be useful to see it from the other side:

> When I first set out in private practice I got a lot of requests from student counsellors looking to get their personal therapy hours. I think initially this was

(Continued)

because as I was new to private work my prices were quite low, and it struck me that many of them were very concerned over the cost of the sessions. I aimed to work in the most boundaried and supportive way with them to ensure that they could get what they needed from the sessions, but without expecting a high level of ongoing commitment in case they weren't at that sort of place yet.

Some of the students I worked with were incredibly open to the process and obviously had done a lot of personal work on their self-awareness already. They were a joy to work with, as they understood what the therapy was for and openly engaged with it to the utmost. If anything, I sometimes had to go to my own supervision to explore how much I enjoyed working with people who were so well prepped for therapy that they pretty much did it all themselves. They reflected so fluently that I started to doubt whether I was being hoodwinked! Of course I don't think I was, it was just the side effect of being immersed in the world of counselling training that made them so 'ready' to explore their own stuff.

The other end of the spectrum was there as well though. Sometimes I could feel a heavy resistance from certain students, particularly those who stated outright that they resented being 'forced' into therapy simply to pass a course. In terms of engaging with these students I must admit it was tough at times, though obviously the work is no less valid. To enable them to look at the reasons behind their resistance was absolutely vital to allow them to move forwards. I was always mindful of holding a non-judgemental space, and not to view them as a 'lesser' potential counsellor than those who engaged easily. We all have our challenges through our training, and for some people the process of stepping out of the counsellor role into the vulnerable place of client is incredibly hard to do. But if they are able to move through it they will have the most amazing perspective on how clients can also find it hard to begin to trust and open up to a counsellor. They may end up the better counsellors for it.

WHAT IF IT DOESN'T WORK OUT?

The process of personal therapy for trainee counsellors may not always run smoothly. Here we will look at an example of what could go awry in the relationship and consider how best to address these sorts of issues.

Q I've been going to see my chosen counsellor for four sessions now, and we're about to do a midway review in my next session. It's been 'okay' but I'm really not sure if it's what I expected. Once I got my head around the idea of going it seemed like it would be a 'done deal' once I got in the room but I have a niggling feeling that this counsellor isn't the one for me. How do I know if it's right to continue?

A It sounds like it's really timely to do a review at this point. Can you tell me more about what your 'niggles' are?

Q Well first off although they say that they work to the same theoretical orientation as me, I keep finding myself questioning their style of work, and they say and do things I would never do in my counselling sessions. For example, the other day they suggested that I talk to my estranged mother about some of my childhood stuff, and gave me a template letter to fill in to help me get my thoughts out onto paper. It just felt really directive and like it came out of nowhere really. I'm left not knowing what to do.

A So for you this intervention felt not only out of place in your personal process, but also left you doubting the counsellor's adherence to their therapeutic approach?

Q Yes, I think it might fit in with other styles of working, but it really didn't feel like something I would want to do, and it wasn't really what I signed up for. They have done similar things along the way too, little hints of advice giving and direct suggestion which have left me feeling a bit judged and patronised to be honest. I've only got a few sessions left though before I hit my minimum amount, so is it ok to just stick it out until then?

A Well that really depends on how you see it benefiting you. One option could be to say nothing and stick it out, but does that really sound like a good idea to you? What other options are there?

Q I could say something about it I suppose. Say that it feels like they're being too directive and it doesn't match up with my expectations. That might open up some discussion about how we work together. But what if it doesn't? What if they feel judged or attacked by me saying that? What if it becomes a confrontation?

A Hmm, I wonder where this insecurity is coming from? It sounds like in this relationship with your counsellor you are finding it hard to say what you are truly feeling to them. Is this something that is coming into the room from their side, some 'power base' that implies that they shouldn't be questioned? Or is this something more familiar to you?

Q Good point! I don't find that I often feel like this. It really reminds me of what I'm like with my parents though. Perhaps we've somehow slipped into an odd parent/child dynamic.

A That's a powerful insight. So it may be that there is some dynamic developing in your therapeutic relationship. I guess my original question still stands; what options are available to you?

Q I do need to bring this up. It might be coming from me and I might be bringing my own insecure child into the room, and they might then be able to help me explore that. But if I were to share my feelings and they reacted badly then it would help me to decide whether I could continue with this particular counsellor anyway.

A Great, that feels like a breakthrough. It's important to remember two things; one – sometimes counselling doesn't run perfectly on its own, it takes two people engaged in working on it and mutually exploring what is going on in the room to really get the most out of it. And two – if it really doesn't feel right then there is no shame or harm in deciding to end a counselling relationship and look at where else your needs might be met.

Q So, if I don't like how it's going I can address it and try to make it better, or move on. Does that sound right?

A Yes, though obviously in moderation.

Q Moderation?

A If you're the client and you're frequently telling the counsellor they are doing something you don't feel comfortable with, it might be that they aren't as competent as you would have hoped. If you are always the one trying to resolve issues then it might be best to change counsellors and chalk it up to experience. In other words – it might be them.

But alternatively, if you are dissatisfied with every counsellor you see and hop from one to another every time they don't live up to your expectations, perhaps you need to reconsider your expectations, or challenge yourself on why you are finding it hard to settle into the process. In other words – it might be you!

SUMMARY

- Personal therapy is usually a requirement of training for very good reasons – do not underestimate how vital it will be for your development.
- Even if you have had personal therapy before, the impact of it at this stage of training is still important.
- Many counsellors offer a reduced rate for trainees, but don't necessarily just go for the cheapest counsellor you can find.
- Don't be afraid to review how the therapy is going for you, and change counsellors if the relationship isn't working out.
- Enjoy being a client – it holds powerful possibilities!

12 Trainee Self-Care and Avoidance of Burnout

> Counsellors and other helping professions may be more likely than other occupational groups to deny that they are stressed. We may be better models of self-neglect than self-care. In particular we may find it difficult to acknowledge when we need help, and then difficult to ask for it. (Bayne and Jinks, 2010: 149)

In this chapter we look at the importance of trainee self-care as a model to take forward into your work as a counsellor in the future. When engaging in practitioner level training there will be an increase in demands upon your time, challenges to your knowledge and skills, and also challenges to your emotional resilience. Preparing for these demands is just as important as preparing for the academic aspects of the training, possibly even more so.

REFLECTION

- When I say that it is important to ask for help as a counsellor, how does that feel to you?
- When you picture yourself being vulnerable how does that feel to you?
- When people place demands on you that you find overwhelming, who do you prioritise – you or them?

While studying for their practitioner level training a trainee will have varied demands on their time and their emotional resilience. From trying to fit course requirements around a work and home life, to coping with fear of failure and growing self-knowledge, it can be one of the most challenging times in their careers. Learning good skills in self-care at this point will build the foundations of their future.

Q On my lower levels of training I found that I could manage quite well with my course, my homework, my part-time job and looking after my family. However, since I started this diploma my tutors have been asking more and more of me and I'm getting really stressed. I know they said it would take a lot more of time and effort but I think I might have underestimated it all. What can I do to cope?

A It is not unusual for counselling trainees to feel the impact of the extra burden that comes with practitioner level training. It often involves extra levels of commitment and a greater complexity of study than lower levels so it is not surprising that you are feeling stressed and overwhelmed.

There are several ways that counselling trainees can utilise methods of self-care during their training. Good places to start include asking your tutors about self-care resources they use or are aware of, and also reviewing what has worked for you in the past and seeing if you can adapt this to the current situation.

REFLECTION

Think of times in your life when you have felt stressed or overwhelmed. This can be a particular event, or a range of experiences you have had that you can recall.

- What helped you move through these times?
- Is there anything that hindered you from moving forwards?
- What do you feel helps you gain a more positive outlook?
- Are there people you turned to for support?
- What did you gain from these experiences that could help you now?

Using the experiences from your own life is a great way to draw upon your own resources for self-care. Often trainees really do know how to care for themselves at times of stress, but often don't implement these.

Q That's a good idea. I have faced difficult times before and have come through them so maybe I can use those skills now. But once I'm through this, things will get easier right, because I'll be a counsellor and I'll know how to cope with stress?

A If only it were that easy.

EXAMPLE

I remember being in my own counselling trainee placement and feeling full of self-doubt and worry that I wasn't coping well enough. But I avoided asking for help because I felt that it would 'give away my secret' that I wasn't the perfect counsellor yet. I also remember having this strange belief that all counsellors were totally sorted in their own lives, and must be so self-aware that they never suffered with the emotional struggles of 'the common person'. I know I know – crazy isn't it!
What I know now is that, if anything, counsellors are more open to, and more aware of, their own imperfections and personal conflicts than 'the common person' may be. But being aware doesn't mean that they all go away and you become perfect. It simply means that you feel acutely what is going on within yourself, and should more easily ask for help or self-regulate so that it doesn't get too pent up, or spill out all over your clients. I say 'should' with great emphasis because it still isn't always easy. That is why the counselling profession puts great emphasis on the importance of regular supervision and even ongoing personal therapy. My supervisor over the years has often spotted when I'm about to 'crack up' sooner than I have and has helped me through. We owe it to ourselves and to our clients to be gentle with ourselves – physically, spiritually and emotionally.

Q So how do I ensure that I attend to my self-care during my training and once I am working as a counsellor?

A Well there are a lot of different ways to conceptualise it. It is likely that in your training so far you have come across Abraham Maslow's Hierarchy of Needs (see Figure 12.1). While usually considered a model of motivation and developmental growth, this can also be a good model to help you consider whether your personal needs are being met, and also if there are areas that need work.

For example if you are trying to study but your home life becomes disrupted (therefore affecting one of the lower parts of the hierarchy), this will likely have an impact on your ability to focus, self-reflect on your counselling practice and consider your higher needs such as fulfilling your potential. Therefore it's important to prioritise what you need to attend to in order to properly move forwards.

Q Ok. Yes I can see that. So say I suddenly was evicted from my home or had a relationship breakdown or a bereavement, I wouldn't be so easily able to sit and contemplate my counselling theory essay as I'd be too preoccupied? Or even go to placement and see clients for that matter!

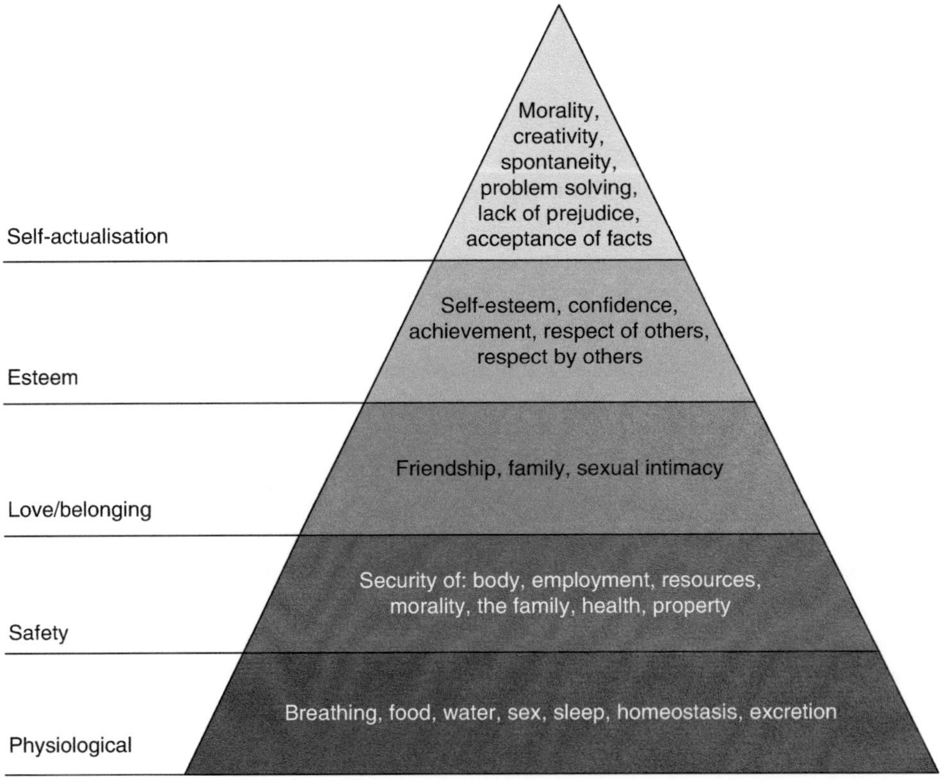

FIGURE 12.1 Maslow's hierarchy of needs

A Exactly. I know that these are some extreme examples, but it highlights that counsellors are not immune to changing life events and must be able to consider ethically what is best for themselves and for their clients.

It is an absolute ethical imperative to take responsibility for our own self-care and wellbeing. It is fleshed out a little more in the BACP *Ethical Framework for the Counselling Professions* (2018):

Care of self as a practitioner

1. We will take responsibility for our own wellbeing as essential to sustaining good practice with our clients by:

    a. taking precautions to protect our own physical safety
    b. monitoring and maintaining our own psychological and physical health, particularly that we are sufficiently resilient and

resourceful to undertake our work in ways that satisfy professional standards

c. seeking professional support and services as the need arises
d. keeping a healthy balance between our work and other aspects of life.

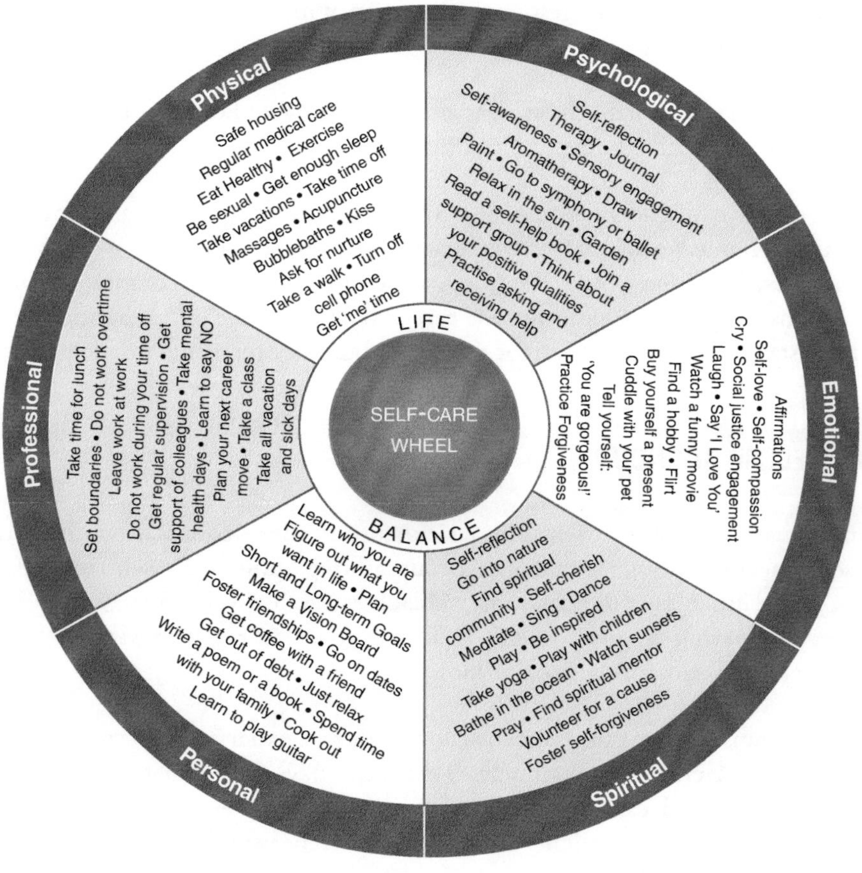

This Self-Care Wheel was inspired by and adapted from 'Self-Care Assessment Worksheet' from *Transforming the Pain: A Workbook on Vicarious Traumatization* by Saakvitne, Pearlman & Staff of TSI/CAAP (Norton, 1996). Created by Olga Phoenix Project: Healing for Social Change (2013). Dedicated to all trauma professionals worldwide. copyright © 2013 Olga Phoenix, All Rights Reserved. www.OlgaPhoenix.com

FIGURE 12.2 Self-care wheel (reproduced with kind permission of Olga Phoenix)

This part of the framework highlights that we must take care of ourselves in order to properly take care of our clients. And that it is more ethical to do so.

Q Ok so how do I take care of myself?

A A wonderful resource to use when considering how to build up your self-care routine is the Self-Care Wheel by Olga Phoenix (see Figure 12.2).

This model allows you to see how your self-care needs can be visualised in six distinct categories; personal, professional, emotional, spiritual, psychological and physical. It then makes suggestions of ways in which you can enhance your life balance in these areas.

Q Great, so I can monitor all these areas as I'm studying and once I qualify as a counsellor and then I will be able to practise effectively?

A Mostly, however sometimes unexpected things can occur in your home life, or in your working world that can take you by surprise and affect your wellbeing. Remember, the earlier note about how even counsellors are not immune to life's ups and downs. So good pre-emptive self-care and a decent life–work balance are great and will stand you in good stead for the future, but not everything can be planned for.

COUNSELLOR BURNOUT

Burnout is a 'syndrome of emotional exhaustion, depersonalisation and reduced personal accomplishment that can occur among individuals who do "people-work"' explains Professor Christina Maslach, the US psychologist widely known for her pioneering research in this field and co-creator of the Maslach Burnout Inventory (Maslach and Jackson, 1986).

When a counsellor or trainee counsellor begins to experience a sense of burnout they may experience this in a range of different ways. It is sometimes called 'compassion fatigue' and can be linked to vicarious trauma – the residual emotional impact of hearing about clients' traumatic experiences and bearing witness to the pain of those with whom you work.

Q So this is what happens when I get home after a day in class and I don't want to talk to my family, I feel like I just want to sleep all evening?

A It's similar to that, but tends to build up over time for those in helping professions. Common symptoms tend to include a reduction in compassion for your clients, a feeling of being overwhelmed by the work and unwillingness to hear your client's problems and feeling irritated or uncaring about their struggles.

It can also include feeling hopeless about your career, or your abilities as a counsellor.

EXAMPLE

I remember getting to a point in my working career when I was seeing five clients a day in my agency, all of whom had been assessed as meeting the high-end criteria required for a referral to the agency to begin with. There was also a risk of redundancies in the company and the counsellors had been asked to re-apply for their own jobs in an attempt to make cutbacks. As you can imagine the environment was quite toxic and a lot of the camaraderie that I was used to had begun to die off.

I had asked my line manager for some support and tried to say that I was finding it hard at the moment but he was too caught up in the internal politics of it all and simply reassured me that everyone was feeling the same, himself included.

I tried to ask my mum for support but she was going through some physical health issues of her own, which meant I didn't want to burden her with my worries.

I began to dread my clients coming in for their appointments. I realised I felt uplifted if one of them cancelled as I'd have at least 50 minutes free from hearing about their lives. One night I went home and put the TV on and it was a dark police drama about childhood abuse. I just turned over and found some light hearted comedy instead. I realised I'd been doing that a lot lately, I couldn't even stomach watching the soaps because I was sick of hearing about all the dramas.

I just felt so tired all the time and all of my previous sense of enjoying my work, or feeling like I was a good counsellor, had just drained away.

Q So in this case something has happened like job cutbacks that is out of my control, and I think it is affecting my work as a counsellor, what would I do?

A It would be important to assess the level of impact upon yourself and whether you have any current clients whom you expect to see. Your supervisor, tutor, and personal therapist can be a great resource in these times to help you assess whether you are fit to practise, and then what you might need to put in place to improve your wellbeing. If you are so diminished by what is going on in your life or in your work, then it may be that you need to take some time out from client work while you rebuild your wellbeing.

Q Oh but I couldn't take time off from client work – think of the clients!

A So let's consider the reasons for and against taking time out when things get tough (see Table 12.1).

TABLE 12.1 Reasons for continuing or taking a break from client work

Reasons to continue client work	Reasons to take a break from client work
• Clients may be disadvantaged by appointments being cancelled or postponed • Clients may be disadvantaged by having to move to another counsellor if the break is extended • Clients may feel let down by the counsellor • Placement agencies may feel let down by the counsellor • Trainees are under pressure to complete allocated placement hours in a specified amount of time • Trainees may risk losing their placement if they take a break • Trainees may not be able to submit pieces of coursework without having access to current clients • Trainees may still be expected to attend and pay for supervision even if they are not seeing clients • Trainee may need to re-sit parts, or all, of their course when they are well again	• Working while unwell or unfit risks harm to the client from a counsellor or trainee intervening inappropriately • Working while unwell or unfit can further diminish wellbeing, and reduce the possibility of full recovery • An ethical agency will respect a counsellor's decision to take time out when done so appropriately • It models good self-respect and compassion • Modelling good self-care and self-respect not only teaches you how to accept yourself in all your forms, at your best and worst, but it allows you to show the same level of compassion and acceptance to your future clients.

Q Wow those reasons to continue working seem pretty compelling and I'm actually very scared of some of those consequences. I can't imagine having put in this much effort to get this far and then making the choice to do something that could jeopardise that. I can see why some practitioners might hide that they are struggling.

A Yes it can be very daunting to admit that you are struggling as a counsellor. Remember that we are talking about the harder end of the self-care spectrum here, which is taking time off entirely. It may just be that self-care activities put into place at the right moment can maintain a consistent level of resilience and help you out of a bad time. Prevention is better than cure.

Q So I just need to ask for help, or take a bit of time out for myself when things get hard to prevent it from escalating. That sounds fine to me.

A Yes, just remind yourself that it is ok to not be ok sometimes. What can sometimes get in the way of asking for help are our own embedded patterns of relating. Those who choose the helping profession are often those who are better at giving help than asking for it. If this feels familiar to you it might be useful to examine what your motivations are for wanting to do this work and consider how they might affect you during times of difficulty.

> Without minimising the external demands of helping others, then, it seems fair to say that some of the factors that wear us down we seem to have brought with us at the outset. Along with a clean shirt, good intentions, and eagerness to serve, we've carried to work a number of needs and expectations. Sometimes burnout is simply our motives coming home to roost (Ram Dass and Gorman, 1985: 191).

Q So are you saying that if I burnout it's my fault for being so terribly defensive about my own vulnerability?!

A Not in those words no. But consider the following motivations for the work, and how these might 'play out' if that person began to ignore their self-care:

- A need to be needed by another person. Perhaps someone who has grown up being relied upon a lot by other family members and has developed a lot of their self-esteem from how much others need them to help them out.
- A need to be perfect all the time. Perhaps someone who got a lot of praise at school and home only when they achieved high grades or pushed through a difficult task without moaning or complaining.
- A need to be powerful over others. Perhaps someone who grew up being told they were worthless and not as good as their peers. Perhaps they are drawn to helping people less fortunate than them because it's the only place where they feel more 'important' and less flawed than those around them.

Q Wow those are some tricky examples but I see what you are saying. I know I can be a bit of a rescuer, so it's hard for me to be rescued by others because that makes me quite uncomfortable. I actually plan to look at where that comes from in my personal therapy.

A Excellent – you sound like you're aware of some of your motivations and are willing to reflect on them. What a great place to start!

SUMMARY

- Practitioner level training can be a demanding and stressful time – attending to your self-care is vital.
- Developing self-care strategies at this time will help you in your future as a counsellor and help avoid burnout.
- Asking for help or support is a strength not a weakness.

13
Writing a Case Study

Q My tutors have told us that we need to write a 'case study' now that we are in practice with clients. I'm unsure what this means, is it like an essay about a client?

A Case studies serve many purposes and are a common element of most practitioner training courses. When you say 'essay about a client' you are close to being correct, but it's important to define a few of those areas more specifically.

A case study is different to a theoretical essay, in that it must incorporate a very personal reflective aspect that is often lacking from purely academic essays. You will probably be asked to draw upon information from outside sources, e.g. quotes from theorists to support the work, but the core part should be a reflection or analysis of your own practice.

The other important distinction is to avoid the starting point of thinking it's 'about your client'. It's about your practice and demonstrating to the assessor that you understand what you are doing in your work and are able to explain that to someone else.

Q Oh but my tutor has always told me that my sessions are 'about my client' so I think I should stick with that.

A Ah that is a bit of misappropriation right there! Yes your sessions are about your client's agenda and what they need, rather than your needs. But to take that piece of advice and apply it to every situation would be hugely inappropriate.

Think of it like your personal therapy; that MUST be about you. Developing your self-awareness through therapy might eventually help your client work. But you can't go to therapy to just discuss your clients – it's the same with your case study. It should be about how you practise, and demonstrate your awareness of safe and competent practice to your tutor so that they are able to pass you on the course. This has the knock on effect that once you are able to analyse your practice and demonstrate competence it will then benefit your clients.

Q Right, ok I get your point. So this is a written piece of work that shows my competence in practice and ability to reflect, and I do this through choosing one client case to reflect upon?

A Yes, exactly that. It is also likely that your tutors will want you to show your theoretical competence through this as well. So bear in mind when writing it that it should have a clear understanding of your theoretical approach running through it, like words through a stick of rock.

Q So how do I begin with this whole process?

A A good place to start is to review the guidance given to you by your tutors. It may be that they have a set of criteria that you need to meet through this piece of work, or they may have a specific structure for the completion of it. That should be your absolute grounding point, and you should keep going back to that at regular intervals to ensure you are meeting the assessment needs of the piece of work.

Q Ok so at some point I suppose I have to choose the right client to use. What is it that makes the client the right client?

A This depends on a few factors, not least of which is ensuring that the client you choose gives their full informed consent to be the subject of a case study.

Q Yes of course. But how on earth do I make a case study fit within the confidentiality contract I set out with clients? I tell them very clearly that what is said in the room stays in the room, with very few legal exceptions. I can't now say 'Oh by the way I'm going to write an essay on you!'

> **REFLECTION**
>
> If you were in therapy and your counsellor asked you to be the subject of their written case study how would you feel?
>
> What sort of explanation would you need from your counsellor to make you feel fully aware of what you were agreeing to?
>
> What would be your concerns?

A Your responsibility here falls into two key areas. First, checking out with a new client (or feasibly an existing one) if they are happy to be used as the subject of a case study. This means telling them all about how their information would be used, their right to see anything that refers to them directly, and their right to withdraw their consent at any point if they change their minds. You would need to be fully transparent about what you are doing, and be open to them saying no, as that is their right. To avoid any future dilemmas, it is advisable to gain their signed written consent.

Secondly, you need to ensure even once consent is gained, that you then create a case study with sufficient anonymity within it that your client isn't immediately identifiable. This is where it being about your practice, and not your client, comes in really handy! Many counsellors will use a pseudonym, a very limited client description, and draw the focus to their practice rather than to an analysis of their client's issues. This is often far more acceptable to a client, and more likely to elicit full informed consent.

Q Ok so I need to be really ethical and above board about this. I get that it would be wrong to write about someone and not let them know, and that it's even more ethical to make sure that it is vague enough that even their family wouldn't realise it was them if they read it. Is that right?

A Perfect!

REFLECTION

What might affect your decision around which client to choose to use for a case study?

- Client consent
- Number of sessions carried out
- Is the client likely to complete or drop-out?
- Are there any key areas of personal learning in the work?
- Any interesting areas of diversity?
- How often you have used supervision to inform this piece of client work
- Have you struggled with your own self-awareness during the work?
- Is there anything in particular that your course criteria requires you to cover?

It is important to also check out what your training course might wish you to focus on in your case study and if they have any particular requirements around consent. They might have a form your client needs to complete to say they consent. Your client should also know their rights in terms of correction and deletion. It would be useful to explore with your training provider where your responsibilities fall in respect of data protection legislation. If your case study contains data on an individual then you may need to be very explicit about how this information is stored and when it will be stored until.

Q This all sounds very complicated.

A It's not the easiest thing to get your head round and you will need to make sure you are up to date with data protection legislation as things can change over the years. But it will stand you in good stead for your future when you need to think about client case notes and data storage.

Q So once I've got a client all set up how do I go about composing my case study?

A It's probably easiest to picture it as a flow diagram (see Figure 13.1)

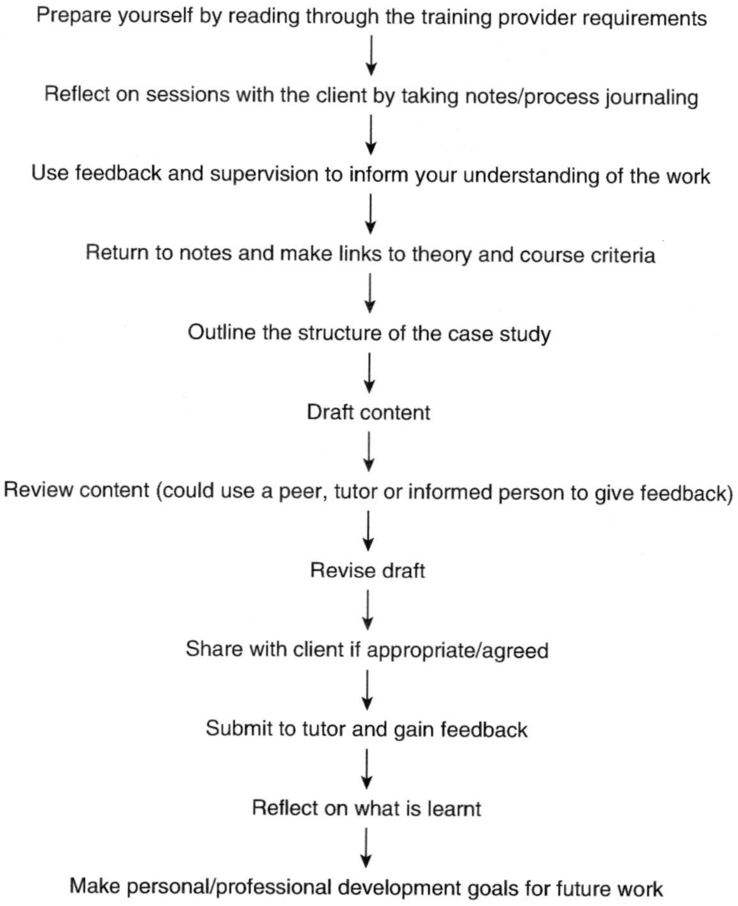

FIGURE 13.1 Completing a case study

Q That seems to give me a good process to follow. I think I have it sorted now.

A Great. It's just one possible way of doing it but will hopefully help guide you on the way to what can be one of the most rewarding aspects of academic work in counselling training – the client case study.

Summative point – Fail to plan – plan to fail!

SUMMARY

- A case study provides an opportunity to reflect on your practice with a certain client, and consider how you might develop.
- Training providers may ask for a range of case study styles – refer back to your guidance when writing.
- Gaining fully informed client consent is of paramount ethical importance.

14
Recording a Counselling Session and Analysing a Transcript

There are a variety of ways in which an individual studying counselling can be asked to demonstrate their proficiency and understanding of their practice. One of these ways is sometimes called a Process Report, in which a student can be expected to record their sessions and then choose a short time period from these sessions to transcribe and analyse. The aim is to demonstrate their understanding of the process of therapy and how their interventions and techniques affect this process.

Q Just when I think I've got the hang of this studying lark my tutor has now thrown in a right curve ball. I have got used to writing essays, case studies, journals, self-reviews, all sorts, and now we have to transcribe a session and write a report about it. Where do I even start with that?

A Ahh yes a Process Report perhaps? This is quite standard for this level of study and though it might seem daunting at first you'll find you gain a whole new world of reflective experience from being asked to do this.

Q I don't really understand what it is for. It seems really similar to a case study to me where we're reviewing our work with a client. How do they differ?

A You're on the right lines but there are some crucial differences. Its purpose is to allow you to reflect on and critique your practice, and to demonstrate your understanding of 'why you do the things you do' and your understanding of the impact of them.

A case study often looks more like an essay, whereas a Process Report includes a written dictation/transcript of what was said in the session with an accompanying annotated analysis. The analysis can be either intermingled with the transcript or a separate document alongside it. We will give you some examples of this later on in the chapter.

Like a case study you will be expected to reflect on your work with a single client, but with this report you will be looking in much greater detail at the 'process level' of a single encounter.

Q Process level?

A Yes, it's really important at any higher level study to differentiate between content and process. Think of it as: content = what is said, process = what is 'going on' for the person who said it and the person who heard it, what did they mean by it, and what is the impact of it in the wider scheme of things.

In a transcribed session this is particularly important and the transcript essentially is the content, so it frees you up to talk about the process. Pretty nifty really.

Q Ok sounds interesting, I think you have got me on board. Where do we start?

AUDIO RECORDING

A The first thing to consider is how to create an audio (or sometimes even video) recording of your counselling sessions, and how you will manage the confidentiality of this.

Q Already I am filled with dread! It took me ages in my introduction training to get over being observed, and now I have to be recorded too, and hear my own voice back on the tape – sounds horrific!

A Yes indeed, it might be a bit challenging. But you're a counselling student, you're up for a bit of challenge right?

And of course many of the 'greats' have done this sort of thing. When you look through Carl Rogers' work you will see endless evidence of sessions being recorded and analysed on a truly microscopic level. Many of the great therapists of our time knew that recordings were essential when considering the subtle nuances of our interventions and critiquing how effective we have been, without being affected by the emotional bias that can occur in the moment of the session.

One of the other things that Rogers also emphasises was that recordings should only be taken with the permission of the client, and that confidentiality was paramount.

Q Yes, this also worries me. If I'm so scared of recording a session I can't imagine how a client would agree. What if none of my clients ever agree to it?

A It is the client's choice whether to be recorded and you must gain their consent. Good ethical practice dictates that you should gain their explicit written consent, and let them know they can withdraw the consent at any time. You will find that it often falls down to how clearly you explain to them the purpose of the recordings, and how their confidentiality will be maintained.

> **EXAMPLE**
>
> So that I am able to fully reflect on our work together to ensure that we can best achieve our agreed goals I would like your permission to make audio recordings of our sessions together. These recordings will help me remember more accurately what we have talked about. As you know I'm a student in training and I can also draw from these recordings to inform my college work if that would be acceptable to you. I can assure you that the recordings will stay confidential, and only I and my course tutor would have access to them. Is this something that you would be ok with?

You can then discuss how your client feels about this and answer any questions they have. Under the General Data Protection Regulations they have the right to not give their consent, or to withdraw their consent and ask for any recordings to be securely destroyed at any point. It is also important to keep these as confidentially as you would your client notes.

Q I would of course be really careful with the recordings. I think I'd also want to be mindful of how obtrusive the Dictaphone, or whatever I use, is in the session. I wouldn't want it to be a distraction.

A Yes good thinking there. You'll want to take care of the practical aspects of recording in advance. For example you don't want to stop a session midway because you didn't check the batteries in the recorder and you just heard a loud CLICK as it turns itself off!

CHOOSING A SESSION

Q Ok so do I just ask one client for permission and take one recording and go from there?

A Ideally you will want to have the choice of many sessions. It might also be worth noting that the reviewing of sessions isn't just for the purpose of the course; it might be useful for your practice overall so perhaps consider making it what you do as standard.

In the case of this report you will want to make an informed choice of session. Listen to a range of your recordings to get a good overview. Things to look for include:

- Is this session representative of my work as a whole?
- Which of these sessions stands out to me? Perhaps because of a dilemma that surfaced, or a challenging moment that you could analyse.
- Does this session show my theoretical approach to its fullest?
- When I think of 'process' rather than 'content', do I feel I can explore this well within this session?

CHOOSING A SECTION

Q Right so next thing to do is to pick a section? How much of a section should I be looking at?

A Your course provider may have specified a length of time, or a length of Process Report. It is typical for this to be around ten minutes long. A ten minute long transcription should provide you with a report around 3,000 words in length.

At this point however, rather than choose a section, you would be better off transcribing the whole session and then looking at the hard copy of the transcription to choose your section.

Q The whole session! But that will take ages!

TIPS

- Set aside plenty of time to transcribe your session. It can take about four minutes to transcribe one minute of tape. So if your session is an hour long, it might take you at least four hours to transcribe it.
- Set aside one block of time, rather than several short time periods. Doing it in one go can really help you recall the flow of the session, and thus make a good choice of which section you wish to use.

> Make it clear in your transcript who is talking when, for example:
>
> *Counsellor*: It sounds like you've really started to think about your relationship with your partner in a new light.
>
> *Client*: Yes, I can't help but think we've come to a new stage of our time together now, and I'm not sure if it's what I really want.
>
> *Co*: So your relationship might not be what you thought it was?
>
> *Cl*: So much has happened in the last year that I don't think I'm who I thought I was, and that has changed how I see them. Does that make sense?
>
> *Co*: It's you that's changed.

Q Ok so let's say I've transcribed the whole session and have it written in front of me, what then?

A Do a full read through and annotate as you go. I'd suggest setting it out with plenty of space in the margins and in between lines. You can then write notes at the end of each line to help you understand the process of what was going on.

Consider the following:

- Intention – what motivated your intervention, or what were you trying to do?
- Impact – how did the client respond, did your intent have the desired effect?
- Tone – remember that your reader cannot hear the tone of voice or emotional expression. It can be helpful to add these notes, e.g. 'whispered', 'gruffly', 'angrily'.
- Metacommunications – What is going on alongside the verbal? Facial expressions, actions, subtle body language, Umms, ahhs, silences.
- Dilemmas – Anything that challenged you, or was unexpected?
- Your process – what were you feeling at the time, how did this affect your interventions, was it managed?

Q Ok that sounds like a mammoth task. But actually really interesting. I've never really thought about a session in this much detail before. I have a feeling it will be really enlightening.

So then I choose my section right?

A Yes. Look over your whole transcript and consider the following:

- Look for a balance between counsellor and client talking. Long chunks of monologue on either side can be hard to analyse.
- Look for something interesting or unique, or an area that stood out to you when you were making your notes.
- Check you have the correct time period, for example, ten minutes worth of text.

WRITING THE REPORT

Q Is that it then? I just hand in my transcript and the notes I've made?

A Not quite so easy unfortunately. The next step is to compose it into a proper analytical report. Your course provider will probably say how they prefer it to be formatted but there are two often used formats that we'll explain here.

The first is to lay out the transcribed text, with regular interspersed comments sections which analyse the interaction above them.

EXAMPLE

Cl: I really can't understand what the point of all this is. I feel so despairing of coming here and talking through my problems with you. How do I actually get anything changed by just talking?!

Co: You really want things to change for you and I hear how frustrated you are talking about it when it doesn't feel like it's making any difference.

[The client had become angrier at this point and glared at me. I tried to hand this back neutrally to the client without becoming defensive of my role as a counsellor, or pushing to explain that counselling could make a difference. I understood it was more important to understand their perspective.]

The other format is to number/label each line of the transcript and then provide an accompanying report which analyses each section in turn.

EXAMPLE

In lines 5–7 the client expressed anger at the lack of change made by the counselling process. In lines 8–9 I tried to paraphrase this neutrally without becoming defensive so the client understood I was not going to dictate to her. Internally I found this a challenge as I felt inclined to justify my approach.

Q That seems a bit complicated. I think if I'm given a choice I'll use the first system as then I can comment on the process as I go along. Anything else?

> **TIP**
>
> Ensure your comments are analytical and provide a critique of your work. Your tutor will want to see that you can critically evaluate your practice more than they want to see your most perfect piece of practice.

A You will also want to shape the report with a clear introduction and an overarching summary at the end. I'd suggest including the following items:

Introduction

- Client profile (being mindful of confidentiality), including briefly their presenting issue
- Outline of counselling approach and theoretical orientation
- Setting, referral, assessment
- Contracting and agreed aims
- Explanation of which number session you have transcribed, which section, and what the context of the section is, e.g. what comes before and after

Main analysis

- Self-critique and line-by-line analysis of the work
- Link to your theoretical orientation
- Explore your own process and how it links to the interventions you made
- Consider how you could improve

Summary

- An overview of the analysis
- Evaluate your work and set it in the context of any future work with the client

You may need to attach references/bibliography, the client consent form, and your audio recording in a secure format.

Q That really sets it out clearly. Thank you for breaking it down like that. I think I could now have a good attempt at it. I'm aware it will be my first one so I guess it's all a learning process, but a valuable one.

SUMMARY

- Leave enough time to do your transcript – it can take a while!
- Remember to differentiate between what is content and what is process. The report should explore the process of the session.
- Decide on a consistent report format and stick with it.
- Use it as a learning process.
- The part of the session you choose doesn't have to be perfect; if it has some flaws it will give you something to critique.

PART III
PROFESSIONAL ISSUES

15
What If?

INTRODUCTION

A How are you feeling at the moment? You've come a long way in your training and personal development.

Q I still don't feel very confident. There seems so much to remember and be aware of. I have had quite a lot of personal therapy over the years and the counsellors I have seen always seem so calm and wise. Most of the time I feel scared and inadequate. Even most of the other trainees on my course seem really together and confident.

In my placement last week, a client was telling me about how she was not sleeping and just pacing all night crying. Her daughter had left for university and she was frightened she would get in with the wrong crowd and take drugs and hurt herself, maybe die. Her brother had done this and she was so terrified it would happen again she couldn't eat or sleep. I remember feeling quite sorry for her only having me.

A I'm reminded of something Wilfred Bion said about the therapeutic relationship.

> In every consulting room there ought to be two rather frightened people: the patient and the psycho-analyst. If they are not, one wonders why they are bothering to find out what everyone knows. (1990: 5)

What do you think about that statement?

Q I guess it is something to do with being congruent, genuine with myself and accepting how I feel without judgement and shame. But actually I think there's something about going into the unknown. When I am with a client, there is no way I can predict what is going to happen. I know I have a set of skills and my theoretical approach to help me understand and relate but what happens within that, within the session is out of my control and that is scary.

A Yes it is.

Q And I am the sort of person that likes to know. Also, I am in a relationship with another person. Of course it is a professional relationship, but we are still two human beings with all our feelings, fears, experiences, differences and similarities. I used to think a counsellor was a bit like a robot.

A And counsellors are very real, flawed human beings.

Q I don't want my insecurities and flaws to hurt my clients though. Despite all my training I still get the urge to make things better for them which I know can actually do more harm than good.

A It can be easy to forget that you are not responsible for your clients. You are not there to fix them, solve their problems or make everything ok. You are there to provide a safe and caring space for them to share their stories and feelings and find a way forward. There is a Latin phrase, 'Primum non nocere' which means 'first, do no harm'. This phrase can be helpful if you are feeling inadequate and not good enough in your role as counsellor. It is much better to do nothing than to take the risk of causing harm. In the British Association for Counselling and Psychotherapy (BACP)'s *Ethical Framework for the Counselling Professions* (2018), the principle of non-maleficence is a commitment to avoiding harm to the client.

Q So it is better for me to feel powerless and useless than to rush in with my own opinions and ideas. I learnt way back on my counselling skills course that I only do that to stop my own uncomfortable feelings rather than to help my client but I still get tempted to do it. I just want to be useful and not sit there like an idiot.

A I'd like to share something with you from when I was doing my counselling training. I was on placement in a domestic violence agency and I was with a client who was in a horrendous situation, I felt totally useless and remember thinking that she really needed to see a counsellor … and then I remembered I WAS the counsellor. How well I remember feeling sorry for the client that she only had me.

Q But look at you now, you've achieved so much. Come so far …

A And now you're trying to rescue me from my old feelings of inadequacy.

Q Oh no! More personal therapy for me I guess.

A Ok. How shall we use the remaining time we have together. What would be helpful for you to help you in your work as a counsellor? What do you need?

Q I still have lots of questions about what to do in certain situations.

A I see, 'what if …' questions.

Q Exactly. There are so many things that spring to mind where I just wouldn't have a clue what the ethical and best thing to do would be. There's probably even more things I haven't thought about.

A The rest of the book can focus on the 'what ifs' then!

TOUCH

Q What do I do if the client asked for a hug?

A This brings us to a very important and very sensitive area, that of touch. Many questions are raised around whether or not it is appropriate to have any physical contact at all with a client.

Q I can't think of anything wrong in giving a caring hug or just reaching out and touching a shoulder or holding a hand. I absolutely agree that exploiting or abusing clients in any way is abhorrent but if I'm coming from a caring, warm place, surely that cannot be harmful or unsafe.

A You are talking about where you are coming from. Let's stop for a moment and reflect on where the client might be coming from.

Q Oh I'd never just reach out and touch, I would always ask if it's ok.

A I'm just wondering what would happen if you asked a client who found it almost impossible to say no, if they wanted a hug.

Q They'd probably say yes even if they didn't want to.

A This could then be replicating other self-defeating relationship patterns but without awareness of the dynamic, this repeating pattern could be ignored.

In psychodynamic counselling an interpretation of the transference could be therapeutic and healing. In Person-Centred Therapy immediacy could be helpful in exploring what was happening.

Q So touch or a hug is something we could discuss in the session?

A Carefully, carefully, tiny tentative steps at the client's pace and only when relevant and appropriate.

Q I see why touch is such a sensitive area.

A Well touch means very different things to different people. For some it is a warm, caring act. Some clients may have been physically or sexually abused and touch will mean something very different. Others may have been manipulated or controlled by touch. Touch can be very loving and also very sexual. Touch can be delightful and can also be terrifying.

Q So what do I do if the client asks me for a hug?

A Again, there are a lot of things to consider. Let's just consider some of the questions we could ask ourselves:

- What led up to the request?
- What was happening in the session at that time?
- What is my relationship with the client like?
- Is gender or sexuality a factor … erotic transference?
- How many times have we met?
- Do I want to give the client a hug?
- What transferential dynamics are or could be present?
- How this will be acknowledged in future sessions e.g. if a hug is offered, does hugging become a part of each session? Is it a one off?
- If you refuse to hug, how can this be worked through with the client?

Whatever happens, hug or no hug, the important thing is to have a strong enough therapeutic relationship that will allow the discussion of and reflection on the issue of touch with the client. To be able to talk about what the hug might mean, how it might impact on future work. Equally, how would rejection feel, how could that be held and explored.

All clients are individual and each relationship we build with each client will be unique. The work needs to be safe and ethical with a clear contract but what is healing for one client could be harmful to another client. So we come back once again to the need for clinical supervision with a supervisor you can be honest with. Someone you don't have to pretend to be a perfect counsellor with. Someone you can share your practice with, warts and all. Also the need for ongoing personal and professional development to ensure self-awareness and insight, ensures we focus on the client rather than our own agenda and needs. With solid support and personal development in place we will be better equipped to make choices in line with what each individual client needs and also what we are prepared to offer. Physical intimacy of any kind must be an individual choice and preference.

TIME BOUNDARIES

Q I really struggle around maintaining the time boundary sometimes.

A That's quite a sweeping statement. Can you explain a little bit more? Do you have any specific examples?

Q When the session is nearing the end, I find myself waiting for an opportunity to let the client know there's only a few minutes left but because I feel so anxious about ending properly on time, I almost stop listening as I'm so focused on the time ticking away. I know it's not ok to interrupt the client and I should just wait for them to finish but when there's no space to prepare for the ending, I don't know what to do. It just feels too horrible to jump in and what if the client's crying or in the middle of something?

A It seems as if there are several different things happening here.

You spoke about feeling anxious about ending appropriately. You spoke about feeling horrible about interrupting the client and almost panicking because you're not sure what to do if the client just continues talking or is distressed near the end.

Q Yes and I know I should end on time. In class it is made very clear that boundaries are essential and vital for the client's safety but sometimes I just can't end on time. It doesn't seem to matter that I know I should, I can't.

A You are using the word 'should' a lot and by the sound of it giving yourself a really hard time because your boundaries aren't perfect. The word should is an interesting word. Sometimes it just sets unrealistic expectations, induces guilt and decreases your desire to do what you otherwise would want to do.

Q Yes, I feel so guilty, that I'm doing things wrong, that I'm not good enough blah blah.

A Perhaps some issues are coming up that could be taken to personal therapy?

Q I think I'll be in personal therapy for quite a while! But yes, I have a lot of difficulties around feeling not good enough and I worry a lot about getting in trouble and being punished. I have talked through so many things in personal therapy; I should be sorted now …

A 'Should be sorted', another 'should'.

Q I did it again. Oh no, I even feel bad for doing it again. I shouldn't have said should argh!!!

A I wonder what would happen if you changed the 'sh' in should to a 'c' so the word becomes could. How would that feel?

Q I guess I'd feel less in the wrong. 'Should' is almost an order to do something in a certain way but 'could' almost offers me a choice of how to move forward, gives me options.

A However, you also made some very important comments about what to do at the end of the session if a client is distressed or in the middle of something important. Your anxiety is very understandable as these are very tricky boundary issues.

Have you ever heard the term 'doorknob confession' in relation to counselling?

Q I've not heard of that before.

A A doorknob confession is a term used by some counsellors in relation to the times in therapy when the client decides to divulge something incredibly important or critical in the last few minutes of the session. The content of the 'confession' is likely to cause the session to go on longer than originally planned and may include themes such as: a death in the family, suicidal/self-harming thoughts or actions, a relationship crisis, drastic change in living situation, etc. Essentially, something a client may say with their figurative 'hand on the doorknob' as they're about to leave, that makes the counsellor consider inviting them to stay longer to address it.

So, you can see that the things you mention are well known in counselling work and can be challenging for even the most experienced counsellors.

Q That's a bit of a relief but I'm still not sure what to do when things like this happen. Do I end on time regardless or allow more time and if I allow more time, how much more time?

A Perhaps it's not always as simple as one right way for everyone. Boundaries are of course vital for safety, clarity, openness, containment, etc. and you show clear awareness of their importance but sometimes other factors are involved that can really challenge boundaries and in some cases the boundary might need to be crossed.

Q I can't believe I'm being told to ignore boundaries.

A I don't think that's quite what I said!! I think the key word is safety. Ensuring the client's safety may sometimes mean crossing boundaries but this would be only in exceptional circumstances. Most counsellors would agree that it is important to acknowledge the significance of what the client has just revealed, so that it is present in the room. Be firm that there is not enough time now to do this justice but that you will make it a priority next time if that is what the client would like.

PLACEMENT ETHICS

Q I am on placement at a counselling agency and am very worried about some ethical matters. Some of the other trainee counsellors on placement there sit and chat about their clients over lunch. Sometimes the door to the kitchen is open and they can be heard in the corridor where clients sometimes use the bathroom. I have overheard them talking about clients on several occasions and even heard them laughing about some things clients have said. I would hate to think my own counsellor would laugh about me with other counsellors. I am too scared to say anything in case it jeopardises my placement and also I'm not 100% sure if what they are doing is a breach of confidentiality or even if it is unethical.

What should I do?

A Sounds like a very tricky situation for you. You raise two issues. The first is whether or not confidentiality has been breached and whether or not the counsellors' conversations are unethical. The second issue is your fear of saying anything.

So actually there is one main issue for you and that is around your fear. Fear of getting it wrong, fear of losing the placement, fear of lack of knowledge, fear of speaking out …

Q Yes, fear does seem to be at the root. I am just so shocked that counsellors do this.

A Firstly not all counsellors do this and secondly it is most certainly not ethical. There are also serious risks around breaching client confidentiality.

My initial response is to wonder what's happening at the agency in terms of counsellor support. This sort of thing can sometimes be attributed to counsellor stress, overwhelm or burn out. There could be some challenges around containing the client work, resulting in the work almost spilling over into other aspects of the counsellor's life making the work potentially uncontained and unsafe. It is also an interesting aside to note that often there can be a very dark humour in relation to trauma; humour can be a very powerful defence to some difficult and potentially distressing emotions. Therefore my initial response would be to ask what support and self-care is in place. What clinical supervision is in place for trainees? How does the agency management monitor and support trainees?

Q We don't get supervision from the agency. We have to provide our own. Often the only other person in the office is the administrator who answers the phone and passes on messages from clients.

A Again, you highlight another important issue around appropriate placements for trainees.

Q I know it's not a perfect placement but I really need my hours to complete my diploma and there are very few placement opportunities in this area.

A As you are still completing your diploma, I wonder whether your college or centre could help. Your college/centre does have a responsibility to ensure the placements are appropriate for trainees and that their supervision is appropriate and this is something they might feel is important to follow up. You don't seem to get any support at all from this agency and I don't think this is ethical or appropriate for a trainee counsellor.

Q I could go to my tutor but I'm worried about losing the placement or my tutor telling me to leave.

A A hard choice to make. There are no easy answers either. I'm left with the words 'ethical responsibility'.

What do the words mean to you?

Q When I think of the word responsibility, I break it down to 'the ability to respond'. Therefore I would think it meant the ability to respond appropriately to ensure ethical practice in the profession.

A Exactly.

Q Which means, even though it is not me chatting and laughing about clients, I still have a responsibility to do something about it. ARGH!!

A Let's refer to the BACP *Ethical Framework for Counselling Professions* (EFfCP) for guidance (2018: 6).

- Part of our commitment to clients is to work to professional standards by, 'collaborating with colleagues to improve the quality of what is being offered to clients'.

- We show respect by, 'protecting client confidentiality and privacy'.
- We build an appropriate relationship with clients by, 'respecting the boundaries between our work with clients and what lies outside that work'.
- We maintain integrity by, 'working ethically and with careful consideration of how we fulfil our legal obligations'.

I would also suggest that the Ethics, Values, Principles and personal moral qualities covered in the framework are also relevant.

Q I know you are right but I hate things like this but in my own therapy I've learnt that the only way to grow is to work through my fears. I will do something but I'm still not sure what the best course of action is.

A Some decent insight and self-awareness.

I'm reminded of a quote by Napoleon which is:

> The world suffers a lot. Not because of the violence of bad people but because of the silence of good people.

Of course I'm not suggesting that the other counsellors are bad but they are definitely showing some areas of bad practice.

There is a place for what is happening between the trainees talking in the kitchen and that's group supervision. If what was taking place was boundaried and private, there could be some peer supervision. This would not count towards your clinical supervision hours but it would count towards ethical practice and counsellor support. There could even be a place for laughter and humour in this setting. Laughter does not have to be judgemental; it could be from a wide variety of sources.

Q I'm going to suggest this and I will highlight the lack of boundaries and privacy when talking in the kitchen.

I'm also going to talk to my tutor and ask for support in taking this forward.

A A lot of courage.

Q Hopefully this will be good for me in the long run. I keep hearing that the more difficult something is, the greater the growth for me.

Why the heck does it have to be like that?

I do want it badly enough, so I will take action. I think my own supervisor will be able to support me through this and I can take my fear about it all to personal therapy.

JUDGEMENTS

Q My client says some horrible things about women and I really don't like him and don't know what to do.

A Is this a new client?

Q No, we have had over ten sessions together.

A What was your relationship like with him before?

Q It was ok I think. I felt quite warm towards him and he seemed quite in touch with his feelings and willing to open up.

A So something he has said has completely changed how you view and feel about him.

Q Yes well I didn't realise he was so sexist, saying how women have an easier time than men and yet men get blamed for everything and other stuff.

A Interesting. You feel warm towards your client but have put a lot of emphasis on what he has said. It sounds like this has stirred things up for you.

Have you explored with him what he's saying and tried to understand why he's thinking and feeling that way? His words could be: truth, lie, to annoy you, to shock, to express anger and many more possibilities. We can't possibly know by guessing.

Q He's a single dad and works like crazy for his children. I had so much respect for what he does but now …

A I hear you don't like sexism but it seems your client became that and nothing else. There's an old saying about walking the walk and not just talking the talk. From what you have said, your client is walking the walk and earning your respect but he's not talking the talk. You don't like sexism; I hear that very clearly but your client has become a sexist but nothing else. What's really going on for your client and indeed what's really going on for you?

Q I know his wife left for someone else last year and doesn't even see their children but he said he's come to terms with that.

A Again, all you are listening to are the words. Your client uses much more than words to communicate with you.

Q I hadn't realised but that is the one thing he never talks about and if what we are discussing even touches on his ex-wife he just moves onto something else.

A Is that something you've been able to take to him?

Q I hadn't even realised it until now. Maybe both of us are in denial.

A … and avoiding the pain that is being denied …

You also had a personal reaction to what he said that triggered a response in you.

Q Yes, I suddenly really didn't like him and felt quite angry. I'm pretty sure I know what it is now. My dad left when I was eight. Do you know, up until the day he left, I had no idea anything was wrong. He'd talk about Christmas and future holidays and was just my dad. Nothing special, nothing horrible, just my dad and then suddenly he wasn't there and the few times we met after that it was like he just wasn't my dad anymore. I didn't know who he was.

A Perhaps that eight year old you was in the room when your client made some comments you didn't like. Your client went from being a decent man, caring father to a sexist unpleasant man. I can't help but draw parallels with what happened with your father.

Q Yes, that's exactly what I think. In our next session, if it feels appropriate, we could perhaps revisit his comments and I feel I can be congruent without letting my agenda creep in.

A It sounds as if you don't dislike him quite so much now.

Q True.

A You do open up an interesting topic though – what do we do if our clients' values and beliefs are vastly different to our own?

Q I know that we need to work through our judgements and put them to one side to focus on the client.

A Of course but what do we do when we can't or won't put them to one side? What if we just can't understand?

I'm thinking back to when I hadn't been working as a counsellor for very long. I had a client who had admitted sexually abusing his three-year-old niece and had served a jail sentence. I felt shocked and disgusted by what he'd said but also felt guilty that I couldn't see past the behaviour to the person underneath. What I actually did was be nicer and gentler and warmer than I usually would be. In other words I wasn't congruent and was pretending to be empathic. I overcompensated due to my guilt.

Q I understand that.

A Sounds a bit strange though. 'I was really nice because I didn't like him'. It does however highlight that blocks in empathy can manifest in different ways – over-compensating, punishing, manipulating, assuming, etc.

> **REFLECTION**
>
> Compile a traffic light list of blocks to empathy, understanding and acceptance.
>
> The list is for your eyes only and doesn't have to be shared with anyone. Be as honest as you can and don't try to justify or rationalise your responses … even to yourself.
>
> RED: Issues/areas you feel judgemental about and have no authentic empathy.
>
> AMBER: Issues/areas you feel judgemental about but are able to process and offer authentic empathy.
>
> GREEN: Issues/areas you feel no judgement and authentic empathy is organically present.
>
> Would you feel able to share your traffic light list with anyone?
>
> If you feel unable to share your list, reflect on why this is?
>
> What have you learnt from this exercise?

Q The end of that reflection caught my attention. When I feel judgemental, I don't want to take it to supervision.

A So you won't talk about your judgements in case you are judged.

Often, it's the things we don't want to talk about that need to be explored in supervision. Things are rarely set in stone and experience and reality are tenuous notions. Our own resistance to taking certain things to supervision can also help us understand clients' resistance and reluctance to being able to talk about things they may feel bad, guilty or ashamed about.

CLIENT CHANGING MIND

Q My client keeps changing her mind. Should I remind her of what she said the week before?

A The week before which week?

Q What?

A If a client is literally in two minds, which one do you want to remind her of?

Q The right one.

A If the client is undecided, who decides which the right one for the client is?

Q This is now very confusing and annoying.

A I wonder if it was you who decided what was right for the client and was wondering how to get your client to agree with you.

Q Then what do I do, just ignore it and let her stay stuck?

A Perhaps you could simply hold the two sides up for your client to see more clearly, just hold the two parts (minds) carefully until your client feels ready and/or able to make the choice.

Q What if they don't?

A Then they don't.

Ok if you were working with a couple, whose side would you be on?

Q I wouldn't be on anyone's side, unless one was definitely in the right.

A Ahh and once again, who in the counselling room decides what's right? Another way of asking the question would be, who are you going to collude with?

Q But what if he's hitting her?

A So, we are doing well with difference and diversity today!

How words can change our opinions very quickly and judgement steps in. You made quite a sweeping assumption just now around violence in a relationship coming from a man and therefore as a counsellor you should be on the side of the woman who is right. A lot of very reactive decisions.

Q So what am I meant to do?

A Of course I am not saying violence, abuse and other harmful behaviours are ok. Our work may be around supporting and caring for clients through these areas but our work is not about dragging the client through them, whether they want to or not.

Maybe as counsellors, part of our role is to sit with those awful things, to sit with injustice, hopelessness, terror and brokenness. Maybe the learning for us is how to manage our own feelings when we sit with clients in such distress and pain.

It's so much to do with how we respond and then of course to recognise the triggers to these responses, to ensure our clients' needs stay ahead of our own.

Q I see now. When I said about 'what if he hits her', it just came out, a throwaway comment and I didn't think I meant anything by it but as you were replying, I realised how powerless and frightened I was when my father hit my mum. I was too scared to help her and feel guilty to this day.

A So in a way it's like part of you wants to help your clients like you weren't able to help your mum all those years ago.

Q Of course but I didn't see it at all.

A Supervision
Supervision
Supervision
Supervision
Supervision
Supervision
Once again Bion springs to mind

Q You like Bion don't you?

A I never actually met him but I like his work!!!

Q Good answer

A It would not be good if I made a diversity blunder when responding to a diversity question.

Bion though did coin a beautiful phrase that applies so beautifully to diversity:

> No memory, no desire.

My interpretation is that if we have no memory, we have no stereotypes. If we have no desire, we have no expectation or opinion on outcome.

GIFTS

Q A client came to a session yesterday and brought some flowers for me out of her garden. At college when we covered boundaries, I thought that accepting or giving gifts was wrong but I just couldn't say no when she offered the flowers to me and now I don't know what to do. Should I just forget it or tell her not to bring any more?

A Maybe there's a middle ground in this instance and then we can think about the bigger picture of giving and receiving gifts. It might help us to start by thinking about why people (not just clients and counsellors) give gifts, what's the motivation?

Q Buying someone a gift is a lovely thing to do; it shows care and affection and also values the person the gift is for. It can be to thank someone for their help or it could even be something to cheer someone up after a hard time. A gift can celebrate a birthday or anniversary or any special occasion. A gift can be given to acknowledge someone's achievement, like passing an exam or driving test. A gift can also be by way of an apology, to say sorry. There are lots of reasons.

A You have mentioned a lot of very positive reasons for giving a gift. Could there be any other reasons for giving a gift? Focus on feelings and emotions rather than occasions and situations.

Q To be nice, loving, kind … I'm not sure what you mean.

A Let's play a little game called, 'Have you ever …'

HAVE YOU EVER … given a gift to try and get someone to like you?

HAVE YOU EVER … given a gift to try and get your own way?

HAVE YOU EVER … given a gift because you thought it's the right thing to do?

HAVE YOU EVER … given a gift because you are frightened of someone?

HAVE YOU EVER … given a gift because you don't feel good enough if you don't?

HAVE YOU EVER … given a gift to manipulate a situation?

HAVE YOU EVER … given a gift so others will think you are a nice person?

HAVE YOU EVER … given a gift to appear a nicer person than someone else?

HAVE YOU EVER … given a gift to overcompensate for something you fear you are lacking?

HAVE YOU EVER … given a gift just because you enjoy buying and giving gifts?

HAVE YOU EVER … given a gift as a form of bribery?

HAVE YOU EVER … given a gift and been angry/upset if you received nothing in return?

HAVE YOU EVER … given a gift to try and get someone to be nice to you?

HAVE YOU EVER … given a gift to make someone feel guilty?

HAVE YOU EVER … given a gift because you feel guilty?

HAVE YOU EVER … given a gift to someone you are sexually attracted to?

Q I can relate to buying gifts because I like buying them. It gives me an excuse to go shopping (which I love!!) and also I love seeing people's faces when I give them something lovely. It makes me feel great.

Sadly I also remember buying my mum lots of little gifts when I was a child. I'd spend all my pocket money on her and make things at home and school for her.

A Sadly?

Q Yes, sadly, my mum was an alcoholic and very unstable and volatile. I'd try and make her better by giving her lovely things but most importantly I just wanted her to love me and spend more time with me than with the bottle. When I did give her something she wanted, usually money, she'd be so lovely to me. It was worth it just for those precious moments.

I think I understand more now. My client could be giving me a gift for all sorts of reasons. It could just be a way of saying thank you but it could also be a way of trying to get my approval or to try and get me to like her and not challenge her in any way. She could also be acting out an old pattern from her past. I can still fall into the pattern of buying gifts to try and get people to care and love me, just like I did with my mum all those years ago.

A The Latin phrase – Do Ut des – I give because I expect you to give something back seems relevant. Altruism is actually very unusual!!

What we can be sure of is that giving a gift is a form of communication and as counsellors it is important to listen carefully to all communication and to work hard to understand what the client is trying to say. What can be assumed to be a simple caring act can be fraught with potential risks and difficulties and only by exploring and reflecting on what is happening between counsellor and client can the real dynamics be understood. I am reminded of the following quote spoken by Archbishop Thomas Beckett in the T.S. Eliot verse drama, *Murder in the Cathedral*:

> The last temptation is the greatest treason:
>
> To do the right deed for the wrong reason.

Q I like that quote. At school I used to tell the teacher if anyone else was talking. Of course a quiet learning environment is right and correct but the reason I actually told on the other children was to try and get my teacher to think I was the goodest girl there and like me best.

A That's very honest of you and gives a very clear overview of a complex issue. Gift giving within a counselling relationship is fraught with potential problems and is why many counselling tutors advise students to just not give or receive gifts from clients but actually, at times, there could be some very intimate and healing work around the dynamics of gift giving in a counselling dyad.

It can help to clarify what we mean by a boundary violation in relation to this.

A boundary violation occurs when a therapist crosses the line of decency and integrity and misuses his/her power to exploit and or harm a client for his/her own benefit (Gutheil and Gabbard, 1998).

Counsellors can be understandably nervous around this issue for fear of being accused of breaking boundaries but gift giving is not unusual and the more we can understand, the more we can contribute to our client's healing. It is important to be mindful of both conscious and unconscious intent in relation to gift giving and to explore the meaning with your client and to use personal therapy and clinical supervision to examine your own feelings, motives and any counter transferential issues that may be present, to ensure the client remains the focus and priority of the work. It is also imperative to ensure you do not allow yourself to be manipulated, influenced or coerced by the gift. It should not influence your regard for your client.

Of course the gift itself is an important factor; a bunch of flowers is a very different proposition to a new sports car! It is also important to notice when the client gives a gift – is it at the beginning, middle or end of the work or session? Is it after a difficult period of therapy? Is it before or after a break? Does your client offer gifts often?

The interpretation and exploration of the meaning behind gift giving can enhance the therapeutic work enormously as long as it is managed ethically, appropriately and thoughtfully.

The Merriam-Webster dictionary defines 'gift' as something 'voluntarily transferred' and 'without compensation.'

Q I see that now but what I don't want to do is make the client feel bad for bringing a gift that could be symbolic of something else but could just be a simple thank you.

A Now we come onto what to actually do when given a gift. I agree it is important to not reject or shame a client regardless of the gift. If the gift seems to be a client's way of trying to 'buy love and affection', this can be brought to the client's attention without shame or judgement but as something to be explored and understood as a learnt pattern of relating that can be worked through if the client chooses.

Q So it's ok to accept some gifts.

A It can be, but you may choose not to and if that's the case, you need to let your client know when contracting. That way if the client brings a gift, you can refer back to the contract, rather than just refusing a gift for no apparent reason. As with all things it's about looking for what best serves the client. If a gift is too expensive or inappropriate, you might need to refuse the gift, but the refusal should be sensitive and explain fully to the client that the gift is being rejected but they are not.

In my experience most gifts are given at the end of the work and as an acknowledgement that the relationship is coming to an end. Some clients like to leave something of themselves with you and may find comfort from this.

It's important for you to decide where you stand with gift giving as appearing unsure and hesitant when presented with a gift may not be helpful and could impact negatively on the relationship. As with many things in counselling, one size doesn't fit all and your response to the gift needs to acknowledge that.

Whatever you choose, to accept the gift or not, it is important to convey your thanks and appreciation, even if you aren't accepting the gift. It may be that you agree with the client to keep the 'gift' in the counselling room (as long as it's not an elephant!), so that it stays within your relationship but doesn't enter your private life.

Clients bring us other things too. To be ignorant of that shows an arrogance that belies the nature of a collaborative therapeutic relationship. For a counsellor to acknowledge and be grateful for the things clients bring that heal and enhance the counsellor's life is to acknowledge the true equality of the therapeutic alliance. Although in a counselling relationship there are two people working together on one person's difficulties, there are still also two human beings in the room and within that boundaried and safe environment are still all the fears, anxieties, frailties, complexities and confusions that exist in every human relationship. So we can be grateful for the things that clients bring that mirror and challenge our own experiences. For clients that remind us of selves past and remind us to be tender to those bruised parts inside each of us. For the clients that remind us how deep and dark pain and despair can be and then show us through our work together how resilient we are. How much hurt can be endured and accepted, if not always overcome.

Q You sounded very passionate then.

A You are right. I simply believe that it is important to acknowledge that the therapeutic experience can benefit both the client and the counsellor, and still be boundaried, ethical and professional.

BOUNDARIES OUTSIDE OF COUNSELLING SESSIONS

Q I was in my local pub with some friends, celebrating a birthday when a client walked in. We were quite merry and in retrospect quite loud.

Do I address this in the next session or just ignore it and wait to see if my client mentions it?

A Personally I would certainly address this in the next session and explore with my client what feelings were present for them and how it could have an impact on our relationship and our work together. Other counsellors might wait for the client to bring it up but in my opinion, there is some very powerful work around the therapeutic space meeting the outside world and what that means. There are potentially very important transferential dynamics which could be explored. In that moment you were a real person in your own life and not your client's counsellor. This can be quite challenging, even painful; for a client who sees you in a certain way and that certain way is challenged by a chance encounter, perhaps leaving the client wondering about who you are and who they are in a relationship with.

Q I feel very uncomfortable now. Should I tell her it was a birthday celebration and that I'm usually not a big drinker? I feel I should explain that I'm not usually so raucous and that she can still trust me.

A I think justifying your behaviour might make you feel a little bit better but I cannot see the value for your client. The most important thing here is the client's thoughts and feelings. If this has affected the trust in the relationship, your client should be allowed to express this and any other feelings she might have. Some of this may be difficult for you to hear but there could well be links to your client's patterns of relating or even personal history that could be worked through in your work together. Sometimes quite innocuous comments, meetings, even an ornament in the room, can evoke quite powerful feelings from a client and our role is to support the client to make sense of these feelings.

If introduced carefully and with the client's interests at the centre, this chance meeting could result in some very powerful therapeutic work.

Q I'm a bit scared to do it as I feel a fool but I agree it's important to explore this. I guess this is intimacy.

A Yes, I think it is and a desire for a real and honest discussion.

I wonder how you would have felt and what you would have done if you'd walked into the pub and your client was drunk?

Q That's easy I would have left. I don't think I would have addressed it with the client unless they mentioned it. If I mentioned it, I would be concerned she might feel judged. I would be open to an honest conversation about it but in this instance I think it's for the client to introduce. What the client does outside of a session is none of my business.

A You make some good points and I'd be inclined to agree with you. There are those who would argue that your life outside the counselling sessions is none of your clients' business but actually I believe that is a different dynamic and needs careful reflection and attention.

DUAL RELATIONSHIPS

Q I was dropping my son off at school and one of the other mums approached me and asked me whether I would see her daughter for some counselling sessions. She had heard I am now a fully qualified counsellor. Would this be ok to do?

A This is really something you could usefully be taking to supervision but it raises some important issues that we can explore here.

What do you think about the request?

Q I think there could be some boundary issues but as long as these were made clear from the beginning, I can't see that there would be a problem. I am not a close friend with the mum. We've chatted at the school gates and met at open evenings, etc. but little else. I said to the mum that no matter what was said in the sessions, I couldn't tell her, that the relationship was between her daughter and me and that I couldn't discuss anything with her. The mum had already spoken about the difficulties at home in the past and how her daughter had started self-harming. It sounds like she needs urgent help. Because I am aware of the potential problems, I have also said I'd be prepared to see her daughter for free, no fee for the sessions.

A This is very concerning. You touch on various things and I'd like to break these down and explore each one closely with you.

You say there are some boundary issues but then you go on to justify why it's ok to skip past these. What you don't explain is the potential risks of taking this child as a client. Could the relationship be harmful to anyone and if so, how?

Q I don't think there would be a problem as long as everything's made clear at the beginning. Her daughter Milly is nine years old and really needs urgent help. I would have no personal contact with the mum once the work started.

A So, already you have an agenda. Milly has had no assessment of her needs and you seem to have built a picture of Milly from what her mum has said and yet you haven't yet met Milly.

Q Oh I do know Milly, from school. She's not close friends with my children but they have done trips and parties together. So I wouldn't be a stranger to her which I thought might help in breaking the ice and of course I'd tell her that I wouldn't be speaking to her mum once we started working together.

A This is very unsafe.

You have an existing relationship with a potential client. You assume that this familiarity would help her; you might be right but you don't seem to consider what other feelings might be present. Embarrassment at being counselled by her peer's mother. Fear that they might hear what's been said. I don't know where you are practising but if it is in your home, there could be fear of who might be there. She might feel judged, knowing her mother has told you things about her. She will know you have knowledge about her that hasn't come from her.

Of course, I don't know if any of these things are actual as I haven't met Milly and have no relationship with her but I don't think it's as simplistic as you imply.

Q But I have said that I wouldn't tell her mum anything and of course I wouldn't tell my children.

A I'm sitting here wondering how Milly could be sure you wouldn't tell anyone. You've already discussed her with her mother, how can she now be sure you are trustworthy?

Also, you keep saying you won't tell her mother. How can you be sure of that?

Q Because I won't, I have made that very clear.

A What about safeguarding?

You seem to be assuming a nine-year-old child has the maturity to understand the implications of those decisions without parental consent. That's a very presumptive and dangerous assumption to make.

How would you feel if she disclosed to you sexual abuse in the family home, what could be the implications for all involved and your presence within that? What would you do?

How would you feel if she disclosed her mother was breaking the law? What would you think and feel? What would you do?

Q I think I made another assumption that nothing like that would happen. I don't feel good at all now. I just agreed immediately and brushed away any worries I had.

A I wonder what was happening for you in that moment when you agreed almost without thinking.

Q Do you know, I slip into the same old patterns of relating over and over again; even when I know them, know where they come from, explored and learnt about them in therapy for what seems like a thousand years. I've attended all sorts of workshops and still I fall into the same old trap. My immediate response is to be helpful so that people will approve of me. I want to be the cleverest, the best, the nicest and kindest, all that old stuff. I've tried really hard not to do it but still do. Part of me even knows I'm doing it but still I do it.

A And then after you've agreed, I guess you don't feel too great, like now. I was mindful that you agreed to do the work for no fee too.

Q I think that's all part of the approval and being nice thing. I knew really I was doing the wrong thing. No, I knew I was GOING to do the wrong thing. I'm certainly not going to work with Milly now. I'll briefly explain why to Milly's mum and give her some details of other local counsellors; what I should have done when she first asked me.

A So, although you began following an old pattern, the ending has been different. You explored the issue here and were able to maintain an ethical and safe boundary.

Q Someone on my course said to me a while ago that if I couldn't say 'no', to just not say yes. I really try and remember this.

A Almost like playing for time and giving yourself time to think. That can be helpful for all referrals, taking time to reflect on any boundary, ethical and professional issues prior to beginning the work.

One thing your initial question has highlighted is the whole issue of dual relationships and how that can impact on the therapeutic relationship.

DRESS

Q My agency manager talked to me about how I was dressed and that it wasn't appropriate and looked in her opinion indecent and provocative. I have worked hard to learn to be congruent in my personal therapy and in doing that, I now dress how I please and wear what I want to wear. I had years of doing what others wanted and wearing what others said I had to. I refuse to do that anymore.

A It sounds as if your clothes have become a way of letting the world know who you are.

Q That's exactly it!

A And I guess that means you want your clothes to tell your client who you are and I'm wondering why you need your client to know that?

Q Why should I change?

A This isn't really about changing who you are. Part of your role is about facilitating a safe space, where the focus is on the client – their feelings, issues and difficulties. If how you are dressed takes the focus away from that, there is a risk of failing in your role.

Q I take your point but it could be seen to stereotype gender roles, assume what constitutes appropriate. It reminds me of society's response of 'She asked for it' if a woman dresses in a certain way and gets raped. I refuse to take on beliefs and values around how women should dress to avoid unwanted sexual attention.

A I applaud your journey to congruence and being true to yourself but we aren't talking about unwanted sexual attention here; we are talking about counselling work and the needs of your client.

I am not suggesting a twinset and pearls (although I hasten to add, there is nothing wrong at all with twinset and pearls) but I am agreeing with your agency manager. I'm quite an experienced counsellor but I find the way you are dressed grabs my attention and has taken my focus away from what is being said at times.

I am also aware that there are many counsellors that would disagree with me and loudly support what you are saying, so this is just my opinion but it is also part of the agency policy which you have agreed to.

Q I'd rather leave the agency than change I think. I don't think you have an argument.

A Let's imagine a different scenario

You are in hospital waiting for quite a serious surgical procedure. You are in the operating theatre and have been prepped for surgery. The surgeon walks in with a clown's hair and red nose, a bikini and flip-flops. How would you feel?

Q That's very different.

A I don't think it is.

What we wear as counsellors can communicate a message of competence and professionalism. It can also do the opposite. Non-verbal communication can be more powerful than the spoken word.

REFLECTION

The above dialogue shows two very different opinions. In the table below reflect on your own opinions around how to dress when working as a counsellor. Don't try and look for and write what you think is the correct answer. Write how you personally think and feel and then reflect on what you write. One example has been completed.

It's important to consider the impact of how we present to our clients and what our goal is in dressing the way we do in relation to our clients' process.

Dress remains a contentious issue within the counselling profession. Below are two statements. What is your response to each one?

TABLE 15.1 Presenting to clients

Appearance	Personal opinion	Possible effect on client
Perfume or cologne	I have a favourite scent that I always use and I think that's fine.	If your client doesn't like it, it could be uncomfortable for them. It could remind them of someone or something. If it is very strong it could make them feel unwell
Hair style		
Symbols of wealth		
Dirty or creased clothing		
Revealing clothing		

Appearance	Personal opinion	Possible effect on client
Messages or quotes on clothing		
Jewellery		
Worn out shoes and clothes		
Make up		
Culturally specific clothing		
Having a pet in the counselling room		

1. It is important for a counsellor to dress smartly and quite formally; modesty is important.
2. It is important for a counsellor to be authentic and dress how they please. The counsellor's character needs to shine through.

It is important to remember that the counselling relationship is not about you and your role is not to provide the client with distractions. Your client does not need to know about your personal identity and beliefs but that doesn't mean that you lose them if you don't dress in a certain way. For me congruence isn't about what you wear, it's about who you are.

There are other things to think about in relation to what we wear as counsellors.

FITNESS TO PRACTISE

Q I know that the BACP (British Association for Counselling and Psychotherapy) *Ethical Framework for the Counselling Professions* (EFfCP, 2018) requires me to monitor my own fitness to practise but I'm not confident that I know where that line sits. It worries me even more that I might not even be aware that I'm not fit to practise.

A An interesting area. Let's look firstly at what is meant by the term 'fitness to practise.' For me this means having the skills, knowledge, attitude and personal ability to work safely, ethically and effectively.

Q Yes, I know that fitness to practise is working safely and effectively; I'm just not sure I'd know if the time came when I wasn't fit to practise.

A OK, there are lots of different strands to this. You talk about 'fitness to practise' in quite concrete terms. I had a picture in my mind of you suddenly waking up in the middle of the night, UNFIT TO PRACTISE! As if the plague had descended upon you in the night!

There are quite a lot of strands to this that we can begin to unpick.

The HCPC mention 'skills, knowledge and character to practise their profession safely and effectively'. Skills and knowledge belong mainly in the 'limits of ability' arena. We are asked if we have the skills, knowledge and experience to work with a client's issues and personality. Some clients may present with complex needs and issues, outside of our limits of ability and will need alternative or additional care and support.

This leaves 'character', who we are and how we relate to others, ourselves and our environment. There can be both internal and external stressors and pressures that could impinge on our fitness to practise. It's at this point that the phrase, 'prevention is better than cure', springs to mind.

Q I'm not sure what you mean by that?

A Let's take a car for example. If a car is well looked after, service, MOT, careful driving, etc., it will be safe, comfortable and roadworthy. If a car is not looked after, no checks, driving on wrong terrain, speeding, etc., it is much more likely to become unsafe or breakdown.

Q I see, I can work on optimising my fitness to practise by looking after myself, fostering a healthy lifestyle, not burning the candle at both ends too often. That way I will be able to give my clients my best. If I don't practise self-care, I am more likely to break down or not practise safely just like a car.

A Interestingly, different counsellors will have different needs; different patterns of relating, personality and personal history will impact in different ways. Are you aware of any of the ways you ignore your own needs or allow yourself to become too stressed and dis-eased?

Q I have three children and am on my own with them. I've been studying and working for a few years and find that everyone else's needs seem to come before mine. I am very aware of this pattern but it is so hard to change. I also think that because I'm a single mum, I work extra hard not to fit into any single parent stereotype. I have a clean and lovely home; all my children are doing well at school and attend any clubs or activities they want.

A You have a lot of responsibilities and it sounds as if you have very high expectations for yourself.

Q That's why I tend to worry about my fitness to practise. Sometimes at the end of a day, I could just sit and cry, I feel so tired and drained. I get everything done but feel wrung out at the end of it. I usually just grab the kids' leftovers for tea and then munch on chocolates and crisps as my waist line bears testimony to. I don't want my clients to be affected by my stress.

A I wonder what you would be thinking if a client sat with you and told you what you have just told me. One of the BACP ethical principles seems relevant here: Self-respect: fostering the practitioner's self-knowledge, integrity and care for self.

What care is there for you in the day? Not very much by the sound of it. You seem to be looking for the sweetness in crisps and chocolate, rather than in life; I think your 'car' needs a good service. Self-care is paramount in maintaining fitness to practise and also for a rich and fulfilling life.

EXERCISE

Developing a Self-Care Routine

Fill in Table 15.2 – acknowledge where you do practise self-care and also highlight areas needing work. There are five categories: professional, physical, psychological, emotional and relationships. For each category, comment on how you take care of yourself. This will allow you to see where you need to focus. Examples are given under each category but it's important to also think of what is relevant to you and your lifestyle. You can choose from these or use ideas of your own to compile a personalised self-care plan. Some activities will fall across more than one category.

See what goals you can set to take better care of yourself and in doing so maintain your fitness to practise.

TABLE 15.2 Self-care assessment

Category	What I do now	Things to add
Professional, for example:		
Regular clinical supervision		
CPD		
Work–life balance		
Adequate breaks for food, etc.		
Peer support group		
Make time for admin. Reply to emails, letters, etc.		
Keep up to date with latest developments in field		
Healthy working environment		
Physical		
Diet		
Exercise		
Sport		
Health checks		

(Continued)

TABLE 15.2 (Continued)

Category	What I do now	Things to add
Monitoring existing conditions		
Drug and alcohol use		
Be in nature		
Regular holidays		
Walk		
Take time off when ill		
Get enough sleep		
Psychological		
Stress management		
Be open to not knowing		
Meditate		
Review values and beliefs		
Ensure finances are stable		
Hobbies		
Have goals and dreams		
Believe they can come true		
Turn off TV, internet, etc.		
Make a personal inventory		
Keep a journal		
Emotional		
Personal therapy		
Personal development workshops, etc.		
Loving and supportive relationships		
Self-esteem building		
Express feelings		
Cry		
Watching favourite films, reading favourite books, etc.		
Seek out comforting people, places and things		
Laugh		
Relationships		
Ask for help		
Speak honestly and openly		
Be alone and reflect		
Self-help and support groups		
Acknowledge achievement		
Say no		

Q This really identifies that I come very far down my list of priorities. I certainly need more time and loveliness for myself.

A We have mainly focused on ways of preventing ill health (physical, emotional and psychological) impacting on our work. Sometimes, despite our best efforts at self-care, things out of our control can impact on us, for example, bereavements, divorce, burglary, etc. These can have a significant impact on our fitness to practise.

Q I find these bigger things more straightforward. I would take any 'life events' to supervision and follow my supervisor's guidance.

A Yes. There isn't always a clear line. It might be important to weigh up the potential harm to the client by suddenly ending the relationship or referring versus continuing to work as a counsellor in a fragile or vulnerable state. What might cause someone considerable distress, might be more easily managed by someone else.

Q So, it's important for me to continue reflecting on who I am and how I am and also to use other people as a mirror to reflect how I am and how I am working. And to get my car serviced and taken out for a spin!

ATTRACTED TO CLIENT

Q I think my client is flirting with me. What should I do?

A What are you currently doing?

Q I'm just ignoring it at the moment to be honest.

A Have you brought this to them, explored what the flirting is about, what it means?

Q Oh god, I can't do that.

A That was a very strong reaction to me asking whether you had explored the flirting with them. I wonder what's going on for you in this dynamic. We know how important the relationship between counsellor and client is and yet this is an area that you seem very resistant to working with. What are your fears around this subject?

Q I would feel embarrassed to bring it up. What if I'm wrong and they're not flirting with me? I'd be absolutely mortified. What if they laughed or were shocked at the thought? It would be awful.

A There's some concern around misreading their behaviour but something else is going on. You mention how awful it would be if they laughed or were shocked. There seems to be more focus on your feelings than on your client's.

Q I'd feel like a complete fool. As if someone attractive like them would be flirting with someone like me.

A This sounds more like your self-esteem than a misunderstanding of your client's behaviour and there seems to be a risk of your own sense of self impacting negatively on your work with this client. There is a lot going on in the room but most of it is remaining hidden. How do you feel, when you experience your client flirting?

Q I feel really uncomfortable.

Actually that's not really true. I feel a bit uncomfortable but part of me enjoys it and looks forward to the sessions.

A Mmm there seems to be an attraction between you.

Q But that is so wrong. I know that and I feel really awful. I've been too scared to talk about this with my supervisor because it is such a taboo but I actually really like this client. We have a similar sense of humour and they are very attractive but I shouldn't feel like this.

A So you find them attractive and that has stirred up a lot of feelings, some conflicted. I think we need to be mindful that there is a big difference between thinking, feeling and actually doing.

Q I would never act on those feelings. I would never ever cross that boundary and become personally involved with a client. I would never let my feelings interfere with the work with my client.

A Actually your feelings are interfering with the work. Your feelings are preventing you exploring the nature of this attraction with your client and what it means to them.

Sexual encounters between counsellor and client are not uncommon and yet are never acceptable. Counsellors experiencing unprocessed challenges may literally use the client to self-soothe, raise self-esteem. The counsellor may abuse the power imbalance in the room or be unaware that abuse relationship patterns are manifesting in the room. The client may feel very deeply towards the counsellor and the counsellor may be flattered and seduced by this … the list is long but never acceptable whatever the circumstances. Clients are vulnerable in therapy and need a strong and boundaried container.

Only by being honest in supervision and practising rigorous self-care, including a strong support system, can a counsellor work through these feelings and hold the client safely as they process their experience.

Q As you were talking then, I realised that part of me is ashamed to talk about it in supervision but another part of me doesn't want it to stop. The feelings are very powerful.

A An honest and insightful statement. Have you learnt about erotic transference?

Q I've heard about it but I'm not very sure what it means.

A Sigmund Freud introduced the term to describe how feelings, desires, patterns of relating from earlier relationships can be transferred onto present relationships. In terms of counselling, it means that the dynamics of past relationships are repeated between client and counsellor but the counsellor can interpret the transference or use immediacy to notice and bring to the attention of the client what's happening between then. This is turn can support the client to challenge self-defeating behaviour patterns to find more effective ways of relating.

Erotic transference is when past erotic feelings, desires and patterns of relating are sexually projected onto the counsellor.

Counter transference is when the counsellor's past erotic feelings, desires and patterns of relating sexually are projected onto the client. The counsellor can even start to believe that touching the client and entering into sexual behaviour will help the client in their healing.

Transference and counter transference are generally unconscious processes and part of the counsellor's role is to make these implicit patterns explicit. The problem being of course that there is no one to bring the counsellor's implicit processes to their attention unless there is honesty and openness in clinical supervision.

Q So just saying I'd never act out on my feelings isn't enough because actually already I am acting out on them, albeit subtly, it is still acting out.

A Another consideration is that it is perfectly healthy and natural to feel drawn to someone who is kind, caring and attentive. A counsellor embodies those qualities and will be facilitating a very loving space without even realising it. Most human beings would respond well to such care and attention.

Q But counselling shouldn't be loving. That's the problem. You are right, I do find my client attractive and do really like them but counselling doesn't mean loving a client does it and it doesn't mean the client loving me either.

A There seems to be a problem with the word 'loving' and actually I don't think the issue is about love in this instance. I think what we are avoiding are sexual feelings that may be present between counsellor and client, either one sided or reciprocated.

It has been hard to even name it.

Q Yes because I shouldn't feel this way. It's not ok to fancy a client and vice versa.

A I would say that it's perfectly ok. We feel the way we feel. The danger is when we become ashamed of our feelings and unable to share them with others.

Q So are you saying I should tell my client that I fancy them?

A It would be more appropriate to take those feelings to supervision initially but it seems your shame prevents you doing this.

Q I was scared my supervisor would be shocked and say I shouldn't be working as a counsellor.

A So you try and stay on your best behaviour and only talk about what goes well … mmm.

Q Yes possibly but I feel foolish and immature. I feel quite strongly about my client actually and think about them a lot outside of the sessions. It's like having a crush.

A You've mentioned feeling immature and having a crush. I wonder what is going on in relation to that in the counter transference.

Q I don't know but it is not like me. I'm not the silly love struck type.

A One big clue that you may be experiencing a counter transference is where you find yourself experiencing feelings and/or acting outside of your normal pattern of behaviour towards a client.

How are your boundaries in relation to this client?

Q I am very careful about keeping to boundaries but in the last session I went over time a little. I guess I was enjoying their company.

I feel awful now.

A Being honest about these feelings and behaviours will go a long way to maintaining a safe therapeutic space. As the old saying goes, 'The truth will set us free'.

An unpalatable truth is that a sexual relationship between client and counsellor is not unusual. It is unsafe, unethical and harmful to the client but not unusual. There seems a higher incidence of sexual inappropriateness when the counsellor is having personal problems.

In a study by Holroyd and Brodsky (1977: 843–849), 5.5% of the male and 0.6% of the female licensed PhD psychologists admitted having sexual intercourse with their patients, and an additional 2.6% of the males and 0.3% of the females reported sexual intercourse with patients within three months of the termination of therapy. Of those who had intercourse with a patient, 80% repeated it. When all erotic contact was considered, 10.9% of the males and 1.9% of the females reported such contact with patients.

Q I don't feel so bad now it's off my chest. It just seemed to be getting bigger and I was really starting to panic. Should I refer my client to another counsellor?

A If you feel unable to work safely and appropriately then yes. But if you can use supervision and personal therapy to work through and understand this, it could benefit both you and your client.

Q I think I can now. I felt so ashamed, almost like a pervert. It makes sense now though. It is a caring relationship, so all sorts of feelings will be involved. For goodness sake, when I was a teenager, someone only had to smile at me and I was in love, married with three children within five seconds.

A No comment.

CONFIDENTIALITY AND ASSISTED SUICIDE

Q I have read a lot about assisted suicide recently and wondered what I should do if a client disclosed to me that they had helped someone terminally ill to die.

Should I breach confidentiality? It is a very serious crime after all.

A What does your heart say?

Q It says not to breach confidentiality, to help the client talk about what happened and how they are left feeling and coping with life. This feels far more important than reporting a crime that I don't even think is a crime.

A What about legally? After all, as you say, it is a serious crime.

Q I've learnt about this at college. There is no statutory duty to report crime and a counsellor doesn't even have to answer police questions unless a court order is in place.

A Absolutely but it's important to add that it would be acceptable and ethical for a counsellor to breach confidentiality to report a serious crime if it was felt to be in the best interests of the client and general public.

Now finally – what does your ethical framework say?

Q To be honest I can interpret it either way to make a fit. There are good reasons for breaching confidentiality and good reasons for not.

A There seems to be a conflict between your personal and professional beliefs and values. Who's going to win I wonder?

You have said serious a few times. Does it matter how serious the crime is and if it does, how do we measure 'serious' to decide whether or not the matter should be taken outside of the counselling relationship?

Q Yes, of course it does, I wouldn't dream of breaching confidentiality for not having a TV licence and that's still against the law.

A Ok, let's see what the Department of Health says:

> Murder, manslaughter, rape, treason, kidnapping, child abuse or other cases where individuals have suffered serious harm may all warrant breaching confidentiality. Serious harm to the security of the state or to public order and crimes that involve substantial financial gain and loss will generally fall within this category. In contrast, theft, fraud or damage to property where loss or damage is less substantial would generally not warrant breach of confidence. (DoH, 2003: 35)

Q So I have to breach then.

A I am mindful of the words, 'may all warrant'. It is not a clear instruction.

I also get a sense of urgency and a need to know what to do now and yet, given the nature of the crime and the fact that it has already taken place, there doesn't appear to be an immediate risk and therefore the dilemma around breaching does not need to be immediately resolved.

Q Well what do I do?

A Your decision may not be mine. This is a complex and current issue. Personally, I would get to know my client. He/she may want to tell authorities and may see counselling as helpful in facilitating that. There could have been other issues present. Only by being with my client can I hope to understand the situation.

Of course, if you are working within an agency, you will already have agreed to abide by their policies and procedures and so would follow your agency guidance and of course your supervisor is there as a more experienced counsellor and an objective support for you.

Of course, your contract can cover this, so your client is clearly aware of your limits of confidentiality.

VIRTUAL REALITY, SOCIAL MEDIA, INTERNET, EMAIL, TEXTS

Q My supervisor asked me quite a lot of questions about how I contact my clients and how I store their information. She also asked me about whether I'm on social media, Facebook, etc. Surely that's my business; I thought my private life should be kept separate from my counselling work.

A Ahh the trials and tribulations of the internet, computers and advancing technology.

Q It began when I told my supervisor that I have always used text to communicate with my clients between sessions. She seemed to think that this could be problematic and a possible breach of confidentiality, but I can't see how. Then it opened to a big discussion about what I post on line and send emails and all sorts. We didn't really cover things like this on my course and I feel very uncertain now.

A You started off by mentioning text messages and I wondered how you store your clients' details on your phone and whether or not it is a dedicated client phone or one you use for personal use too.

Q It's just my usual phone. I use just my clients' first name and initial of surname. Nothing else. So in my phone, in my contacts it would read:

Client sally P 079*******2

Client tony L 0789******8

Client victor G 074*******4

A Can you think of any potential difficulties with that?

Q Not really, my phone is password protected, no one else uses it. Surely that's safe enough.

A I'm mindful that if one of your clients sent you a text, it would flash up on your phone automatically and could be viewed by anyone. Although this is unlikely, it does point to a possible breach of confidentiality. Also if your clients are in a long list of contacts it would be easy to call or text the wrong person in error.

I would also be careful how much you send by text. I strongly suggest keeping texts as short as possible and to focus on facts and details, for example, time and dates, rather than any therapeutic work. Also to be aware that the written word can be open to interpretation and so it is important to keep things brief and simple to avoid ambiguity and confusion.

Q Ok I can see that a dedicated phone would be helpful and I'll definitely anonymise my clients.

What about email. Is that ok?

A You are asking me these questions and I'm wondering why you aren't asking your clients. Are they ok receiving texts and emails? Do they need them encrypted or anonymised? Are you ok with them sending texts and emails to you between sessions?

Quid pro quo and all that.

Q I could make it part of my contract how we keep in touch and what is appropriate between sessions.

A That was easy enough.

Q What about social media, Facebook, Twitter, etc. Surely they are my private business and I should be at liberty to post what I like.

A Maybe, maybe not. The reflection below may shed more light on the matter. Take time to consider each of the scenarios and apply any insights to your practice.

CASE SCENARIOS

Johnathon works as a counsellor in private practice. He posts on Facebook how devastated he is that his partner has died. His Facebook has no privacy settings and the post was seen by a client.

- How do you feel about Johnathon's Facebook post?
- How could this impact on the therapeutic relationship and work?
- What ethical issues could be present?
- Should Johnathon address this with the client? If so, how could he do this?

Lucy tweets that her private practice is failing and she is worried she may have to end it. One of her clients is following her under a pseudonym. Lucy realises it is a client who is following her Twitter account.

- How do you feel about Lucy's tweet?
- How could this impact on the therapeutic relationship and work?
- What ethical issues could be present?
- Should Lucy address this with the client? If so, how could she do this?
- Do you feel Lucy should challenge her client around using a pseudonym?

Beverly is a counsellor and is also an internet blogger. She writes about her own therapeutic journey and her recovery from addiction and prostitution. Her blogs are in the public domain and she is happy for her clients to read it.

- How do you feel about Beverly's blog?
- How could this impact on the therapeutic relationship and work?
- What ethical issues could be present?
- Should Beverly bring the blog and her personal experiences into her sessions with clients? What could be the risks and benefits of doing this?

Brian has a personal Facebook account and also one for his counselling work. His personal Facebook account has strict privacy settings and cannot be accessed without his permission. His counselling Facebook account gives details of his practice, experience and training, alongside information on local personal development workshops. He also posts quotes and articles on counselling. This account is in the public domain.

(Continued)

- How do you feel about Brian's Facebook accounts?
- Could this impact on the therapeutic relationship and work?
- What ethical issues could be present?
- Do you think Brian could use his Facebook counselling account to communicate with clients? What could be the risks and benefits of doing this?

Q I can see how easily posting on social media could impact on my client and also on our relationship in so many different ways. I will look again at my privacy settings and also will use a pseudonym, so I won't be recognisable by anyone but my friends. I was starting to feel resentful that my work was overshadowing me and limiting my life but of course it doesn't need to be that way – but I do enjoy a little self-pity!

There are so many things to think about, aren't there?

A Some things only have to be thought about once and then reviewed on occasion, like contracts, internet protocol, fees, room, etc. Other things need to be thought about and revisited on almost a constant basis, like ethics, boundaries, and self-awareness.

This is a new and curious area for counsellors and there has been a lot of resistance to online, Skype and Messenger sessions. Communicating via social media and advertising through the same medium can be a tricky path to tread and will require a lot of ethical decision making to ensure not only safety but also integrity and clarity. It is essential to separate the professional from the personal as cleanly as possible – separate email, mobile phone, Facebook accounts. The less the two worlds meet, the better.

Definition of 'never the twain shall meet' in English:

ACTIVITY

Devise a guidance leaflet or brochure that would be helpful to other counselling students around using technology in relation to counselling work.

Reflect on the following areas: mobile phones, email, Skype, social media, for example, Thou shalt not post pictures of your bare bottom on social media!!

A And as in all situations ask yourself, could your client be significantly or negatively impacted?

If the answer is yes, you know what to do.

SESSION COST

Q I have a client who pays a reduced fee and yet she drives a very expensive car and I know she works full time too. Her clothes are designer makes and her mobile the latest model. When we contracted she said she could only pay the reduced amount and I agreed without knowing her circumstances. We've only had two sessions but I think she should pay more. Should I challenge this?

A Before we think about challenging, perhaps some reflection and discussion around the issue would be helpful.

You sounded quite cross about her asking for a reduced fee. What's going on for you in this?

Q I just don't think it's fair. Some people really can't pay and then can't access counselling because people like my current client are taking their places.

A How are you working with this client, with such strong personal feelings around payment?

Q I am aware I was thinking about it a lot in the last session, which is why I felt I should challenge her and sort it out.

A It is only you who wants to sort it out. Your client has negotiated the fee she wants to pay and is happy with that.

Q But it's not fair.

A But … the 'not fair' is your agenda, not your client's.

At some point in the work, it may be very helpful and therapeutic to explore issues around payment, money, value, etc. but at the moment, you have only just met. It feels unsafe and harmful to start challenging your client, especially as, in essence, you are calling her a liar.

Q Well she said she can't afford it and she can. Therefore, the word liar does actually spring to mind.

A You are making a lot of assumptions and judgements. There are certainly things here around injustice, but this seems related to your experience at the moment.

Q You're right. I really do hate injustice. I really wanted to say, 'but doesn't everyone' then but I knew you'd get on your high horse and tell me I was making generalisations to avoid my feelings.

A Are you avoiding your feelings? There's something here touching on something really tender and raw I think.

Q I know I sound like a pious goody goody but I've worked since I left school and I fund this course and see clients, etc. whilst still working full time. I also have my own home, but I have a big mortgage and have sacrificed a lot for it. I have to pay my own therapy and supervision, there are no discounts for me. I haven't got a car, can't afford one.

A There are similarities between you and your client then, but she seems better off than you but you think you are paying more than her, in lots of different ways.

Q It reminds me of my ex brother and sister in law. Neither of them work, they are on disability benefits, but I certainly can't see any disability. All their bills are paid. They have holidays and a car, a lovely home. They have more than me for doing nothing and it's not fair.

A You sound upset.

Q I just feel that I battle on and battle on and others just seem to float through life. I envy my brother and sister in law, I really do.

A Do you envy your client …?

Q Do you know … that's really odd … I think I do envy her but what I just thought of was that I envy her for asking for a fee reduction. I wouldn't have been able to do that. I'm not very good at asking for help.

A So although part of you is very judgemental of your client, part of you envies her being able to voice and get her needs met.

What you said also helps us appreciate that things aren't always as they seem.

You would pay full price for a counselling session because although you actually do need a fee reduction, you don't feel able to ask.

Your client on the other hand, appears to not need a fee reduction but managed to ask for one.

From what you've said about your own situation, I can understand your reaction to your client. However now we need to think about how to respond.

Q Yes. I see now that there could be many different things going on for her. Maybe it's all an act, the suave and polished exterior, I actually know very little about her. Maybe she's got a lot of debt. Maybe she's an addict. Maybe, maybe, maybe …

A I like the way you are thinking now. There are also the emotional and psychological dynamics. Issues around deprivation can cause such fear around not having enough; there can be a poverty of spirit that in some cases drives people to collect, gather and hoard but no matter how much is amassed, it is never enough to quieten the internal fear and anxiety.

> **REFLECTION**
>
> What relationship do you have with money, possessions, etc.? Is your relationship with money reflected in any of your other relationships?

Q I remember in college one day, there was a discussion about people not able to give good things to themselves. Perhaps they felt not worth it or not deserving or spent their money on others rather than themselves. Counselling was an act of self-love and they couldn't value themselves highly enough to pay for that.

A Yes, some people aren't able to give to themselves.

Q I relate to that. Sadly, I also realise that part of me just waits for someone to rescue me and sort everything out for me.

A Like a cross between a mum and Mary Poppins?

Q Yes, I also know my thinking is seriously flawed. How can anyone rescue me, when they don't even know there's anything wrong?

A We are very strange creatures aren't we?

REFLECTION

Look at the list of character traits and feelings on the left hand side of Table 15.3 and reflect on how each thing could have an effect on how much a client says they are able to pay for a counselling session.

Some examples have been given.

TABLE 15.3

Trait/feeling	Thought/belief
Pride	Pretends to be able to afford high cost.
Fear	Worries about terrible things that might happen and so wants to hold onto everything… just in case. I'll pay anything, I can't carry on like this.
Shame	I'm not good enough for counselling. I'm too embarrassed to let you know I have no money.
Anger	Why should I pay anything, I haven't done anything wrong.
Self-esteem	
Power	
Confidence	
Envy	Why should I pay a counsellor all that money? They're ok with their posh job and everything.
Unmet emotional needs	
Control	I want to decide how this will work.
Security	
Anxiety	

What have you learnt from engaging with this activity?

Q Anything could be going on with my client. It's that old jumping to conclusions thing. I know when I start doing that, my own feelings are definitely getting in the way.

A There is another strand to this. How much do you charge and how do you manage the financial aspect of the client and counsellor relationship?

Q I agreed a lower fee with my client, but I didn't really want to. For me, it's about believing I'm good enough for people to pay.

REFLECTION

The questions below are designed to raise your personal awareness of the financial issues that can impinge and impact on the counselling relationship and counselling work.

- How much do you or would you charge per session?
- Why did you choose this amount?
- What would you do if a client said they couldn't afford it?
- What would you do if at the end of the session, a client started to leave without paying?
- What would you do if a client said at the end of the session that they couldn't find their money and must have lost it?
- A client pays by bank transfer and a payment is overdue. Do you continue seeing them for counselling sessions?
- A client you have been working with for several months breaks down and says she can't afford the sessions. She asks if you will see her free of charge for a few weeks. What do you say?
- How do you feel about raising your fees?
- What are your feelings towards money as a whole?
- You forget to ask a client for the fee. Do you contact them to remind them?
- In your contract you ask for payment if a session is cancelled less than 48 hours before the session. A client cancelled an hour before but says they can't remember you saying about the cancellation fee. What do you do?
- Have you been able to be honest when answering these questions and if not, why not?

Q Money seems to be tied up with so many things: power, control, security, safety. I certainly won't be challenging my client, but I do think there could be good work around exploring some of these things … for both of us.

SUMMARY

It is impossible to cover all professional issues and challenges that can arise as the possibilities are endless. It is, though, important to:

- Use an ethical decision-making model when faced with challenges and difficulties.
- Use clinical supervision to work things through.
- Access CPD to address gaps in learning and understanding.
- Engage with personal therapy to maintain self-awareness and insight into own practice and relating styles.
- Practise self-care and foster resilience.

16
What Next?

PRIVATE PRACTICE

Q Ok, I'm now a qualified counsellor. I've got a lot of agency experience and am currently the senior counsellor at one agency, where I am responsible for assessment and referral of clients to appropriate counsellors. I feel ready to take the next step and move into private practice. I'm just not sure where to start.

A I agree, there are a lot of things to think about. Let's make a start. Firstly, what makes you feel drawn towards setting up in private practice and what are the pros and cons?

Q To be honest, up until now I have worked in a voluntary capacity as an agency counsellor and I'd like to earn some money. After all I've spent a lot of time, money and energy becoming qualified and I want to make a career from it. I haven't been able to find many full-time counselling jobs, so maybe it's time to create one for myself. Also I would be able to fine tune my practice to work more creatively, using different tools and techniques to encourage healing and recovery. I can better do this when I am my own boss.

A You sound ready to take the step. There will be losses though. Up until now you have had the protection and support of an agency. You will have had colleagues, senior staff, managers, your supervision could be provided. Policies and procedures will have been in place already, alongside an established client base. Premises were provided and no need to advertise or promote yourself to get clients.

Q I have thought about all of this and although I agree, there are also a lot of benefits. I will be able to fit my work around other aspects of my life; I'll be my own boss and have the autonomy that affords. Also, there are some things I disagree with in my agency and I wouldn't have to conform to others' ethics and working practices.

I do know though, that there is an awful lot to think about and I can't work out how to get started; there are so many areas to consider.

EXERCISE

Draw a spider diagram with things that need to be considered when setting up private practice.

Put the items identified in order of personal importance to you and take time to reflect on your list.

The order you place things may help you identify the areas for which you need further information and support.

Q There is a lot to think about and it makes sense to go through each one, almost like a checklist.

I'm still not sure about priorities, they all feel equally important and sort of blur together.

Time to get started then. I just hope I'm up to the job.

> Our deepest fear is not that we are inadequate. Our deepest fear is that we are powerful beyond measure. It is our light, not our darkness, that most frightens us. We ask ourselves, 'Who am I to be brilliant, gorgeous, talented, fabulous?' Actually, who are you not to be? You are a child of God. You're playing small does not serve the world. There is nothing enlightened about shrinking so that other people won't feel insecure around you. We are all meant to shine, as children do. We were born to make manifest the glory of God that is within us. It's not just in some of us; it's in everyone. And as we let our own light shine, we unconsciously give other people permission to do the same. As we are liberated from our own fear, our presence automatically liberates others. (Williamson, 1992: 90)

A We can check that out. I'm wondering how you can best utilise the skills and qualities you already have.

Q It helped to identify clearly what needs doing and also what skills and qualities I'm bringing.

These are the main areas that concern me at the moment.

- Setting up a business and all that entails
- Setting and room
- The law and ethics
- Cost and finances

- Promotion and advertising
- Website. Professional or own design?
- Tax and insurance
- Professional will
- Safeguarding
- Supervision

EXERCISE

Transferable Skills

Complete Table 16.1 by listing your personal and professional skills and qualities, and in the second column, think about how they can be utilised in setting up in private practice.

Some examples are provided

TABLE 16.1 Transferable skills

Skill/quality	Application
Organisational skills	
Tenacity and determination	
Marketing skills	

I haven't put them in any order but they are the main areas for me I think.

A Firstly I would suggest doing some research. Talk to other counsellors about working in private practice. Find out how they work and what they charge. Look at websites and get ideas for your own. Check out how many counsellors are practising in your area, etc.

Q I'm not even sure what setting up a new business actually means. Do I have to register as a business with anyone or do I need to tell anyone I'm working from home?

A I am a counsellor not a business person. To that end, I would suggest seeking help and information around setting up in private practice as a new business. There are many organisations geared to helping people start up a new business and many of them offer support and incentives.

Business Link is an organisation with a mine of information and guidance. It offers free support and guidance in many areas, for example, advertising, marketing, finances, taxes, and start up, grants. It is for small businesses only and will help not only in setting up your private practice but also in growing your practice. They can be contacted on 0845 6009006 or on www.businesslink.gov.uk.

There are many such companies and as a free resource the support and guidance is invaluable.

Q That will be my first step.

I know ethics are more important but I'd really like to think about the setting. I'm really looking forward to getting my room ready.

A I can hear that. You're taking a big step and the room you work from is important. Where the room is located is also important. Earlier you said you would be working from home.

Q Yes, I have like a sun room at the back of my house. It's a light room and a perfect size.

A In relation to working from your own home, what potential challenges can you think of?

Q This has been very much on my mind and I find myself walking around my home, looking at things with fresh eyes. The garden room obviously looks out on the garden and that's where my washing line is. I will definitely need to remember that. I don't want my client coming face to face with my underwear.

Also I have children and so will be working mainly in school hours. I think I would rather my client come face to face with my underwear than face to face with my three year old in a tantrum. I've thought about school holidays too and how I could make that work.

A Neighbours?

Q Neighbours?

A Yes, what are your neighbours like. Are they noisy or quiet? If they are noisy, is it at any particular time? Could the noise disturb the sessions?

Q Most of the time it's fine but there do tend to be barbeques in the summer and people sitting outside. That might be a little noisy but hopefully manageable.

A You said the room is at the back of the house. What is the access to the room like?

Q My client would just need to walk through my kitchen into the room. There's a downstairs toilet they could use. It will mean I'll have to be very organised. I also don't want a client to have to walk into a house full of cooking smells or any other unpleasant smells for that matter.

A It's also useful to look around for personal photos, etc. that might not be appropriate. Some counsellors do leave some personal items and photos on show and that's something you will need to come to a decision about.

Q I'm lucky that there aren't any stairs to my house and so clients with mobility problems can gain access safely.

A We've talked about the clients' safety but what about yours?

Q I am talking it all through with my supervisor. In fact, I wouldn't be even considering this if she didn't believe I was ready.

A What about safety in your home? A new client is a stranger and a stranger that will be invited into your home. Instances of any harm to counsellors is extremely rare but it is important to be aware and remain vigilant.

Q I'm not sure what to do about that. I can't have a panic button or personal alarm can I?

A There are things you can do. Perhaps an initial telephone conversation could allow the seeds of the relationship to be planted and also give you the opportunity to get to know them a little. When meeting a new client, perhaps someone else could be in the house in another part of the house, or you could contract with a friend to call as soon as the session ends. To help you find a way that works for you, the Suzi Lamplugh Trust offers guidance and support to lone workers (www.suzylamplugh.org/training/lone-workers/).

Now onto the room itself. What do you have in mind?

Q This is where I'm undecided. I want my room to talk about the kind of work I do but I don't want it to be all about me. I don't want a cold clinical room that's for sure.

Maybe somewhere in the middle.

EXERCISE

On a piece of paper, design your ideal counselling room for your private practice. Be as detailed as you can. Include the following:

Heat, light, seating, furniture, colour scheme, ornaments and pictures, therapeutic tools.

As you plan, think about why you are doing things the way you are.

Are you happy with it?

What would you like your clients to think and feel as they enter the room?

A One thing I forgot to ask; is it a dedicated room?

Q It hasn't been but I could make it that way if necessary or just get really good at removing items that shouldn't be there, for example, kids, cats, odd socks and teaspoons!!

A You said you wanted your room to speak about how you work and didn't want a stark plain clinical space.

Q I like to work creatively and symbolically and so would like to have pens, crayons and pencils in the room. I have some pictures that I want to put in the room and some other things that I think are quite special. If my client noticed one of them, we could perhaps make it part of the work, exploring what it means to them and how they feel towards it. Of course it's important that a client feels safe and comfortable in a room but it is even more important to facilitate a space where a client can talk about not feeling safe and comfortable in a non-judgemental space.

A You really have given a lot of thought.

What about ethical and legal considerations. What might they be?

Q I'm a member of BACP and I've read through the *Ethical Framework for the Counselling Professions* (EFfCP) and that has really helped me to think about things. My supervisor uses an ethical decision-based model, based on the framework and I find that really helpful. My main concerns around the law and ethics are around safeguarding. This has always been an area that frightens me. It feels like a huge responsibility.

A It is a responsibility. If you haven't had any safeguarding training, it's something I'd strongly suggest as CPD. If nothing else, it will hopefully allay some fears and give you confidence, when working with vulnerable people. You mentioned your supervisor; is setting up in private practice something that you've discussed in supervision? It is important that your supervisor feels you are ready for private practice and is willing to support you and work with you in setting up.

Q Yes, we have been discussing it for some time and I have her backing.

A You mentioned things like tax, insurance, advertising and promotion. Again, I am not an expert in these areas and would suggest consulting specialists in each area. An accountant, web designer and small business support will all be able to provide relevant information and services.

Q Advertising is very important to me and I definitely need a website.

A When you advertise, ask yourself, what do you want your prospective clients to know about you and the type of counselling you offer? What message do you want these people to hear? What can you offer that's different to other counsellors in your area?

Before we continue, there is one important area we need to cover – that of a professional will.

Q A professional will? I've never heard of that.

A It prepares for the unexpected. If anything happens to you when working in private practice, your clients would be left high and dry. A professional will would name a counsellor willing to work with your clients. This is something some supervisors are willing to do. Your professional will could simply name someone who would be responsible for the ethical management of your practice if you were unavailable. It is not generally a legal document, more a set of instructions, including specific information regarding location of and access to records and client information, to a trusted colleague who will be able to ensure appropriate care for your clients.

In my opinion, this should be an ethical consideration for all counsellors.

Q I agree. I can't imagine how awful I'd feel if I became incapacitated and couldn't work and my clients are just left in the dark. I would find having a professional will reassuring.

A Below is an example. It is important to remember that you need your client's consent.

Take time to reflect on your personal thoughts and feelings around having a professional will.

REFLECTION

Professional Will

I ....

Address ....

....

Declare this to be my professional will.

This is not a legal document. It consists of detailed instructions on how to manage my professional practice and to offer care and support to my clients in the event of my death or incapacitation.

My professional body is..

Membership number..

Professional insurance details..

Clinical supervisor's details..

Name and contact details of professional executor..

I hereby grant my professional executor authority to act on my behalf.

My specific instructions are:

To notify current and past clients appropriately.

To offer current clients a choice of referral options.

To notify relevant professionals.

To appropriately store client records and notes.

To forward notes and details to new counsellor if appropriate and with client consent.

To bring the practice to a close; practically and financially.

Signed..

Name..

Date..

Witness signature ....

Name..

Date..

A We have explored some areas around setting up in private practice but it would be impossible to cover everything. Private practice can be isolating and lonely, so it can be very helpful to join local networking groups for counsellors and engage as much as possible with CPD.

Overall I believe the most important thing is for you to value yourself, your experience and what you have to offer. Do not undersell yourself. It can take time to build any new business and a counselling practice is no different. It can be tempting to lower session costs to try and build a client base but this can undervalue what you have to offer. Believe in yourself and your profession and put the legwork in. Then … let go …

PROFESSIONAL REGISTERS

Q I've heard about professional membership associations and voluntary registers and colleagues have said that I should be on one or more but I'm not sure what they are and which one if any to try and get on.

A This is a very confusing area for a lot of counsellors.

In the UK counselling has no statutory regulation and no statutory register recognised by the government. Voluntary registers have been set up by professional bodies.

The professional standards authority oversees the voluntary registers to protect the public. Their role is to ensure that counsellors on a voluntary register work safely and ethically to an agreed standard. The voluntary registers are monitored to ensure their integrity and relevance remains current.

Below is a list of bodies on the Professional Standards Authority's (PSA) accredited register (last updated on 1 September 2016). Please note that for some professions, there is more than one register. The list is changeable.

- Association of Child Psychotherapists
- Association of Christian Counsellors
- British Association for Counselling and Psychotherapy
- British Association of Play Therapists
- British Psychoanalytic Council
- COSCA (Counselling & Psychotherapy in Scotland)
- Genetic Counsellor Registration Board
- Human Givens Institute
- National Counselling Society
- National Hypnotherapy Society
- Play Therapy UK
- UK Council for Psychotherapy

The requirements for each register is different. It is important to look into these in more detail if you plan to become registered.

ACTIVITY

For each of the voluntary registers, research the entry requirements and then assess whether or not you are eligible to apply for entry to any of them. Which do you feel drawn towards? Why?

TABLE 16.2 Voluntary registers

Name of register	Requirements	Personal eligibility
ASSOCIATION OF CHILD PSYCHOTHERAPISTS		
ASSOCIATION OF CHRISTIAN COUNSELLORS		
BRITISH ASSOCIATION FOR COUNSELLING AND PSYCHOTHERAPY		
BRITISH ASSOCIATION OF PLAY THERAPISTS		
BRITISH PSYCHOANALYTIC COUNCIL		
COSCA (COUNSELLING & PSYCHOTHERAPY IN SCOTLAND)		
GENETIC COUNSELLOR REGISTRATION BOARD		
HUMAN GIVENS INSTITUTE		
NATIONAL COUNSELLING SOCIETY		
NATIONAL HYPNOTHERAPY SOCIETY		
PLAY THERAPY UK		
UK COUNCIL FOR PSYCHOTHERAPY		

Q As I'm a student member of BACP, it makes sense to try and join their register. Is joining the register the same as BACP accreditation?

A No. As you are a student member of BACP, it makes sense to look at the different membership categories they have and what your next steps are after qualifying.

Student membership: As you know, you need to be in training on an appropriate course.

Individual member: For appropriately qualified counsellors in practice.

Registered member MBACP: A registered member represents the minimum recommended standard a client can expect from a counsellor. To become a member of the BACP register you need to have graduated from a BACP accredited course or passed their Certificate of Proficiency.

Registered member MBACP (Accred): Accreditation is a quality standard for practising counselling and is widely recognised within the profession. It is an acknowledgement that your practice exceeds minimum requirements. It is quite an in-depth process that requires you to be able to provide a rationale for your practice alongside other assessment requirements.

Other categories are senior accreditation and retired member but both of those are a long way away yet.

If you need further information, I suggest you contact BACP directly at: www.bacp.co.uk.

Q There's a lot more to it than I thought but I like the steps as they seem like an acknowledgement of achievement.

A Exactly.

Q You mentioned above that when I apply for accreditation, I will need to provide a rationale for my work. What do you mean by that?

A Basically it's the what and why of your practice. It requires you to explain your approach and to be able to reflect on your work. What you do and why you do what you do.

REFLECTION

Provide a rationale for your work by writing about your knowledge and understanding of your practice.

(Continued)

> As you write, reflect on:
>
> - The theory or theories that underpin your work. If you are an integrative counsellor, it is important to describe how the different theories integrate to provide a coherent approach. It is not enough to just describe the individual theories.
> - The link between theory and practice.
> - What interventions do you make in line with your approach?
> - If you work with different groups, how do you tailor your approach to meet their needs?
> - Give some examples from your practice to illustrate your rationale.
>
> Finally, explain why you have chosen to work the way you do.

CONTINUED PERSONAL AND PROFESSIONAL DEVELOPMENT (CPD)

Q Well here I am, a qualified counsellor. I can hardly believe it; what a journey it's been. It has been very different to what I expected. I look back and remember how much I wanted to help and sort everybody out. I had no idea that I'd have to take a look at myself first. It was a big step for me to admit that part of me wanted to be a counsellor to feel important and clever. One thing this training has taught me is to be honest about what I think and feel. Before I used to be so ashamed of the way I thought and felt that I pretended to think and feel completely differently, so I appeared nice and kind and understanding.

A Sounds a bit like the Waltons to me.

Q I realise that now. So many of us hide who we are – for approval, love, acceptance. Life then appears like a hall of mirrors with no true reflection.

A It is very important not to judge your insides with other people's outsides.

Q I used to look at magazines and TV and think that's what real life was and that's how everyone lives. So I pretended. It never occurred to me that other people were pretending too. For me counselling is a place to learn to stop pretending.

I guess that was my long winded way of saying thank you for accompanying me on this journey and goodbye.

A Goodbye?

Q Well, this was what I set out to achieve. A qualified counsellor.

A So what happens next?

Q I continue working in my placement until my private practice builds and then concentrate on that.

A I was wondering about your personal and professional development.

Q I think I've done enough personal development.

A What about professional development? Is that something you feel you have done enough of?

Q Was that a little bit of sarcasm I can hear?

Of course I haven't finished learning.

A So you haven't finished learning about counselling but you have learnt all there is to know about yourself.

I actually find it difficult to completely separate personal and professional development. For me they are intertwined and in dynamic relationship with each other. It concerns me that you see them very separately. My sense is you see one as knowledge and one as feeling and at the moment prefer knowledge. For me just that view suggests a need for further personal development. Personal development is an ongoing process. We are not static beings. We change, adapt, learn and our awareness needs to keep in line with that. It's not just self-awareness; it's also other-awareness and being able to engage with the changing dynamics and transferential issues. As such, personal development will involve professional development to become both education and growth, so both training and personal therapy are relevant as is supervision, group process, reflection on client work, workshops, seminars, webinars and many other mediums.

It is also a very personal thing. A unique, evolving process of discovery.

Q I see what you mean. Maybe I need to start looking.

A Or planning.

ACTIVITY

Prepare a personal and professional development plan for the forthcoming year. This can be very simple.

(Continued)

TABLE 16.3 Continuing personal development

Areas for growth	Personal or professional activity and date completed
For example: Lacking knowledge around eating disorders	Webinar on the Complexity of Hungry Need 6 June
Being congruent with clients rather than colluding with their defences	Why I am I frightened of the truth Tom Drew Workshop, 9 November

It can be more detailed and specific.

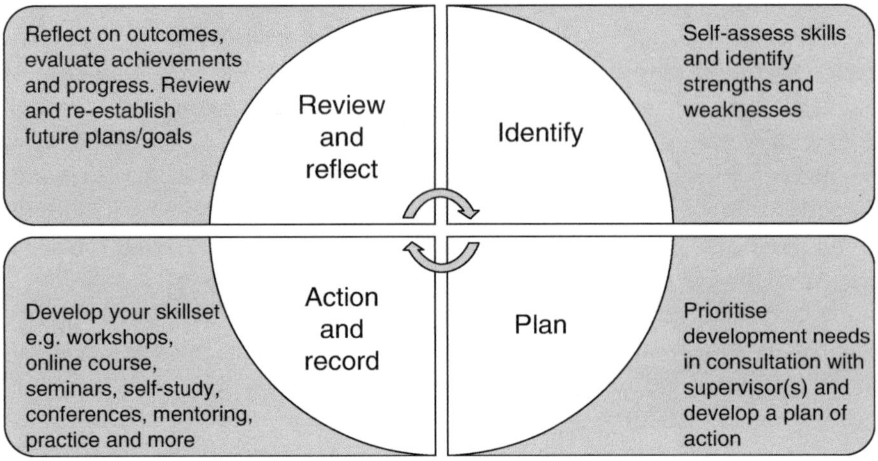

FIGURE 16.1 Personal development planning

Q An ongoing journey.

A If that is the case, then perhaps, counselling is not the learning of facts but the training of the mind to understand and the heart to feel.

Why am I here?
I am here to listen …
… Not to work miracles.
I am here to help you discover what you are feeling …
… Not to make things go away.
I am here to help you identify your options …
… Not to decide for you what you should do.
I am here to discuss steps with you …
… Not to take the steps for you.
I am here to help you discover your own strength …
… Not to rescue you and leave you still vulnerable.
I am here to help you discover that you can help yourself …
… Not to take responsibility for you.
I am here to help you choose …
… Not to make it unnecessary for you to make difficult choices.
I am here to provide support for your change.

Source: Adapted from an anonymous poem from Texas Council on Family Violence. Reproduced in BACP publication *The Independent Practitioner*

SUMMARY

Once qualified and working, whether in an agency, organisation or private practice, there is ongoing maintenance and development required.

- Be clear about how you work and also why you work the way you do.
- Remember ethical principles build a practice.
- Continue to look at self and work towards personal care and growth.
- Continue being curious.
- Enjoy not knowing!!!

References

Baldwin, M. (2000) 'Interview with Carl Rogers on the use of self in therapy', in M. Baldwin (ed.), *The Use of Self in Therapy*, 2nd edn. New York: Haworth Press. pp. 29–38.

Bayne, R. and Jinks, G. (2010) *How to Survive Counsellor Training – An A–Z Guide*. London: Palgrave Macmillan.

Bion, W.R. (1990) *Brazilian Lectures: 1973 São Paulo; 1974 Rio de Janeiro/São Paulo*. London: Karnac Books.

British Association for Counselling and Psychotherapy (BACP) (2016) *Ethical Framework for the Counselling Professions*, 2nd edn. Lutterworth: BACP.

British Association for Counselling and Psychotherapy (BACP) (2018) *Ethical Framework for the Counselling Professions*. Available at: www.bacp.co.uk/events-and-resources/ethics-and-standards/ethical-framework-for-the-counselling-professions/ (accessed 15 April 2019).

Castonguay, L.G. and Beutler, L.E. (eds) (2006) *Principles of Therapeutic Change That Work*. New York: Oxford University Press.

Clarkson, P. (2003) *The Therapeutic Relationship*, 2nd edn. London: Whurr.

Cooper, M. (2008) *Essential Research Findings in Counselling and Psychotherapy: The Facts are Friendly*. London: Sage.

Cooper, M. and McLeod, J. (2015) *Pluralistic Counselling and Psychotherapy*. London: Sage.

Cooper, M. and MacLeod, J. (2007) 'A pluralistic framework for counselling and psychotherapy: Implications for research', *Counselling and Psychotherapy Research*, 7(3).

Department of Health (DoH) (2003) NHS Code of Practice, confidentiality: Gateway ref:1656.

Gutheil, T.G. and Gabbard, G. (1998) 'Misuses and misunderstandings of boundary theory in clinical and regulatory settings', *American Journal of Psychiatry*, *155*(3): 409–414.

Hawkins, P. and Shohet, R. (2012) *Supervision in the Helping Professions*, 4th edn (originally published 2006). Maidenhead: Open University Press.

Holroyd, J. and Brodsky, A. (1977) Psychologists' attitudes and practices regarding erotic and non erotic physical contact with patients. *American Psychologist*, *32*(10), 843–849

Inskipp, F. and Proctor, B. (1993) *The Art, Craft and Tasks of Counselling Supervision, Part 1: Making the Most of Supervision*. Twickenham: Cascade Publications.

Inskipp, F. and Proctor, B. (1995) *The Art, Craft and Tasks of Counselling Supervision, Part 2: Becoming a Supervisor*. Twickenham: Cascade Publications.

Johnstone, L. and Boyle, M. with Cromby, J., Dillon, J., Harper, D., Kinderman, P., Longden, E., Pilgrim, D. and Read, J. (2018) *The Power Threat Meaning Framework: Towards the Identification of Patterns in Emotional Distress, Unusual Experiences and Troubled or Troubling Behaviour, as an Alternative to Functional Psychiatric Diagnosis*. Leicester: British Psychological Society.

Klass, D., Silverman, P.R. and Nickman, S. (1996) *Continuing Bonds: New Understandings of Grief (Death Education, Aging and Health Care)*. London: Routledge.

Kugler, P. (ed.) (2012) *Jungian Perspectives on Clinical Supervision*. Einsiedeln: Daimon.

Macran, S. and Shapiro, D.A. (1998) 'The role of personal therapy for therapists: A review', *British Journal of Medical Psychology*, *71*: 13–26.

Maslach, C. and Jackson, S. (1986) *Maslach Burnout Inventory Manual*, 2nd edn. Palo Alto, CA: Consulting Psychologist Press.

McLeod, J. (2003) *An Introduction to Counselling*, 3rd edn. Maidenhead: Open University Press.

Norcross, J.C. (ed.) (2011) *Psychotherapy Relationships That Work: Evidence-Based Responsiveness*. New York: Oxford University Press.

Oxford English Dictionary (2016) Oxford: Oxford University Press. Available at: www.oxforddictionaries.com/definition/english/ (accessed 9 May 2019).

Page, S. and Woskett, V. (1994) *Supervising the Counsellor: A Cyclical Model*. London: Routledge.

Ram Dass and Gorman, P. (1985) *How Can I Help?* London: Rider.

Rogers, C.R. (1942) *Counseling and Psychotherapy: Newer Concepts in Practice*. Boston, MA: Houghton-Mifflin.

Rogers, C.R. (1961) *On Becoming a Person: A Therapist's View of Psychotherapy*. Boston, MA: Houghton-Mifflin.

Ronnestad, M.H. and Skovholt, T. (2012) *The Developing Practitioner*. New York: Routledge.

Rothschild, B. (2006) *Help for the Helper*. New York: Norton.

Rowan, J. (1993) *The Transpersonal: Psychotherapy and Counselling*. London: Routledge.

Stoltenberg, C. and Delworth, U. (1987) *Supervising Counsellors and Therapists: A Developmental Approach*. San Francisco, CA: Jossey-Bass Wiley.

Trott, A. and Reeves, A. (2018) 'Social class and the therapeutic relationship: The perspective of therapists as clients', *Counselling & Psychotherapy Research Journal, 18*(2).

Wampold, B. and Imel, Z. (2015) *The Great Psychotherapy Debate*, 2nd edn. New York: Routledge.

Williamson, M. (1992) *A Return to Love: Reflections on the Principles of 'A Course in Miracles'*, 1st edn. London: Thorsons.

Wosket, V. (1999) *The Therapeutic Use of Self*. London: Routledge.

WEBSITES

ACC – www.acc-uk.org

BABCP – www.babcp.com

BACP – www.bacp.co.uk

CORE – www.coreims.co.uk

CPCAB – www.cpcab.co.uk

DSM – www.psychiatry.org/psychiatrists/practice/dsm

GAD-7 – www.phqscreeners.com/select-screener

NCS – www.nationalcounsellingsociety.org

PHQ-9 – https://patient.info/doctor/patient-health-questionnaire-phq-9

SWOT analysis – https://en.wikipedia.org/wiki/SWOT_analysis

UKCP – www.psychotherapy.org.uk

Index